"THE PERFECT GIFT FOR A NEW MOM AND FAMILY . . .

Every aspect of care for mom and baby is covered, with interesting charts and clear references. There are many good books on baby care . . . but this book possesses unusual tenderness and heart, and it respects babies as people, albeit little ones."

—*Library Journal*

"The extent of Tracy's knowledge on all things baby-related is truly hard to comprehend. She combines this with extraordinary intuition, and most importantly, makes it accessible to everyone."

—CHRISTA MILLER
Actress, *The Drew Carey Show*

"Tracy Hogg's book, full of her trademark warmth and wisdom, should be mandatory reading for all expectant and new parents. Even more than teaching what to expect, she teaches how to deal with all the things you don't expect."

—SUSANNAH GRANT
Screenwriter, *Erin Brockovich* and *Pocahontas*

"While I read countless how-to books throughout my pregnancy, only Tracy's offered genuine tools for loving, respecting, and nurturing a happy baby. Reading *Secrets of the Baby Whisperer* eased my anxiety about motherhood and helped build my confidence. It is a gift I would share with any expecting parent."

—DANA WALDEN
President, 20th Century Fox Television

Also by Tracy Hogg
Published by The Random House Publishing Group

Secrets of the Baby Whisperer for Toddlers

Books published by The Random House Publishing Group
are available at quantity discounts on bulk purchases for
premium, educational, fund-raising, and special sales use.
For details, please call 1-800-733-3000.

SECRETS OF THE BABY WHISPERER

HOW TO CALM, CONNECT, AND COMMUNICATE WITH YOUR BABY

TRACY HOGG

WITH
MELINDA BLAU

BALLANTINE BOOKS • NEW YORK

2005 Ballantine Books Mass Market Edition

Published in the United States by Ballantine Books, an imprint of The Random House Publishing Group, a division of Random House, Inc., New York.

Originally published in hardcover in the United States by Ballantine Books, an imprint of The Random House Publishing Group, a division of Random House, Inc., in 2001.

ISBN 0-345-47909-2

Cover photograph: Tony Bakhtiar/Mere Images Photography

Printed in the United States of America

www.ballantinebooks.com

OPM   30 29 28 27 26 25 24 23 22 21

To
Sara and Sophie

Contents

Acknowledgments

I want to thank Melinda Blau for interpreting the work I do, for bringing her writing expertise to this wonderful project, and for making my voice ring true throughout the book. I knew from our first conversation that she totally understood my philosophy about babies. I am grateful for her friendship and her hard work.

Thank you, Sara and Sophie, my wonderful daughters. I have you to thank for awakening my gifts in the first place and for helping me relate to infants on a deeper, intuitive level.

I owe a debt of gratitude as well to my large extended family, especially my Mum and my Nan, for their patience, continuing support, grounding, and constant encouragement.

I appreciate beyond words the families who over the years have given me the opportunity to share their joys and their precious time. A special thanks to Lizzy Selders whose friendship and daily support I shall never forget.

Finally, I am grateful to the people who have helped me negotiate the new terrain of the publishing world: Eileen Cope of Lowenstein Associates, who stepped up to the plate and did such a good job seeing this project through; Gina Centrello, president of Ballantine Books, for believing in my work; and our editor, Maureen O'Neal, for her ongoing support.

—*Tracy Hogg*
Encino, California

Watching Tracy Hogg do her magic has been a delight. Although I've interviewed many parenting experts and am a parent myself, her insights and strategies never fail to amaze me. I thank her for her patience with my endless questions and for letting me into her world. Thanks, too, to Sara and Sophie for loaning their mum to me.

I also am grateful to those of Tracy's clients who welcomed me into their homes, allowed me to meet their babies, and helped me understand what Tracy has done for their families. A bow of appreciation as well to Bonnie Strickland, Ph.D., the consummate networker, for putting me in touch with Rachel Clifton, Ph.D.; to Rachel, in turn, who opened the doors to a whole world of infant research; and to other professionals who gave me their input.

I am always grateful to Eileen Cope, of the Lowenstein Literary Agency, for listening carefully, judging wisely, and standing by me, and to Barbara Lowenstein, for her many years of experience and guidance. Sincere thanks to Gina Centrello, Maureen O'Neal, and the rest of the crew at Ballantine, who championed this project with unprecedented enthusiasm.

Finally, I must express my gratitude to two wise mentors, my octogenarian pen pal Henrietta Levner, and Aunt Ruth, who is more than a friend or a relative; both women truly appreciate what writing is and have always cheered me on. And I want to thank Jennifer and Peter, who were planning their wedding as this book was being written, for loving me even when I said, "Sorry, can't talk now." To the others who are close to my heart—Mark, Cay, Jeremy, and Lorena—you all must know how endlessly grateful I am for our "family apart." If not, I'm telling you now.

—*Melinda Blau*
Northampton, Massachusetts

Foreword

One of the most common questions asked of me by prospective parents is, "What books do you recommend we obtain for guidance?" My dilemma has never been with the choice of a medically-based text, but rather with a solid volume presenting practical, simple, and yet individualized advice about early infant behavior and development. Now my dilemma is solved.

In *Secrets of the Baby Whisperer*, Tracy Hogg has given new (and even experienced) parents a great gift—the ability to develop early insight into their child's temperament, a framework for interpreting a baby's early communication and behavior, and as a result, a set of very practical and workable solutions for remedying typical infant problems such as excessive crying, frequent feedings, and sleepless nights. One can't help but appreciate Tracy's sensible "English" banter—the book is comfy, often chatty, humorous but practical and intelligent. It is an easy read—not overbearing but full of useful content applicable to even the most difficult of baby temperaments.

For many new parents, information overload from well-meaning family members, friends, books and the electronic media creates confusion and anxiety, even before a baby is born. Current publications dealing with typical newborn problems are often too dogmatic or, worse yet, too loose in philosophy. Barraged with these extremes, new parents often develop a style of "accidental parenting," well-intentioned, but likely to produce even more problems with Baby. In this book, Tracy emphasizes the importance of a structured routine to help parents fall into a predictable rhythm.

She suggests an "E.A.S.Y." cycle of eating, activity, and then sleep in order to detach the expectation of eating from sleeping, and thus time is created for the parent—You. As a result, babies learn to self-soothe and settle without a breast or bottle association. Cries or behavior observed after a baby is well fed are then able to be interpreted more realistically by new parents.

In a new parent's zeal to multi-task and integrate parenting into a "pre-baby" world, Tracy encourages you to "S.L.O.W." down. She gives very useful suggestions for surviving the postpartum adjustment all family members must make, how to anticipate problems and simplify this most tiring of periods, and therefore how to capture the most subtle, yet most important of cues— the new baby's desire to communicate. Tracy teaches care givers to observe Baby's body language and responses to the real world, and to use this knowledge to help interpret an infant's basic needs.

For parents who pick up this book late into their baby's infancy, helpful suggestions are brought forth to untangle and resolve ongoing difficulties—take heed, old habits can still be corrected. Tracy walks you patiently through the process and will instill in you confidence that parenting (and sleep, and fussiness) can get back on a livable track. For all parents, *Secrets of the Baby Whisperer* will become the dog-eared, well-loved reference we have all been waiting for. Enjoy!

—*Jeannette J. Levenstein, M.D., F.A.A.P.*
Valley Pediatric Medical Group
Encino, California
Attending Pediatrician at
Cedars Sinai Medical Center,
Los Angeles, California, and
Children's Hospital of Los Angeles

Becoming the Baby Whisperer

> The best way to make children
> good is to make them happy.
> —Oscar Wilde

Learning the Language

Let me tell you straightaway, luv: *I* didn't dub myself "the baby whisperer." One of my clients did. It's a lot better than some of the other affectionate names parents have come up with—names like "the witch," which is a bit too scary, "the magician," which is too mysterious, or "the Hogg," in which case I fear they have my appetite in mind as well as my last name. So, the baby whisperer I have become. I have to admit, I kind of like it, because it does describe what I do.

Perhaps you already know what a "horse whisperer" does, or possibly you've read the book or seen the movie of the same name. If so, you might remember how Robert Redford's character dealt with the wounded horse, advancing toward it slowly and patiently, listening and observing, but respectfully keeping his distance as he pondered the poor beast's problem. Taking his time, he finally approached the horse, looked it straight in the eye, and talked softly. The entire time, the horse whisperer stayed steady as a rock and maintained his own sense of serenity, which, in turn, encouraged the horse to calm down.

Don't get me wrong, I'm not comparing newborns to horses (although both are sensate animals), but it's pretty much the same with me and babies. Despite the fact that parents think I have some special gift, there's really nothing mysterious about what I do, nor is it a talent that only certain people possess. Baby whispering is a matter of respecting, listening, observing, and interpreting. You can't learn it overnight—I've watched and whispered to over five thousand babies. But any parent can learn; every parent should learn. I understand infants' language, and I can teach you the skills you'll need to master it, too.

How I Learned My Craft

You could say I've spent my life preparing for this job. I grew up in Yorkshire (and make the world's best pudding, by the way). My greatest influence was Nan, my mum's mum—she's eighty-six today and still the most patient, gentle, and loving woman I've ever met. She, too, was a baby whisperer, able to cuddle and calm the crankiest infant. She not only guided me and reassured me when my own daughters (the other two greatest influences in my life) were born, but also was a significant figure in my childhood.

Growing up, I was a jiggling, jumpy little thing, a tomboy who was anything but patient, but Nan could always manage my high energy with a game or a story. For example, we would be waiting on a queue at the cinema, and I, a typical little kid, would be whining and pulling at her sleeve. "How long till they let us in, Nan? I can't wait anymore."

Now, my other grandmum, whom I called Granny—she's no longer living—might have given me a good swat for such insolence. Granny was a true Victorian, believing children should be seen and not heard. In her day, she ruled with an iron hand. But my mum's mum, Nan, never had to be stern. In response to my grousing, she'd just glance at me with a twinkle in her eye and say, "Look what you're missin' by moanin' and just payin' attention to yourself." And with that, she'd fix her gaze in a particular direction. "See that mum and baby over there?" she'd say, pointing with her chin. "Where do you think they're goin' today?"

"They're goin' to France," I'd say, immediately catching on.

"How do you think they're goin' to get there?"

"A jumbo jet." I must have heard the phrase somewhere.

"Where will they sit?" Nan would continue, and before I knew it, not only had our little game taken my mind off the waiting, but we had woven a whole story about that woman. My Nan constantly challenged my imagination. She'd notice a wedding dress in a store window and ask, "How many people do you think it took to get the dress there?" If I said, "Two," she'd keep on pressing me for more details: How did they get the dress to the shop? Where was it made? Who sewed on the pearls? By the time she was through with me, I was in India, picturing the farmer who planted the seeds that eventually turned into the cotton used in that dress.

In fact, storytelling was an important tradition in my family, not just with my Nan, but for her sister, their mum (my great-grandmum), and my own mum. Whenever one of them wanted to make a point with us, there was always a tale to go with it. They passed on that gift to me, and in my work with parents today, I often use stories and metaphors: "Would *you* be able to fall asleep if I put your bed on the freeway?" I might say to a parent whose overstimulated baby is having trouble settling down for a nap with the stereo blaring. Such images help parents understand why I make a particular suggestion, rather than my simply saying, "Do it this way."

If the women in my family helped me develop my gifts, it was Granddad, Nan's husband, who saw how I might apply them. Granddad was the head nurse in what they then called a lunatic asylum. I remember one Christmas when he took my mum and me to visit the children's ward. It was a dingy place, with weird sounds and smells and, to my young eyes, disjointed-looking children sitting in wheelchairs and lying on pillows that were scattered about the floor. I couldn't have been any more than seven, but I still have this vivid image of the look on my mum's face, tears of horror and pity streaming down her cheeks.

I, on the other hand, was fascinated. I knew most people were afraid of the patients and would just as soon never set foot near the place, but not I. I repeatedly begged Granddad to take me back, and one day, after many subsequent visits, he took me aside and said, "You should think about doing this kind of nursing yourself, Tracy. You've got a big heart and a lot of patience, just like your Nan."

That was just about the greatest compliment anyone had ever given me, and, as it turned out, Granddad was right. When I was eighteen, I went to nursing school, which in England is a five-and-a-half-year course. I didn't graduate at the top of the class—I admit, I was a last-minute crammer—but I really excelled in patient intervention. We call it "the practicals," which in my country is a very important part of the coursework. I was so good at listening, observing, and displaying empathy that the Nursing School Board gave me the Nurse of the Year award, bestowed annually to the students who demonstrated outstanding patient care.

And so I became a registered nurse and midwife in England, specializing in children with physical and mental disabilities—children who often had no means of communication. Well, that's not quite true; like babies, they had their own way of conversing—a sort of nonverbal communication expressed through their cries and body language. To help them, I had to learn to understand their language and to become their interpreter.

Cries and Whispers

Caring for newborns, many of whom I brought into the world, I came to realize that I could comprehend their nonverbal language, too. So when I came here from England, I specialized in infant care, becoming a newborn and postpartum care giver, which you Yanks refer to as a baby nurse. I worked for couples in New York and Los Angeles, most of whom described me as a cross between Mary Poppins and the Daphne character on *Frasier*—apparently her accent, at least to American ears, sounds just like my Yorkshire burr. I showed these new mums and dads that they, too, could whisper to their babies: learn to hold back a bit and read their little ones and, once they knew what the problem was, calm them.

I shared with these mums and dads what I believe all parents should do for their babies: give them a sense of structure and help them become independent little beings. I also began to promote what I've come to call a whole-family approach—little ones need to become part of the family rather than the other way round. If the rest of the family—parents, siblings, even pets—is happy, then the baby will be content, too.

I feel very privileged when I'm invited into someone's home, because I know this is the most treasured time in parents' lives. It's a time when, along with the inevitable insecurities and the sleepless nights, mothers and fathers experience the greatest joy of their lives. As I watch their drama unfold and am called upon for help, I feel that I add to that joy because I help them step out of the chaos and relish the experience.

Nowadays, I sometimes live in with families, but more often I work as a consultant, dropping by for an hour or two over the first few days or weeks after the baby arrives. I meet lots of mothers and fathers in their thirties and forties, who are used to being in control of their lives. When they become parents and are put in the uncomfortable position of being beginners, they sometimes wonder, "What have we done?" You see, whether a parent has a million pounds in the bank or two shillings in her purse, a newborn, especially a first baby, is the great equalizer. I've been with mums and dads from all walks of life, from people who are household names to those whose names are known only in their own neighborhood. And let me assure you, luv, having a baby brings out fear in the best of them.

Most times, in fact, my beeper goes off all day long (and sometimes in the middle of the night) with desperate calls such as these:

"Tracy, how come Chrissie seems hungry all the time?"

"Tracy, why does Jason smile at me one minute and burst out crying the next?"

"Tracy, I don't know what to do. Joey's been up all night, crying his head off."

"Tracy, I think Rick is carrying the baby around too much. Would you tell him to stop?"

Believe it or not, after twenty-odd years of working with families, I can often diagnose problems over the phone, especially if I've already met the baby. Sometimes, I ask the mum to put the baby near the phone, so I can hear her crying.* (The mum is often crying, too.) Or I might pop in for a quick visit, and, if necessary, stay the night to observe what else is going on in the household that might be upsetting the baby or disrupting her routine. So far, I haven't found a baby I don't understand nor a problem I can't make better.

Respect: The Key to Unlocking a Baby's World

My clients often say, "Tracy, you make it all look so easy." The truth is, for me it *is* easy, because I connect with infants. I treat them as I would any human being: with respect. That, my friends, is the essence of the whispering I do.

Every baby is a person who has language, feelings, and a unique personality—and, therefore, deserves respect.

Respect is a theme you'll hear throughout this book. If you remember to think of your baby as *a person*, you'll always give her the respect she deserves. The dictionary definition of the verb is "to avoid violation or interference with." How violated do *you* feel when someone speaks over or at you instead of *with* you, or

---

*Throughout this book, when I talk about a baby, the pronouns *he* and *she* are alternated to give a balanced representation of gender.

touches you without your consent? When things are not explained correctly or when someone treats you with disregard, how angry or hurt do you feel?

It's the same for a baby. People tend to speak over babies' heads, sometimes acting as if the infant is not even there. I often hear parents or nannies say, "The baby did this" or "The baby did that." That's so impersonal and disrespectful; it's as if they're talking about an inanimate object. Even worse, they tug and pull at the sweet darling without a word of explanation, as if it's an adult's right to violate an infant's space. That's why I suggest drawing an imaginary boundary around your baby—*a circle of respect,* beyond which you cannot go without asking permission or telling your baby what you're about to do (more about this in Chapter 5, pages 151–154).

Even in the delivery room, I immediately call babies by their rightful names. I don't think of that little being in the crib as "the baby." Why not refer to an infant *by her proper name?* When you do, you tend to think of her as the tiny person she is, not a helpless blob.

Indeed, whenever I initially meet a newborn, whether at the hospital, a few hours after he gets home, or weeks later, I always introduce myself and explain why I'm here. "Hi, Sammy," I say, looking into his big blue eyes. "I'm Tracy. I know you don't recognize my voice, because you don't know me yet. But I'm here to get to know you and to find out what you want. And I'm going to help your mummy and daddy understand what you're saying."

Sometimes a mum will say to me, "Why are you talking to him like that? He's only three days old. He can't possibly understand you."

"Well," I say, "we don't know that for sure, do we, luv? Imagine how terrible it would be if he *does* understand me and I *don't* talk to him."

In the last decade especially, scientists have found out that newborns know more and understand more than we ever dreamed they did. Research confirms that babies are sensitive to sounds and smells and can tell the difference between one type of visual input and another. And their memories start to develop within the first few weeks of life. Therefore, even if little Sammy doesn't quite understand my words, he can surely *feel* the difference between someone who moves slowly and has a reassuring voice and someone who just breezes in and takes over. And if he does understand, he will know that right from the beginning, I'm treating him with respect.

Whispering Isn't Just Talking

The secret of baby whispering involves remembering that your infant is always listening and, on some level, understands you. Now, virtually every book about child care tells parents, "Talk to your babies." That's not enough. I tell parents, "Talk *with* your baby." Your baby may not actually *talk* back, but he communicates by cooing, crying, and making gestures (more about decoding baby language in Chapter 3). Thus, you're really having a *dialogue*, a two-way conversation.

Talking *with* your baby is another way of showing respect. Wouldn't you converse with an adult you were caring for? When you first approached him, you would introduce yourself and explain what you were there to do. You'd be polite, peppering your conversation with "Please" and "Thank you" and "May I." And you'd probably keep talking and explaining. Why not give the same consideration to your baby?

It's also respectful to find out your baby's likes and

dislikes. As you will learn in Chapter 1, some babies easily go with the flow, and others are more sensitive or contrary. Some also develop at a slower pace. To be truly respectful, we must accept our babies *as they are,* rather than compare them to a norm. (That's why you won't find any month-to-month descriptions in this book.) Your baby has a right to *his unique reactions* to the world around him. And the sooner you begin to have a dialogue with this precious being, the sooner you will understand who he is and what he wants from you.

I'm sure all parents want to encourage their children to become independent, balanced human beings whom they will respect and admire. But this starts in infancy; it's not something you begin teaching when a child is fifteen, or even five. Remember, too, that parenting is a lifelong process and that, as a parent, you are a role model. By listening, and giving your baby respect, she will in turn grow up to be a person who listens and gives respect to others.

If you take the time to observe your baby and to learn what she's trying to say to you, you're going to have a baby who's content and a family that isn't dominated by a distressed baby.

Babies whose parents do the best they can to acknowledge and attend to their needs are secure babies. They don't cry when they're put down, because they feel safe on their own. They trust that their environment is a safe place—if they're troubled or in pain, someone will be there for them. Paradoxically, such babies ultimately need *less* attention and learn to play on their own more quickly than infants who are left to cry or whose parents consistently misread their cues. (By the way, it's normal to miss a *few* cues.)

What Parents Need: Self-Confidence

It gives parents a sense of security to feel they know what they're doing. Sadly, the pace of modern living works against mums and dads, who often get caught up in their own hectic schedules. They don't realize they have to slow *themselves* down before trying to calm their baby. Part of my job, then, is getting Mum and Dad to slow down, tune in to their baby, and—just as important—listen to their own inner voice.

Regretfully, many parents today are victims of information overload. When they're expecting, they read magazines and books, do research, scour the Internet, listen to friends and family and specialists of all sorts. These are all valuable resources, but by the time the baby comes along, new parents are often more confused than when they started. Worse still, their own common sense has been drowned out by other people's ideas.

Granted, information is empowering—and in this book I intend to share with you all the tricks of my trade. But of all the tools I can give you, your own self-confidence about parenting will serve you best. To develop it, though, you have to figure out what works for you. Every baby is an individual, and so is every mum and dad. Hence every family's needs are different. What good would it do for me to tell you what I did with my own daughters?

The more you begin to see that you *can* understand and meet your baby's needs, the better you become at it. And I assure you, it *will* get easier. Every day I spend teaching parents how to be aware and how to communicate, not only do I see the baby's understanding and abilities grow, but I also see the parents themselves become more proficient and more confident.

What Makes a Good Parent?

In one of the infant-care books I skimmed, I read, "In order to be a good mother, you have to breastfeed." Rubbish! Parenting shouldn't be judged by how you feed or diaper your child or how you put your baby to sleep. Besides, we don't become good parents in the first weeks of a baby's life. Good parenting develops over years, as your children grow and you get to know them as individuals, which later encourages them to come to you for advice and support. However, the foundation of good parenting begins when you

- Are **respectful** of your baby
- Know your baby as a **unique individual**
- **Talk with**, not at, your baby
- **Listen** and, when asked, meet your baby's needs
- Let your baby know what's coming next by providing a daily dose of **dependability**, **structure**, and **predictability**

You *Can* Learn This from a Book!

Baby whispering *can* be learned. Indeed, most parents are amazed at how quickly they start to understand their babies *once they know what to look and listen for.* The real "magic" I perform is the reassurance I give new mums and dads. All new parents need a supportive figure, and that's where I come in. Most simply aren't prepared for the adjustment period, when there seem to be a million and one questions and no one around to answer them. I sort out their concerns. And I tell them, "Let's start with a plan." I show them how to implement a structured routine, and then I show them everything else I know.

On a day-to-day basis, parenting is a tough, sometimes scary, constantly demanding, and often unrewarding job. I hope this book will help you to have a sense of humor about it all and, at the same time, give you a realistic portrayal of what you're in for. Here's what you can expect from this book:

• An understanding of what kind of baby you have and what you can expect from her temperament. In Chapter 1, you'll find a checklist to help you see what particular challenges you might encounter.

• An understanding of your own temperament and adaptability. Life changes when Baby arrives, and it's important to find out where you stand on what I call the Wing It/Plan It continuum (Chapter 2)—whether you're someone who normally flies by the seat of your pants or someone who likes to plan things down to the most minute detail.

• An explanation of my E.A.S.Y. plan, which helps give structure and routine to your day in this order: Eat, Activity, Sleep, Your time. E.A.S.Y. enables you to tend to your baby's needs *and* rejuvenate your mind and body, whether by taking a nap, a hot bath, or a jaunt round the block. You'll find an overview of E.A.S.Y. in Chapter 2, and detailed discussions about what each of the letters stand for in Chapters 4 through 7—4 is about eating; 5 about activities, 6 is about sleep issues, and 7 about what you can do to keep yourself physically *and* emotionally healthy and strong.

• Skills that will help you whisper to your baby— observe and understand what she's trying to tell you, calm her when she's upset (Chapter 3). I'll help you hone your own powers of observation and self-reflection as well.

• The special circumstances that accompany unusual conceptions and deliveries, and the parenting issues that arise: when one adopts or uses a surrogate mother; when babies arrive early, have problems at birth, and/or can't come home from the hospital right away; the joys and challenges of multiple births (Chapter 8).

• My Three-Day Magic (Chapter 9), a troubleshooting technique that can help you change bad patterns into beneficial ones. I will explain what I call "accidental parenting," in which parents unwittingly reinforce negative behavior in infants, and teach you my simple ABC strategy for analyzing what went wrong.

I've tried to make this book fun to read, because I know that parents tend to use books about infants on an as-needed basis rather than plodding through them cover to cover. If they want to know about breastfeeding, they'll look in the index and read those pages only. If they're having sleep problems, they'll turn to the chapter on sleep. Given the demands of most parents' daily lives, I can understand that approach. However, in this case I urge you to read at least the first three chapters, which lay out my basic philosophy and approach. That way, even if you just read portions at a time of the remaining chapters of the book, you will understand my ideas and advice in the context of the larger issue of always treating your baby with the respect she deserves and, at the same time, not allowing her to take over your household.

Having a baby is by far the most life-changing event you'll ever experience—bigger than marriage or a new job or even the death of a loved one. Just the thought of having to adapt to a very different kind of life is scary. It's also very isolating. New parents often think they're the only ones who feel incompetent or have problems with breastfeeding. Women are sure that other mothers are instantly "in love" with their babies, and they wonder why they don't feel that way. Men are sure other fathers are more attentive. Unlike England, where a home health aide nips over every day during the first fortnight and several times a week for the next two months, many new parents in America don't have anyone around to guide them through the early days.

Dear reader, I can't come into your living room, but I hope you'll hear my voice in this book and let me be a reassuring guide, doing for you what my Nan did for me when I was a young mother. You need to know that the sleep deprivation and your sense of being overwhelmed won't last forever and that, in the meantime, you're doing the best you can. You need to hear that this happens to other parents, too, and that you'll get through it.

I hope that the philosophy and skills I share with you—my secrets—will wend their way into your head and heart. You might not have a smarter baby in the end (then again, you might), but you surely will have a happier, more confident one—without giving up your own life in the bargain. Perhaps most important, you'll feel better about your own parenting abilities. For I truly believe—and have seen firsthand—that inside every new mum and dad lies a caring, confident, and competent parent—a baby whisperer in the making.

CHAPTER ONE
Loving the Baby You Gave Birth To

> I just can't get over how much
> babies cry. I really had no idea what
> I was getting into. To tell you the
> truth, I thought it would be more
> like getting a cat.
>
> —Anne Lamott in
> *Operating Instructions*

Oh My God, We Have a *Baby*!

No event in an adult's life equals both the joy *and* the terror of becoming a parent for the first time. Fortunately, it's the joy that carries on. But in the beginning, insecurity and fear often take over. Alan, for example, a thirty-three-year-old graphic designer, vividly remembers the day he picked up his wife, Susan, from the hospital. Coincidentally, it was their fourth anniversary. Susan, a writer, age twenty-seven, had had a fairly easy labor and birth, and their beautiful blue-eyed baby, Aaron, nursed easily and rarely cried. By day two, Mum and Dad were eager to leave the hubbub of the hospital to start life as a family.

"I whistled as I walked down the hall toward her room," Alan recalls. "Everything seemed perfect. Aaron had nursed right before I got there, and now he was sleeping in Susan's arms. It was just as I imagined it would be. We went down in the elevator, and the nurse let me wheel Susan out into the sunlight. When I ran for the car door, I realized I'd forgotten to set up the infant seat. I swear it took me half an hour to get it in right. Finally, I gently slid Aaron in. He was such an angel. I helped Susan into the car, thanked the nurse for her patience, and then climbed into the driver's seat.

"Suddenly, Aaron started making little noises from the backseat—not really crying, but sounds I didn't recall hearing in the hospital or maybe hadn't noticed. Susan looked at me, and I looked at her. 'Oh, Jesus!' I exclaimed. 'What do we do *now?*' "

Every parent I know has a what-now moment like Alan's. For some it comes in the hospital; for others it arrives on the trip home, or even on the second or third day. There's so much going on—the physical recovery, the emotional impact, the reality of caring for a helpless infant. Few are prepared for the shock. Some new mothers admit, "I read all the books, but nothing prepared me." Others recall, "There was so much to think about. I cried a lot."

The first three to five days are often the most difficult because everything is new and daunting. Typically, I'm bombarded by queries from anxious parents: "How long should a feeding take?" "Why does she pull her legs up like that?" "Is this the right way to change him?" "Why is her poop that color?" And, of course, the most persistent question of all time: "Why is he crying?" Parents, particularly mums, often feel guilty because they think they're *supposed* to know everything. The mother of a one-month-old said to me, "I was so afraid I'd do something wrong, but at the same time, I didn't want anyone to help me or tell me what to do."

The first thing I tell parents—and keep telling them—is to slooooooow down. It takes time to get to know your baby. It takes patience and a calm environment. It takes strength and stamina. It takes respect and kindness. It takes responsibility and discipline. It takes attention and keen observation. It takes time and practice—a lot of doing it wrong before you get it right. And it takes listening to your own intuition.

Notice how often I repeat "it takes." In the beginning, there's a lot of "take" and very little "give" on your baby's part. The rewards and joys of parenting will be endless, I promise. But they won't happen in a day, darlings; rather, you'll see them over months and years. What's more, everyone's experience is different. As a mother in one of my groups, looking back on her first few days home, observed, "I didn't know if I was doing things right—and, besides, everyone defines 'right' differently."

Also, every *baby* is different, which is why I tell my mums that their first job is to understand the baby they have, not the one they dreamed about during the past nine months. In this chapter, I'll help you figure out what you can expect from *your* baby. But first, a quick primer on your first few days at home.

Coming Home

Because I see myself as an advocate for *the whole family,* not just the new baby, part of my job is to help parents gain perspective. I tell mums and dads right from the start: This won't last forever. You *will* calm down. You *will* become more confident. You *will* be the best parent you can be. And at some point, believe it or not, your baby *will* sleep through the night. For now, though, you must lower your expectations. You'll have good days and not-so-good days; be prepared for both. Don't strive for perfection.

Homecoming Checklist

One of the reasons my babies do well is that everything is ready for them a month *before* the due date. The more prepared you are and the quieter it is in the beginning, the more time you'll have to observe your baby and to get to know him as the individual he is.

✓ Put sheets on the crib or bassinet.

✓ Set up the changing table. Have everything you need—wipes, diapers, cotton swabs, alcohol—in easy reach.

✓ Have baby's first wardrobe ready. Take everything out of the packages, remove any tags, and wash in a mild detergent that has no bleach.

✓ Stock your refrigerator and freezer. A week or two before you're due, make a lasagna, a shepherd's pie, soups, and other dishes that freeze well. Make sure you have all the staples on hand—milk, butter, eggs, cereal, pet food. You'll eat better and cheaper and avoid frantic trips to the store.

✓ Don't take too much to the hospital. Remember, you'll have several extra bags—*and* the baby—to bring home.

> **TIP:** *The more organized you are before you come home, the happier everyone will be afterward. And if you loosen the tops of bottles and tubes, open boxes, and take all new items out of their packages, you won't have to fiddle with such things with your new baby in hand! (See "Homecoming Checklist" above.)*

I usually need to remind mothers, "It's your first day home—the first you're away from the security of the hospital, where you get help, answers, and relief at the push of a button. Now you're on your own." Of course, a mother is often happy to leave the hospital. The nurses may have been brusque or given her conflicting advice. And the frequent interruptions from hospital personnel and visitors probably made it impossible for her to rest. In any case, by the time most mums come home, they are usually either scared, confused, exhausted, or in pain—or maybe all of the above.

Therefore I advise a slow reentry. When you walk

through the door, take a deep, centering breath. Keep it simple. (You'll be hearing that a lot from me.) Think of this as the beginning of a new adventure, and you and your partner as explorers. And by all means, be realistic: The postpartum period *is* difficult—a rocky terrain. All but a rare few stumble along the way. (More about Mum recuperating during the postpartum period in Chapter 7.)

Believe me, I know that the moment you get home, you'll probably feel overwhelmed. But if you follow my simple homecoming ritual, you're less likely to feel frantic. (Remember, though, this is just a quick orientation. Later on, as indicated, I go into greater detail.)

Start the dialogue by giving your baby a tour of the house. That's right, luv, a tour, as if you're the curator of a museum and she's a distinguished visitor. Remember what I told you about respect: You need to treat your little darling like a human being, as someone who can understand and feel. Granted, she speaks a language you may not yet understand, but it's nevertheless important to call her by name and to make every interaction *a dialogue,* not a lecture.

So walk around with her in your arms and show her where she's going to live. Talk *with* her. In a soft, gentle voice, explain each room: "Here's the kitchen. It's where Dad and I cook. This is the bathroom, where we take showers." And so on. You might feel silly. Many new parents are shy when they first start to have a dialogue with their baby. That's okay. Practice, and you'll be amazed at how easy it becomes. Just try to remember that this is a little *human being* in your arms, a person whose senses are alive, a tiny being who already knows your voice and even what you smell like.

While you're walking around, have Dad or Grandma make chamomile tea or another calming beverage. Tea, naturally, is *my* favorite. Where I come from, the moment a mum gets home, Nelly from next door nips over and puts on a kettle. It's a very English, very civilized tradition, which I've introduced to all my families here. After a nice cuppa, as we call it, you'll want to really explore this glorious creature you've given birth to.

Limit Visitors

Convince all but a few very close relatives and friends to stay away for the first few days. If parents are in from out of town, the greatest thing they can do for you is cook, clean, and run errands. Let them know in a kind way that you'll ask for their help with the baby *if* you need it, but that you'd like to use this time to get to know your little one on your own.

Give your baby a sponge bath and a feed. (Information and advice about feeding is in Chapter 4, sponge bathing on page 177.) Keep in mind that you're not the only one in shock. Your baby has had quite a journey himself. Imagine, if you will, a tiny human being coming into the bright light of a delivery room. Suddenly, with great speed and force, that little body is rubbed, poked, and pricked by strangers whose voices are unfamiliar. After a few days in a nursery, surrounded by other tiny beings, he then has to travel from the hospital to home. If you adopted him, the trip was probably even longer.

> **TIP:** *Hospital nurseries are kept quite warm, almost womblike, so make sure the temperature in the baby's new "woom" is around 72 degrees.*

This is a perfect opportunity for you to pore over your miracle of nature. It may be the first time you see your baby naked. Get acquainted with his bits and pieces. Explore each tiny finger and toe. Keep talking with him. Bond with him. Nurse him or give him a bottle. Watch him as he gets sleepy. Start him off right, and allow him to fall asleep in his own crib or bassinet. (I have lots of sleeping tips in Chapter 6.)

Take Small Bites

You've got a lot on your plate; don't heap on any additional pressures. Rather than being angry at yourself because you haven't gotten the announcements addressed or sent thank-you notes, give yourself a manageable daily goal—say, five instead of forty a day. Prioritize your tasks by creating piles marked "urgent," "do later," and "can wait till I feel better." If you're calm and honest when you assess each chore, you'll be surprised at how much goes in that last pile.

"But her eyes are open," protested Gail, a hairdresser whose two-day-old daughter seemed to be staring contentedly at a photo of a baby propped up on the crib bumpers. I had suggested that Gail leave the room and get some rest herself, but Gail said, "She's not asleep yet." I've heard the same protest from many new mums. But I'm going to tell you straightaway that your baby doesn't have to be asleep for you to put her down and walk away from the crib. "Look," I said to her, "Lily's hanging out with her boyfriend. Now *you* go lie down."

Take a nap. Don't unpack the bags, don't make phone calls, and don't look around the house and think of all the things you've got to get done. You're exhausted. When the baby sleeps, luv, take advantage of it. In fact, you've got one of the great miracles of nature on your side. Babies take a few days to recuperate from the shock of birth. It's not unusual for a one- or two-day-old newborn to sleep for six hours at a stretch, which gives you a little time to recuperate from your own trauma. Beware, though: If your baby seems good as gold, this may be the calm before the storm! He may have absorbed drugs from your system or at the very least is probably tired from squeezing his way through the birth canal, even if you had natural childbirth. He's not quite himself yet, but, as you will read in the pages that follow, his real temperament will soon emerge.

A Word About Pets

Animals can get jealous of new babies—after all, it's like bringing another child home.

DOGS: You can't actually talk to your dog to prepare it, but you can bring home a blanket or diaper from the hospital to get it used to the baby's smell. When you come home from the hospital, have Rover meet the new arrival *outside* the house, *before* you go in. Dogs are very territorial and likely not to welcome a stranger. It helps if they've gotten used to the baby's smell. All the same, I advise parents *never* to leave a baby alone with any pet.

CATS: It's an old wives' tale that cats like to lie on babies' faces, but cats *are* attracted to that little lump of warmth. Keeping it out of the nursery is the best way to prevent your cat from jumping into the crib and curling up with your baby. Your baby's lungs are very tender. Cat hair as well as fine dog hair, such as that on a Jack Russell, can cause an allergic reaction, and even bring on asthma.

Who Is *Your* Baby?

"He was such an angel in the hospital," Lisa protested on Robbie's third day. "Why does he cry so much now?" If I had a quid for every new mum or dad who uttered those words, I'd be a rich woman. This is the moment when I have to remind Mum that the baby she thought she knew rarely acts like the same baby once he's home.

The truth is, all babies—just like all people—differ in the way they eat, sleep, and respond to stimulation, and in the ways that they can be soothed. Call it temperament, personality, disposition, nature—it starts to emerge somewhere around day three to day five, and it indicates the type of person your baby is and will be.

I know this from firsthand experience, because I stay in touch with many of "my" babies. As I watch them grow into children and teenagers, I invariably see kernels of their infant selves in the way they greet people, how they handle new situations, even the way they interact with their parents and peers.

Nature or Nurture

Harvard researcher Jerome Kagan, who studies temperament in babies and young children, notes that, like most twentieth-century scientists, he was trained to believe that social environment could override biology. However, his research over the last two decades tells a different story:

"I confess to an occasional sadness," he writes in *Galen's Prophecy* (after the second-century physician who first categorized temperament), "over the recognition that some healthy, attractive infants born to affectionate, economically secure families begin life with a physiology that will make it a bit difficult for them to be as relaxed, spontaneous, and capable of hearty laughter as they would like. Some of these children will have to fight a natural urge to be dour and to worry about tomorrow's tasks."

Davy, a scrawny, red-faced infant who surprised his mum and dad by arriving two weeks early, needed shelter from noise and light and quite a bit of extra cuddling to feel safe. Now a toddler, he is still a bit shy.

Anna, a bright-faced little girl who slept through the night at eleven days, was such an easy baby that her mum, a single mother who had conceived her through donor insemination, told me she didn't need me after the first week. At age twelve, Anna still welcomes the world with open arms.

Then there are the twins, two boys who couldn't have been more different from each other—Sean easily took his mother's breast and smiled on cue, while Kevin had trouble breastfeeding for the first month and seemed to be perpetually angry at the world. I lost touch with that family when Dad, an oil executive, was transferred overseas, but I'd wager that Sean still has a sunnier disposition than Kevin.

My clinical observations aside, many psychologists have documented the consistency of temperament and have come up with ways to describe various types. Jerome Kagan of Harvard (see sidebar on page 25) and other psychological researchers have documented that, in fact, some infants *are* more sensitive than others, some more difficult, some grumpier, some sweeter, some more predictable. Such aspects of temperament affect how a baby perceives and manipulates her environment and, perhaps most important for new parents to understand, what comforts her. The trick is to see your baby clearly and to get to know and accept her for who she is.

Let me assure you, luv, temperament is an *influence*, not a life sentence. No one is saying your handful of a baby will still be spitting milk at you when he grows up, or that your seemingly fragile little one will be a wallflower at her first dance. We dare not nullify nature—brain chemistry and anatomy do matter—but *nurture* still plays a vital role in development. Still, to fully support and nourish your baby, you need to understand the package he has brought with him into the world.

In my experience, I've found that infants generally fit into one of five broad temperamental types, which I call

Angel, Textbook, Touchy, Spirited, and *Grumpy.* I describe each below. To help you look at your baby, I've made up a twenty-item multiple-choice test that applies to healthy babies from five days old to eight months. Bear in mind that during the first two weeks, there may be apparent changes in temperament that are actually quite temporary. For example, circumcision (often done on the eighth day) or any type of birth abnormality such as jaundice, which makes babies sleepy, may obscure a baby's true nature.

I suggest that both you *and* your partner answer the questions . . . separately. If you're a single mum or dad, enlist the cooperation of your own parent, a sibling or other relative, a good friend, a child-care worker—in short, anyone who has spent time around your baby.

Why have *two* people fill it out? First of all, especially if it's you and your spouse, I guarantee that each of you has a different view. After all, no two people see *anything* exactly the same way.

Second, babies do act differently with different people. That's simply a fact of life.

Third, we tend to project ourselves onto our babies, and we sometimes identify quite strongly with their temperament—and see only what we want to see. Without realizing it, you may be overly focused on, or blind to, certain traits in your baby. For example, if you were shy and maybe even teased as a child, you might make too much of the fact that your baby cries in the presence of strangers. It is a bit painful to imagine that your child will have to endure the same social anxiety and taunts you did, isn't it? Yes, ducky, we do project *that* far in advance when it comes to our babies. And we identify. The first time a wee lad picks up his head by himself, Dad's likely to say, "Look at my little football player." And if the boy is easily quieted by music, Mum, who's been playing the piano since she was five, is bound to say, "I can already see that he has my good ear!"

Please, please don't argue about your answers if they're different. This isn't a contest to see who's smarter or who knows the baby better. It's meant as a way for you to understand this little human being who has come into your lives. After you score your answers according to the directions below, you'll see which description best fits your baby. Naturally, some babies display a bit of this and a bit of that. The idea here is not to typecast your baby—that's just so bloody impersonal—but rather to help you cue in to some of the things I look for in a baby, such as crying patterns, reactions, sleep patterns, and disposition, all of which ultimately help me determine what that baby needs.

The Know-Your-Baby Quiz

For each of the following questions, pick the *best* answer—in other words, the statement that describes your child *most of the time*.

1. My baby
   A. rarely cries
   B. cries only when she's hungry, tired, or overstimulated
   C. cries for no apparent reason
   D. cries very loudly, and if I don't attend to it, she quickly gets into a rage cry
   E. cries a lot of the time

2. When it's time for him to go to sleep, my baby
   A. lies peacefully in his crib and drifts off to sleep
   B. generally falls asleep easily within twenty minutes
   C. fusses a bit and seems to be drifting off, but then he keeps waking up
   D. is very restless and often needs to be swaddled or held
   E. cries a lot and seems to resent being put down

3. When she wakes up in the morning, my baby
   A. rarely cries—she plays in her crib until I come in
   B. coos and looks around
   C. needs immediate attention or she starts crying
   D. screams
   E. whimpers

4. My baby smiles
   A. at everything and everybody
   B. when prompted
   C. when prompted but sometimes starts to cry within minutes of smiling
   D. a lot and is also very vocal, tending to make very loud baby noises
   E. only under the right circumstances

5. When I take my baby on any kind of outing, he
   A. is extremely portable
   B. is okay as long as where I take him isn't too busy or unfamiliar
   C. fusses a great deal
   D. is very demanding of my attention
   E. doesn't like to be handled a lot

6. When confronted by a friendly stranger cooing at her, my baby
   A. immediately smiles
   B. takes a moment and then usually smiles fairly quickly
   C. is likely to cry at first, unless the stranger can win her over
   D. gets very excited
   E. hardly ever smiles

7. When there's a loud noise, like a dog barking or a slamming door, my baby
   A. is never rattled
   B. notices it but isn't bothered
   C. flinches visibly and often starts to cry
   D. gets loud himself
   E. starts to cry

8. When I first gave my baby a bath
   A. she took to the water like a duck
   B. she was a little surprised at the sensation, but liked it almost immediately
   C. she was very sensitive—she shook a little and seemed afraid
   D. she was wild—flailing about and splashing
   E. she hated it and cried

9. My baby's body language is typically
   A. relaxed and alert almost always
   B. relaxed most of the time
   C. tense and very reactive to external stimuli
   D. jerky—his arms and legs are often flailing all over the place
   E. rigid—arms and legs are often fairly stiff

10. My baby makes loud, aggressive noises
    A. once in a while
    B. only when she's playing and is highly stimulated
    C. hardly ever
    D. often
    E. when she's angry

11. When I change my baby's diaper, bathe him, or dress him
    A. he always takes it in stride
    B. he is okay if I do it slowly and let him know what I'm doing
    C. is often cranky, as if he can't stand being naked
    D. wriggles a lot and tries to pull everything off the changing table
    E. he hates it—dressing is always a battle

12. If I suddenly bring my baby into bright light, like sunlight or fluorescent light, she
    A. takes it in stride
    B. can sometimes act startled
    C. blinks excessively or tries to turn her head away from the light
    D. becomes overstimulated
    E. acts annoyed

13a. If you bottle-feed: When I feed my baby, she
- A. always sucks properly, pays attention, and usually eats within twenty minutes
- B. is a little erratic during growth spurts but generally a good eater
- C. is very squirmy and takes a long time to finish the bottle
- D. grabs at the bottle aggressively and tends to overeat
- E. is often cranky and feedings take a long time

13b. If you breastfeed: When I feed my baby, he
- A. latches on immediately—it was a snap right from day one
- B. took a day or two to latch on properly, but now we do fine
- C. always wants to suckle but goes on and off the breast, as if he's forgotten how to nurse
- D. eats well as long as I hold him the way he wants me to
- E. gets very annoyed and restless, as if I don't have enough milk for him

14. The comment that best describes the communication between my baby and me is
- A. she always lets me know exactly what she needs
- B. most of the time her cues are easy to read
- C. she confuses me; sometimes she even cries at me
- D. she asserts her likes and dislikes very clearly and often loudly
- E. she usually gets my attention with loud, angry crying

15. When we go to a family gathering and lots of people want to hold him, my baby
- A. is very adaptable
- B. is somewhat selective about whom he'll go to
- C. cries easily if too many people hold him
- D. might cry or even try to lurch out of someone's arms if he doesn't feel comfortable
- E. refuses anyone's arms except Mummy's or Daddy's

16. When we come home from any kind of outing, my baby
- A. settles in easily and immediately
- B. takes a few minutes to get acclimated
- C. tends to be very fussy
- D. is often overstimulated and hard to calm down
- E. acts angry and miserable

17. My baby
    A. can amuse herself for long periods by staring at anything, even the slats in the crib
    B. can play on her own for around fifteen minutes
    C. finds it hard to be amused in unfamiliar surroundings
    D. needs a lot of stimulation to be amused
    E. is not easily amused by anything

18. The most noticeable thing about my baby is how
    A. incredibly well-behaved and easy he is
    B. much he is developing precisely on schedule—just like the books said he would
    C. sensitive he is to everything
    D. aggressive he is
    E. grouchy he can be

19. My baby seems to
    A. feel utterly safe in her own bed (crib)
    B. prefer her bed most of the time
    C. feel insecure in her bed
    D. act feisty, like her bed is a prison
    E. resent being put down into her bed

20. A comment that best describes my baby is that
    A. you hardly know there's a baby in the house—he's good as gold
    B. he's easy to handle, easy to predict
    C. he's a very delicate little thing
    D. I fear when he begins crawling, he's going to get into everything
    E. he's an "old soul"—he acts like he's been here before

To score the self-test above, write A, B, C, D, and E on a piece of paper and next to each one, count how many times you've used each letter, which denotes a corresponding type.

A's = Angel baby
B's = Textbook baby
C's = Touchy baby
D's = Spirited baby
E's = Grumpy baby

Zeroing in on Your Baby's Type

When you tally up your letters, chances are that you'll have picked predominantly one or two. As you read the descriptions below, remember that we're talking about a way of being in the world here, not an occasional mood or a type of behavior associated with a difficulty, such as colic, or a particular developmental milestone, like teething. You'll probably recognize your baby in the following thumbnail sketches, or perhaps she's a bit like this, a bit like that. Read all five descriptions. I've exemplified each profile with a baby I've met who fits it almost exactly.

The Angel baby. As you might expect, this is the kind of baby every first-time-pregnant woman imagines herself to have: good as gold. Pauline is such a baby—mellow, eternally smiling, and consistently undemanding. Her cues are easy to read. She's not bothered by new surroundings, and she is extremely portable—in fact, you can schlepp her anywhere. She feeds, plays, and sleeps easily, and usually doesn't cry when she wakes up. You'll find Pauline babbling in her crib most mornings, talking to a stuffed animal or just amusing herself by staring at a stripe on the wall. An Angel baby often can calm herself down, but if she gets a little overtired, perhaps because her cues were misread, all you have to do is snuggle her and tell her, "I can see that you're overtired." Then, turn on a lullaby, make the room nice and dim and quiet, and she will put herself to sleep.

The Textbook baby. This is our predictable baby, and as such, he's fairly easy to handle. Oliver does everything on cue, so there are few surprises with him. He reaches all the milestones right on schedule—sleeps through the night by three months, rolls over by five, sits up by six. He'll have growth spurts like clockwork—periods during which his appetite will suddenly increase because he's putting on extra body weight or making a developmental leap. Even as young as a week, he can play on his own for short periods—fifteen minutes or so—and he'll coo a lot and look around. And he smiles when someone smiles at him. Though Oliver has normal cranky periods, just like the books describe, he's easy to calm. It's not hard to get him to sleep, either.

The Touchy baby. For an ultrasensitive baby like Michael, the world is an endless array of sensory challenges. He flinches at the sound of a motorcycle revving outside his window, the TV blaring, a dog barking in the house next door. He blinks or turns his head away from bright light. He sometimes cries for no apparent reason, even at his mother. At those moments, he's shouting (in his baby language), "I've had enough—I need some peace and quiet." He often gets fussy after a number of people have held him, or after outings. He'll play on his own for a few minutes, but he needs the reassurance that someone he knows well—Mum, Dad, a nanny—is close by. Because this type of baby likes to suck a lot, Mum may misread his cues and think he's hungry when he'd do just as well on a pacifier. He also nurses erratically, sometimes acting as though he's forgotten how. At nap time and at night, Michael often has difficulty falling asleep. Touchy babies like him easily get off schedule, because their systems are so fragile. An extra-long nap, a skipped meal, an unexpected visitor, a trip, a change in formula—any of these things can throw Michael for a loop. To calm the Touchy baby, you have to re-create the womb. Swaddle him tightly, snuggle him into your shoulder, whisper a rhythmic *sh . . . sh . . . sh* sound (like the splashing of fluid in the womb) close to his ear, and pat his back gently, mimicking a heartbeat. (This, by the way, will calm most babies, but it works especially well with a Touchy baby.) When you have a Touchy baby, the quicker you learn his cues and his cries, the simpler life is. These babies love structure and predictability—no hidden surprises, thank you.

The Spirited baby. This is a baby who seems to emerge from the womb knowing what she likes and doesn't like, and she won't hesitate to let you know it. Babies like Karen are very vocal and even seem aggressive at times. She often screams for Mum or Dad when she gets up in the morning. She hates lying in her own pee or poop, and she says "Change me" by boisterously vocalizing her discomfort. Indeed, she babbles a lot and loudly. Her body language tends to be a bit jerky. Karen often needs swaddling to get to sleep, because her flailing arms and legs keep her up and overstimulated. If she starts crying and the cycle is not interrupted, it's like a point of no return, and her crying leads to more crying until she's reached a fever pitch of rage. A spirited baby is likely to grab for her bottle at an early age. She'll also notice other babies before they notice her, and as soon as she's old enough to develop a good, firm grasp, she'll grab their toys as well.

The Grumpy baby. I have a theory that babies like Gavin have been here before—they're old souls, as we call them—and they're not all that happy to be back. I may be wrong, of course, but whatever the reason, I assure you this type of baby is downright mardy, as we say in Yorkshire—he's mad at the world and lets you know it. (My coauthor informs me that the Yiddish equivalent is *farbissiner.*) Gavin whimpers every morning, doesn't

smile much during the day, and fusses his way to sleep
every night. His mum has a lot of trouble keeping baby-
sitters, because they tend to take this little guy's bad
humor personally. He hated baths at first, and every
time anyone tried to change or dress him, he was fidgety
and irritable. His mother had tried to breastfeed him,
but she had a slow letdown (the pace of milk working its
way down and through the nipple), and Gavin was impatient. Even though she switched him to formula, feeding is still difficult because of his cranky disposition. To
calm a Grumpy baby, it usually takes a patient mum or
dad, because these babies get very angry and their cries
are particularly loud and long. The *sh . . . sh . . . sh* has
to be louder than the cry. They hate to be swaddled, and
they certainly let you know it. If a Grumpy baby has
reached a major meltdown, instead of shushing say, "It's
okay, it's okay, it's okay," in a rhythm while gently
swaying front to back.

> **TIP:** *When you rock any type of baby, sway back and
> forward, not side to side or up and down. Before your
> baby was born, she sloshed around front to back inside
> you as you walked, so she's used to, and comforted by,
> that kind of movement.*

Fantasy Versus Reality

I'm sure that you recognized your baby in the above descriptions. Maybe he's a cross between two types. In
either case, this information is meant to guide and en-
lighten you, not to alarm you. Also, it's less important to
figure out a label per se than to know what to expect
and how to deal with your baby's particular temperament.

But wait a minute . . . you say this wasn't the baby you dreamed about? He's harder to soothe? Squirms more? Seems more irritable? Doesn't like to be held? You're confused, even a bit angry. You might even have regrets. You're not alone. During nine months of pregnancy, virtually all parents come to have an image of the baby they're expecting—what she looks like, what kind of child she'll grow into, what kind of person she'll eventually be. This is especially true of older mums and dads who have had trouble conceiving or who have waited until their thirties or forties to start a family. Sarah, thirty-six, who had a Textbook baby, admitted to me when Lizzie was five weeks old, "In the beginning, I only enjoyed around twenty-five percent of my time with her. I really thought I didn't love her as much as I should." Nancy, a lawyer in her late forties who used a surrogate mother to conceive Julian—an Angel baby at that—was nevertheless "stunned to see how difficult it was and how instantly I felt, 'I can't do this.' " She recalls looking down at her four-day-old son, pleading, "Sweetie, please don't kill us!"

The period of adjustment may last the first few days or weeks, or maybe even longer, depending on what life was like before Baby arrived. However long it takes, all parents (I hope) will get to the point where they accept

Love at First Sight?

Eyes meet across the room and you're instantly in love—or at least that's how it happens in Hollywood. But it's not like this for many real couples. It's the same way with mothers and their babies. Some mums are instantly in love, but for many it takes a while. You're exhausted, shocked, and frightened, and perhaps most difficult of all, you *want* it to be perfect. It rarely is. So don't get down on yourself. Loving your baby takes time. Just as it happens with adults, true love comes as you get to know the person.

the baby they have—and the life that goes with it. (Very neat parents may have trouble reconciling the mess, and very organized folks may flounder in the chaos; more about that in the next chapter.)

> **TIP:** *Mum, it helps to talk to anyone who can remind you that the ups and downs are normal—good friends who've been through it, sisters, and your own mother if you have a good relationship with her. Dad, talking to your guy friends might not be as helpful. Men in my "Daddy-and-me" groups tell me that new fathers tend to compete with one another, especially over lack of sleep and sex.*

Interestingly, it almost doesn't matter what type of baby is involved. There's so much riding on parents' expectations that no child, not even an Angel baby, could possibly fit the bill. For instance, Kim and Jonathan were working parents, both with a lot of responsibility. When little Claire came along, I couldn't imagine a better baby. She fed well, played independently, and slept soundly, and her cries were easily recognizable. I figured I'd be out of a job in quick order. Believe it or not, though, Jonathan was worried. "Isn't she a little too passive?" he asked. "Should she be sleeping so much? If she's so placid, she's certainly not going to take after my side of the family!" I suspect, too, that Jonathan was a bit disappointed that he couldn't compete against his buddies in the All-American Sleep Deprivation Marathon. I assured him, though, that he ought to count his blessings. Angel babies like Claire are utterly enjoyable. Who wouldn't want one?

Of course, more often the shock comes when parents hoped for and envisioned a quiet, gentle baby but have quite a different experience. During the first few days, while their newborn is still sleeping it off, they actually believe that their dream came true. Then, all of a sudden, everything changes and they have a vigorous, impulsive baby on their hands. "What did we do?" is the first response. "What *can* we do?" comes next. The first step is to acknowledge their disappointment—and then adjust their expectations accordingly.

> **TIP:** *Think of your baby as the bearer of a wonderful life challenge. After all, each of us has a host of lessons to learn in life, and we never know who or what is going to be the teacher. In this case, it's your baby.*

Sometimes, parents aren't conscious of the letdown. Or if they are, they may feel too ashamed to verbalize their disappointment. They don't want to admit that their baby isn't as adorable or well behaved as they'd envisioned or that this isn't the love-at-first-sight experience they'd imagined. I can't count the number of couples I've seen go through this. But it might make you feel better to hear some of *their* stories.

Mary and Tim. Mary is a pleasant, mild-mannered woman who moves with grace and has a wonderful disposition. Her husband is also a very calm, even-tempered, and grounded person. When their daughter Mable was born, she seemed like an Angel baby for the first three days. The first night she slept for six hours, the second night almost as long. When they came home, however, Mable's true personality began to emerge. She slept more sporadically, was difficult to quiet, and often had a very hard time dropping off. But that wasn't all. She jumped at the slightest noise and cried. She squirmed and whined when visitors tried to hold her. Often, in fact, she seemed to cry for no apparent reason.

Mary and Tim couldn't believe they had produced a

high-strung baby. They kept talking about friends' babies who took naps easily, could amuse themselves for long periods, and could be schlepped about in cars. This was definitely not Mable. I helped them to see Mable for who she really was—a Touchy baby. Mabel liked predictability because her central nervous system was not fully developed; she therefore needed her parents to take their time and to be exceptionally calm around her. In order for her to adjust to her environment, Mary and Tim needed to be gentle and patient. Their little girl was a delicate person who had her own unique manner. Her sensitivity was not a problem, but rather her way of teaching them about her. And, given her mum's and dad's temperaments, I suspected that the apple hadn't fallen that far from the tree. Like Mary, Mable needed a slower pace. Like her dad, she craved serenity.

Those insights and a bit of encouragement helped Mary and Tim accommodate the real child they were living with rather than continue to wish that Mable would act more like their friends' children. They slowed the tempo around her, restricted the number of people who held her, and started to observe her more closely.

Mary and Tim discovered, among other things, that Mable gave them very clear cues. When she started to feel overwhelmed, she would turn her face away—from whomever was looking at her or even from a mobile. In her baby way, Mabel was telling her parents, "Enough stimulation!" Mum noticed that if she quickly acted on those cues, it would be easier to get Mable to take a nap. But if she missed that window, Mable would start to wail, and it would invariably take a long time to calm her. One day when I happened to drop by for a visit, Mary, in her eagerness to share her news about Mable, inadvertently ignored the cues, and Mable started to cry.

Fortunately, her mum respectfully told her, "I'm sorry, honey. I wasn't paying attention to you."

Jane and Arthur. This lovely couple, one of my favorites, had waited seven years to have a child. James, too, seemed like an Angel baby in the hospital. When they got home, though, he cried when he was changed, cried when he was bathed, cried, cried, and cried some more, seemingly at the drop of a hat. Now, Jane and Arthur are fun-loving people with great senses of humor, but they couldn't even muster a crooked smile for James. He seemed so miserable all the time. "He cries so much," Jane said, "and he's impatient at my breast. I have to admit we look forward to his nap time."

Even saying those words aloud worried them both. It's hard to acknowledge that your baby seems to have a dark cloud over him. Like many parents, Jane and Arthur believed it had something to do with them. "Let's step back and look at James as an individual," I suggested. "What I see is a little boy who is trying to say, 'Hey, Mum, get a move on when you're changing me' and 'Oh, no, not feeding time again' and 'What? Another bath?'" Once I gave their Grumpy baby a voice, Jane and Arthur's sense of humor kicked in. I told them my "old souls" theory about Grumpy babies. They laughed knowingly. "You know," said Arthur, "my dad is like that—and we love him for it. We just think of him as a character." Suddenly little James no longer seemed like a little monster who had come along to willfully disrupt their lives. He was James, a person with a temperament and needs, just like everyone else—a human being who deserved their respect.

Now when it came to giving him a bath, rather than dreading it, Jane and Arthur slowed themselves down, gave James more time to get used to the water, and talked him through the experience: "I know you don't find this fun," they'd say, "but someday soon you'll cry when we take you *out* of the bath." They also stopped swaddling him. They learned to anticipate his needs and knew that if they could avoid a meltdown, everyone would be better off. James at six months still has a tendency to sulk, but at least his parents accept this as his nature and know how to head off his more severe moods. Little James is lucky to be understood at such a tender age.

Stories like these illustrate two of the most critical aspects of baby whispering: respect and common sense. Just as you can't apply blanket prescriptions to all people, the same is true with babies. You can't conclude that because your sister's son liked to be held a certain way when she nursed him or liked to be swaddled when she put him down, your little boy will, too. You can't assume that because your friend's daughter has a sunny disposition and easily takes to strangers, your baby girl will. Forget about wishful thinking. You must deal with the reality of who your child is—and know what's best for *your* child. And I promise that if you watch and listen carefully, your baby will tell you precisely what he needs and how to help him through difficult situations.

Ultimately, that kind of empathy and understanding will make your child's life a bit easier, because you'll help him build on his strengths and compensate for his weaknesses. And here's the good news: No matter what kind of baby you have, all infants do better when life is calm and predictable. In the next chapter, I'll help you get started straightaway with a routine that will help your whole family thrive.

CHAPTER TWO
E.A.S.Y. Does It

Eat when you're hungry. Drink
when you're thirsty. Sleep when
you're tired.
—Buddhist saying

I had a sense that she'd be happier
if she had a structured beginning.
Besides, I saw how it worked for my
friend's baby.
—Mother of a Textbook baby

Rx for Success: A Structured Routine

Every day I get phone calls from parents who are anxious, confused, overwhelmed, and, most of all, sleep-
deprived. They bombard me with questions and beg me
for solutions because the quality of their family life is
suffering. No matter what the specific problem, I always
suggest the same remedy: *a structured routine*.

For example, when Terry, a thirty-three-year-old advertising executive, called me, she truly believed that
five-week-old Garth was a "bad eater." She told me,
"He won't breastfeed properly. It takes him almost an
hour to eat, and he keeps bobbing off my breast."

The first thing I asked was, "Do you keep to a regular
routine?"

Her hesitation told me the answer—a loud and clear
no. I promised Terry I'd drop by later that day to have a
look and a listen. But I was fairly sure that, even from
such a tiny jot of information, I already knew what was
happening.

"A schedule?" questioned Terry when I later offered my solution. "No, no, not a *schedule*," she protested. "I've worked all my life, and on every job I've had to keep to a very tight timetable. I quit work to be with my baby. Now you're telling me I have to put *him* on a schedule?"

I wasn't suggesting rigid deadlines or strict disciplinary boundaries—rather, a solid but flexible foundation that would change as Garth's needs changed. "I'm not talking about a *schedule* as you're imagining it," I clarified, "but a structured routine—a plan that involves a framework and regularity. I'm not saying that you must live by a clock—far from it. But you need to bring consistency and order into your baby's life."

I could see that Terry was still a bit skeptical, but she started to come round when I reassured her that not only would my method solve Garth's so-called problem, it would also teach her to understand her son's language. Feeding him every hour or so, I explained, meant that she had to be misinterpreting his cues. *No normal baby needs to eat every hour.* I suspected that Garth was probably a more efficient feeder than his mum had imagined. His bobbing off the breast meant "I'm finished," but she kept trying to make him suckle. Wouldn't *she* fuss under those circumstances?

I could also see that *Terry* wasn't thriving. She was in her bloomin' pajamas at four o'clock in the afternoon. Obviously she had no time for herself, not even fifteen minutes to shower. (Yes, I know, luv, if you've just had a baby, you're probably still in *your* jammies at four o'clock, too. But I hope that won't be the case by the time your baby is five weeks old.)

Now let's stop right here. (Later, I'll tell you how Terry fared.) Perhaps helping Terry establish a routine seems like a too-simple solution. But believe it or not, no matter what the particular presenting issue—feeding problems, irregular sleep patterns, or misdiagnosed colic—a structured routine *is* often all it takes to solve the problem. And if by chance you're still having a difficult time, at least you've taken a step in the right direction.

Terry was unwittingly ignoring Garth's cues. She was also letting *him* set the pace instead of establishing a routine that he could follow. Yes, I know that following a baby's lead is all the rage today—perhaps a backlash against the strict schedules American babies were once raised on. Unfortunately, that philosophy gives parents the mistaken impression that *any* kind of structure or routine will inhibit their baby's natural expression or development. But I say to these mums and dads, "She's only a *baby,* for goodness' sake. She doesn't know what's good for her." (Remember, luv, there's a big difference between respecting your baby and allowing her to be in charge.)

Besides, because I'm an advocate of a whole-family approach, I always tell parents, "Your baby is part of *your* life, not the other way round. If we allow an infant to set the pace, eating and sleeping whenever he likes, within six weeks your household will be in chaos. Hence, I always suggest starting *right from the beginning* to create a safe, consistent environment and to set a pace that Baby can follow. I call it E.A.S.Y., because it actually is.

Going E.A.S.Y. on Everyone

E.A.S.Y. is an acronym for the structured routine that I begin to establish with all my babies, ideally *from day one.* Think of it as a recurring period, more or less three hours long, in which each of the following segments occurs in this order:

E—*Eating.* Whether your baby is fed by the breast, the bottle, or both, nutrition is his primary need. Babies are little eating machines. Relative to their body weight, they eat two to three times the calories an obese person does! (In Chapter 4 I go into eating issues in greater detail.)

A—*Activity.* Before the age of three months, your baby will probably be eating and sleeping 70 percent of the time. When she's not, she'll be on the changing table, in the tub, cooing in her crib or on a blanket, in her carriage for a stroll, or looking out the window from her infant seat. Doesn't sound like much activity from our perspective, but it's what babies *do*. (More about activities in Chapter 5.)

S—*Sleeping.* Whether they sleep like a dream or in fits and starts, all babies need to learn how to get themselves to sleep *in their own beds* (to promote their independence). (See Chapter 6.)

Y—*You.* After all is said and done—that is, when Baby is sleeping—it's *your* turn. Sound impossible or unreasonable? It's not. If you follow my E.A.S.Y. program, every few hours there will be "you" time to rest, rejuvenate, and, once you've started to heal, to get things done. Remember that in the first six weeks—the postpartum period—you will need to recover physically and emotionally from the trauma of childbirth. Mothers who try to rush back to life as they once knew it, or whose on-demand feeding schedules don't allow them any time to rest, pay the piper later on. (More on this in Chapter 7.)

Compared to many other baby-care regimens, E.A.S.Y. is a sensible and practical middle ground, a welcome relief to most parents from the wild pendulum swings in parenting fashions, which seem to alternate between two extremes. On the one side are tough-love experts who believe that "training" babies right involves a struggle: You need to let 'em cry it out and be a little frustrated some of the time. You don't "spoil" babies by picking them up each time they cry. You keep them on a strict schedule and make them fit into *your* life, live by *your* needs. On the opposite side, representing the currently more popular view, are follow-the-baby advocates, who tell mums to feed "on demand," a term that I believe speaks for itself—you end up with a demanding

---

An E.A.S.Y. Timetable

All babies are different, but from birth to 3 months, the following routine is fairly typical. As your baby becomes a more efficient feeder and is content to play independently for longer periods, don't be afraid to adjust it a bit.

Eating: 25 to 40 minutes on breast or bottle; a normal baby, weighing 6 pounds or more, can go 2½ to 3 hours to the next feed

Activity: 45 minutes (includes diapering, dressing, and, once a day, a nice bath)

Sleep: 15 minutes to fall asleep; naps of half an hour to an hour; will go for progressively longer periods through the night after the first two or three weeks

You: An hour or more for you when the baby is asleep; this time is extended as baby gets older, takes less time to eat, plays independently, and takes longer naps

---

baby. Proponents of this doctrine believe that to have a well-adjusted child, you've got to meet its every need . . . which, if followed slavishly, translates into giving up your own life.

In truth, luv, neither approach works. With one, you're not respecting your baby; with the other, you're not respecting yourself. What is more, E.A.S.Y. is central to a whole-family approach, because it ensures that every member's needs are met, not just the baby's. You listen and observe carefully, respecting your baby's needs, *and,* at the same time, you acclimate him or her to family life. (For a bird's-eye view of the way E.A.S.Y. differs from on-demand or a rigid feeding schedule, see the chart opposite.)

Why E.A.S.Y. Works

Humans, at any age, are habitual creatures—they function better within a regular pattern of events. Structure and routine are normal to everyday life. Everything has a logical order. As my Nan says, "You can't add eggs to the pudding after it's baked." In our homes, our workplaces, our schools, even our houses of worship, there are systems set in place that make us feel secure.

Think about your own daily routines for a minute. Without consciously realizing it, you probably perform recurring rituals every morning, at dinner, and at bedtime. How do you feel when one of those is interrupted? Even if it's something as minor as a plumbing problem that causes you to skip your morning shower, a roadblock that forces you to take a different route to work, or a slight delay in your usual mealtime, such disruptions can throw off your whole day. So why should it be any different for babies? They need routines as much as we do, which is why E.A.S.Y. works.

A Bird's-Eye View of the E.A.S.Y. Method

On Demand	E.A.S.Y.	Schedule
Following whatever Baby demands—feeding 10 to 12 times a day as Baby cries	Flexible but structured routine that spans a 2½-to-3-hour period of eating, activity, sleep, and "you" time	Clock-watching to conform to a predetermined timetable of regular feedings, usually 3 to 4 hours apart
Unpredictable—Baby takes the lead	Predictable—parents set a pace that Baby can follow, and Baby knows what to expect	Predictable but anxiety-provoking—parents set a schedule, which Baby may not follow
Parents don't learn to interpret Baby's signals; many cries misinterpreted as hunger	Because it's logical, parents can anticipate Baby's need and therefore are more likely to understand the different cries	Cries may be ignored if they don't match schedule; parents don't learn to interpret Baby's signals
Parents have no life—Baby sets the schedule	Parents can plan their lives	Parents are ruled by the clock
Parents feel confused; there is often chaos in the house	Parents feel more confident about their own parenting because they understand their child's cues and cries	Parents often feel guilty, anxious, even angry if Baby doesn't conform to the schedule

Babies don't like surprises. Their delicate systems do best when they eat, sleep, and play pretty much at the same time every day, and in the same order. It may vary slightly, but not by much. Children, especially infants and babies, also like to know what's coming up next. They tend not to be good about hidden surprises. Consider the groundbreaking visual perception research of Dr. Marshall Haith at the University of Denver. He noted that babies' eyes, though slightly myopic in the first year, are very coordinated, even from birth, and when presented with predictable patterns on a TV screen, they begin to look for things that are going to happen *before* they happen. By tracking babies' eye movements, Haith has demonstrated that "when an image is predictable, a baby more readily forms expectations. When you fool them, they get upset." Can this be generalized? Absolutely, says Haith; babies need and prefer routine.

E.A.S.Y. gets your baby used to the natural order of things—food, activity, and rest. I've seen parents put their infants to bed right after eating, often because the baby falls asleep on the breast or bottle. I don't advise this for two reasons. One, the baby becomes dependent on the bottle or breast, and soon needs it to fall asleep. Two, do *you* want to sleep after every meal? Unless it's a holiday and you've eaten a huge turkey dinner, probably not. More often, you eat a meal and then go off to an activity. Indeed, our adult days are organized around a morning meal; going off to work, school, or play; lunch; more work, school, or play; then dinner, bath, and bedtime. Why not offer the same natural progression to your baby?

Structure and organization give everyone in the family a sense of security. A structured routine helps parents set a pace that their baby can follow and create an environment that helps him know what's coming. With E.A.S.Y., there is no rigidity—we listen to Baby and respond to his specific needs—but we keep his day in logical order. *We*, not Baby, set the stage.

For instance, in the evening, for the five or six o'clock feed (the *E*), Baby is given the breast or a bottle in the nursery or at least in a quiet corner of the house reserved for his meals, away from kitchen odors wafting in the air, loud music, and the hubbub of other children. We then move into the activity phase (the *A*), which in the evening means giving him his bath. It's done the same way each time (see pages 179–182). With his jammies or nightshirt on, it's finally time for bed (the *S*), so we lower the lights in his bedroom and put soothing music on.

The beauty of this simple plan is that with each step, Baby knows what's coming next, and so does everyone else. That means Mum and Dad can also plan *their* lives, too. Other siblings don't get pushed into the background. In the end, everyone gets the love and attention he or she needs.

E.A.S.Y. helps parents interpret their baby. Because I've handled so many babies, I know their language. When a baby cries, "I'm hungry—feed me," it sounds far different to me than "My diaper's dirty—change me" or "I'm tired—help me calm down and get to sleep." My goal is to help parents learn *how* to listen and observe so that they, too, can understand the language of infancy. But this takes time, practice, and a bit of trial and error. In the meantime, with E.A.S.Y., you can make intelligent guesses about what your baby wants even *before* you become fluent in baby language. (In the next chapter, I'll explain more about interpreting babies' gestures, cries, and other sounds.)

For instance, let's say your baby has been fed (the *E*) and for the last twenty minutes has been lying on a blanket in the living room staring at black and white wavy lines (her way of playing, hence the *A*). If she suddenly starts to cry, you can be fairly sure she is probably getting overtired and is ready for what comes next: sleep (the *S*). Rather than shoving something in her mouth, taking her for a car ride, or putting her in one of those bloody vibrating chairs or swings (which will only make her more miserable—I explain why on page 204), you put her to bed, first setting the mood, and then—presto!— she falls asleep on her own.

E.A.S.Y. establishes a solid but flexible foundation for your baby. E.A.S.Y. sets up certain guidelines and routines that parents can adapt according to their baby's temperament and, just as important, according to their own needs. For example, I had to help little Greta's mum, June, through *four* different versions of E.A.S.Y. June breastfed only for the first month and then switched Greta to formula. Such a change in feeding method often requires a change in routine. Moreover, Greta was a Grumpy baby, and her mum had to learn how to accommodate her very definite preferences. Complicating matters further, June was a clock-watcher who felt very guilty when Greta didn't respond exactly as she had planned. Given all these factors, it's understandable that we needed to modify and adjust accordingly.

Although the same order—eat, activity, and sleep—is always maintained, changes also occur as a baby gets older. On page 47, I've given a typical E.A.S.Y. timetable for a newborn, which generally lasts until around the age of three months. At that point, most babies start to stay up longer, have fewer naps during the day, suckle more efficiently, and, therefore, take less time to eat. But by then you know your baby, and it's a simple matter to adjust your routine.

E.A.S.Y. facilitates cooperative parenting—with or without a partner. When the primary caretaker of a newborn—usually Mum—doesn't have time for herself, she's likely to moan about it or resent her partner for not sharing the burden. I see these difficulties crop up in so many of the households I visit. There's nothing more infuriating to a new mother who is trying to vent her frustrations to her spouse than to hear, "What are you complaining about? You've only got the baby to look after."

"I've had to walk her around all day. She's been crying for two hours," Mum says.

What she really wants is to have a good moan and then it will be over. But her partner has solutions on the brain and wants to fix the situation, so he comes back with a suggestion like "I'll buy you a sling" or "Why didn't you take her for a walk?" Eventually, she gets angry and feels underappreciated. He gets frustrated and feels harassed. He has no idea what her day was really like; all he can think is, *What does she want from me?* What he wants to do most right now is hide behind a newspaper or turn on the telly to watch his favorite basketball team. At that point, she's likely to get madder than a wet hen, and instead of the two of them dealing with their baby's needs, they're immersed in their own drama.

E.A.S.Y. to the rescue! When a structure is in place, Dad knows what Mum's day was like and, just as important, he can be part of the routine. I've found that men do best when they have concrete tasks. So if Dad knows he'll be home by six, you just look at your routine and decide what jobs he can take over. Many men love to do the bath and evening feeds.

It's far less common, but in close to 20 percent of all families with young children, Dad is at home all day, and Mum is the one who comes home after work. Either way, I suggest that when whoever has been out of the house returns, the three of you spend half an hour together. Then encourage the one who's been home all day to go out for a walk—just to chill out.

> **TIP:** *When you come home from work, you should always change out of your work clothes, even if you're in an office all day. Clothing retains smells of the outside that can upset Baby's delicate senses (and you don't have to worry about getting them messed up).*

In Ryan and Sarah's case, E.A.S.Y. cut down on their frequent arguments about what was "best" for baby Teddy. Ryan was traveling a lot when I first helped Sarah get Teddy on a routine. When he came home, he understandably wanted to spend lots of time holding and jostling his little boy. It didn't take long for little Teddy to get used to Dad's carrying him around, and by the time he was three weeks old, it was virtually impossible for Sarah to lay him down. Dad had unwittingly trained Teddy to expect a great deal of holding, especially before naps and bedtime. When she called me, I explained to Sarah that she just had to reprogram Teddy to sleep without a human "prop," as I call them (see pages 195–197), especially because her hubby was about to go on a trip again, leaving poor Mum to do the carrying about. It only took two days for us to get Teddy on track because he was so young. Luckily, Ryan understood E.A.S.Y., so when he came home from his trip this time, he and his wife worked together.

What about single mums and dads? Admittedly, they often have a hard time at the beginning, because no one's waiting in the wings to relieve them. But, apart from being emotionally overwhelmed at times, Karen, age thirty-eight, actually thought she had it better than some couples. "There's no one to fight with over what to do or how to do it," she observed. Putting Matthew on E.A.S.Y. actually made it less complicated for Karen to call upon others for help. "Because I had written everything down," she recalls, "whenever friends or

TIP: *If you're a single parent, friends are a lifeline. For those who can't or don't want to help with child care, enlist their support to help with the housework or do grocery shopping and other errands. Remember that you have to ask. Don't expect others to read your mind and then become resentful when they don't.*

family members baby-sat for me, they knew exactly what Matthew needed, what time his naps were, when he played, and so on. There just wasn't any guesswork."

Start as You Mean to Go On

I realize that the idea of a structured routine may fly in the face of what you have heard from your friends or read in other books. The idea of planning the day for a tiny infant is not popular in most quarters—some even think it cruel. And yet many of those same books, as well as your relatives and friends, usually suggest establishing some kind of routine at three months. By then, the reasoning goes, you know that your baby has gained the weight he needs and has displayed a fairly regular pattern of sleeping.

Codswallop, I say! *Why wait?* Pandemonium usually sets in by that time. Besides, nothing reflexive automatically occurs at the age of three months. It's true that most infants will have made certain developmental strides by then, but a routine is not a phenomenon of age—it's something learned. Some babies, usually Angel or Textbook types, will put themselves on a schedule long before that. Others may not. By three months, instead of settling in, they will have developed what are construed as eating or sleeping "problems"—*difficulties that could have been avoided altogether or at least minimized had they been given a structure in early infancy.*

With E.A.S.Y., *you* guide your baby and, at the same time, get to know his needs. By the time he's three months old, you'll already know his patterns and understand his language. And you can build good habits straightaway. As my Nan taught me, *start as you mean to go on.* That is, imagine what you want your family to look like, and begin that way when your baby comes home from the hospital. Let me put it this way: If you want to embrace my idea of whole-family parenting, in which Baby's needs are met and, at the same time, he or she is immediately integrated into your family's life, use my E.A.S.Y. method. If you choose another approach—that's your prerogative.

But the problem is that parents often don't realize they're making the choice—they get into what I call "accidental parenting." They don't think past the first few weeks to decide whether that's what they really want, or they may not be conscious of how their behavior and their attitudes affect the way they relate to their baby. They don't start as they mean to go on. (More about accidental parenting and solving the problems it can cause in Chapter 9.)

Truth be told, it's usually adults, not babies, who create difficult situations. As a parent, you must always take the lead. After all, you know better than your baby does! Despite the fact that infants come in with their own unique temperament, parents' actions *do* make a difference. I've seen Angel babies and Textbook babies turn into mardy little munchkins because they are confused by the turmoil. Regardless of your baby's type, remember that the habits he or she develops are in *your* hands. Think through what you do.

It's also helpful to think in terms of your *own* routines. What happens to you when your day is thrown off by an unexpected event or a barrier to your usual regimen? You get irritable and frustrated, and perhaps you even lose your temper, which in turn can affect your appetite and the quality of your sleep. Your newborn is no different, except that he can't set his own routine. *You have to do it for him*. When you create a sensible plan

Mindful Parenting

Buddhists refer to a state of "mindfulness," which means fully attending to your surroundings and being totally present in every moment. I suggest applying this idea to parenting your newborn. Try to make yourself more conscious of habits you might be setting up.

For example, I recommend to parents who carry their infants around in order to get them to sleep that they try doing that for half an hour with a twenty-pound sack of potatoes. Is that what you want to be doing a few months from now?

To those who endlessly hover over babies to keep them amused, I ask, "What do you want your life to look like when he's a bit older?" Whether you're planning to go back to work or stay home, will you be happy if he constantly needs your attention? Don't you think it would be nice to have some time for yourself? If so, you need to take steps now to support his independence.

that Baby can follow, it will make him feel more secure and you less overwhelmed.

Wingers and Planners

Parents sometimes initially reject the *idea* of a structured routine. When I say, "We're going to immediately introduce structure into your baby's day," they gasp in horror.

"Oh, no!" a mother or father might exclaim. "The books say we have to let the baby lead, and make sure all her needs are met. Otherwise, she'll be insecure." They somehow have the mistaken notion that getting a baby on a routine means either ignoring her natural rhythms *or* letting her cry. They don't realize that just the opposite happens: Using E.A.S.Y. helps parents become even better at interpreting and meeting their infant's needs.

Some parents also discount the idea of a structured routine because they're convinced it will take all the spontaneity out of their *own* lives. I recently visited a young couple who felt that way. Everything about their lifestyle—which was typical of many couples in their twenties and thirties who embrace what they view as "natural" parenting—told me that they didn't want to be fenced in. Chloe, a former dental hygienist, had given birth at home with a midwife assisting. Seth, a computer whiz, had purposely taken a flexible job, which allowed him to work at home much of the time, so that he could share in child care. And when I asked questions such as "When does little Isabella usually breastfeed?" and "What time does she nap?" the two of them looked at me, confused. After a moment, Seth finally answered, "Well, it depends on what *our* day is like."

Couples who initially resist E.A.S.Y. tend to fall on opposite ends of what I call the Wing It/Plan It continuum. Some wingers cherish their off-the-cuff style, as Chloe and Seth did. Others may be naturally disorganized and feel they *can't* change. (That's simply not true, as you are about to learn.) Or they might be like Terry—parents trying to change a formerly structured lifestyle into a much looser arrangement. In any case, when I say "structured routine," they *hear* "schedule" and they *think* timetables and clock-watching. They erroneously believe that I'm asking them to abandon all vestiges of spontaneity in their life.

When I meet parents who are either totally disorganized or quite laissez-faire in their own lives, I tell them honestly, "You have to have good habits yourself before you can transmit them to a child. I can teach you how to interpret your baby's cries and how to meet his needs, but you're never going to give this baby a sense of security and calm unless you also take at least some steps to provide a proper environment."

At the opposite end of the continuum are the planners, by-the-book parents like Dan and Rosalie, both high-profile executives in Hollywood. Their home is as neat as a pin; their own time is measured out in precise minutes. During Rosalie's nine months, they envisioned their baby fitting right in. But a few weeks after little Winifred arrived, things weren't working out as they had anticipated. "Winnie is usually good about keeping on her schedule—but sometimes she wakes up earlier or takes longer to eat," Rosalie explained. "Then our whole day is thrown off. Can you teach me how to get her back on track?" I've tried to get it across to Rosalie and Dan that although I underscore the importance of consistency, I also believe in flexibility. "You must tune in to your baby's cues," I told them. "She's just getting used to the world. You can't expect her to be on *your* time."

Most parents eventually get it. I'm not at all surprised when, after several weeks or months of trying it their way, mothers and fathers who initially rejected E.A.S.Y. call me back, either because their life is a shambles or because they have a cranky baby on their hands and don't know what he needs—or both. If a mum was a planner, highly organized and efficient in the past, and has tried to fit her baby into her old life, she usually doesn't understand why it's not working. Or if she's a winger who has gone the route of following her baby, she's let a helpless infant take charge and now wonders why she can't find time to take a shower, to get dressed, to even breathe! She hasn't had a conversation or a meal with her mate in weeks. My answer in either case: *Turn the chaos into calm—or let go of some of your need to control—with E.A.S.Y.*

What's Your WPQ?

Of course, some of us are planners by nature, others like to live on the edge and totally wing it, and most are somewhere in the middle. What about *you*? To find out, I've devised a brief questionnaire that can help you figure out where you fall on the Wing It/Plan It continuum. Each item is based on what I've seen in the homes of the many different families I've met over the last twenty years. By observing how parents keep house and conduct their daily lives, I can pretty much tell how well

---

WPQ (Wing It/Plan It Quotient)

For each question, circle the number that best describes you. Use the following key:

5 = Always
4 = Usually Yes
3 = Sometimes
2 = Usually No
1 = Never

I live by a schedule.	5	4	3	2	1
I prefer people to call before they drop in.	5	4	3	2	1
After shopping or laundry, I immediately put everything away.	5	4	3	2	1
I prioritize my daily and weekly tasks.	5	4	3	2	1
My desk is very organized.	5	4	3	2	1
I shop weekly for the food and other supplies I know I'll need.	5	4	3	2	1
I hate it when people are late.	5	4	3	2	1
I am careful not to overbook myself.	5	4	3	2	1
Before starting a project, I lay out whatever I'm going to use.	5	4	3	2	1
I clean out and organize my closets at regular intervals.	5	4	3	2	1
When I finish a chore, I put away whatever I was using.	5	4	3	2	1
I plan ahead.	5	4	3	2	1

they'll adapt to a structured routine once the baby arrives.

To find out your WPQ (Wing It/Plan It quotient), add up your scores and divide by 12. Your total score will range somewhere between 1 and 5, which indicates where you fall on the continuum. Why is this important? If you're too much at either extreme, you might be one of those parents who initially has trouble with my E.A.S.Y. method, either because you're a bit on the rigid side or too laissez-faire. That doesn't mean you *can't* implement a structured routine, only that you might have to give a little more thought and patience to E.A.S.Y. than parents who fall somewhere in the middle. The descriptions below explain your score and what challenges you might face:

5 to 4: You're probably a very organized person. You have a place for everything and like everything in its place. I'm sure you have no trouble with the *idea* of a structured routine—you even welcome it. You might find it difficult, though, to incorporate flexibility into your day and/or to make changes in your usual practices that factor in your baby's temperament and needs.

4 to 3: You're fairly organized, although you tend not to be a fanatic about neatness or structure. Sometimes you let the house or your office space get a bit cluttered, but you eventually put things away, straighten up, file, or do whatever else is needed to restore order. You probably will have a relatively stress-free time putting your baby on E.A.S.Y. And because you seem to be somewhat flexible already, you won't have trouble adapting if your baby has other ideas.

3 to 2: You tend to be a little scattered and disorganized, but you're far from a lost cause. To manage a structured routine, you may actually need to *write down* your routine so that you don't lose track. Note the exact times every day when your baby eats, plays, and sleeps. You might also want to make lists of things you need to do. (On page 71, I've provided a form to help you.) The good news for you is that you're already used to a little chaos, so life with Baby might not be *that* much of a surprise.

2 to 1: You're a real winger, a fly-by-the-seat-of-your-pants type. Managing a structured routine is going to be somewhat of a challenge. You *definitely* have to write everything down, which means a radical change in your lifestyle. But guess what, luv? Having a baby *is* just that radical!

Changing Their Spots

Luckily, parents aren't like leopards. With the exception of a few rare cases (see sidebar opposite), most of us *can* change our spots. I find that parents who fall in the middle of the continuum catch on right away, perhaps because by nature they're the most flexible group. They can appreciate the benefits of organization and, at the same time, tolerate a little chaos.

If they can liberate themselves from their own striving for perfection, parents who are overachievers or very fastidious can find relief in the method, too, because it's managerial and organized. They often have to work a bit on being more flexible, though. To my delight, I've also seen the most disorganized parents grasp the logic and the benefits of E.A.S.Y.

When E.A.S.Y. Seems Hard

It's rare, but some parents have a great deal of trouble establishing a structured routine. Usually it's for one of the following reasons:

- **They have no perspective.** In the greater scheme of things, infancy lasts but a moment. Parents who view E.A.S.Y. as a life sentence moan and groan and never get to understand or enjoy their baby.

- **They're not committed.** Your routine may change over time, or you may have to make adjustments because of your particular child or your own needs. Still, every day you must try to keep this structure pretty much as it is—eat, activity, sleep, and time for yourself. It's a bit boring, luv, but it works.

- **They can't take a practical middle road.** Either they believe in making Baby conform to their needs or they embrace an all-baby-all-the-time philosophy in which Baby (and chaos) rule the household.

Hannah. Hannah, whose WPQ was 5 when I first met her, has come a long way. When I say she fed her baby by the clock, I mean literally. A confirmed rule follower, Hannah was told in the hospital to feed little Miriam ten minutes on each breast (which I emphatically do *not* believe in; see page 120), and that is exactly what she did. She set a timer whenever she nursed her baby. At the sound of that dreadful bell, she would detach Miriam from her breast and change sides. Ten minutes later, the bell would ring again, and Miriam would be off the breast and taken swiftly to her room for a nap. To my horror, Hannah then set the timer again, explaining, "I go in every ten minutes. If she's still crying, I reassure her. Then I leave her for another ten minutes, and I repeat the whole thing until she finally falls asleep." (Mind you, it didn't matter whether Miriam cried for *nine* out of those ten minutes; the timer ruled.)

"Throw away that damn timer!" I said, in as tactful and sensitive a tone as I could muster. "Let's listen to

Miriam's cries and find out what she's trying to say. We'll observe her feeding, watch her little body, and let her cues tell us what she needs." Straightaway, I explained my E.A.S.Y. routine and helped Hannah establish it. It took a few weeks for Mum to get used to it (Miriam, of course, was instantly relieved), but soon Miriam fed and played for a bit on her own. Only when she showed signs of fatigue did Hannah head toward Miriam's crib.

Terry. Even though she was initially appalled by the idea of a structured routine, Terry was a 3.5 on the continuum. Personally, I think she might have been closer to 4, because she had spent so many years as a high-powered executive. Perhaps her answers to the questions reflected the way Terry *wanted* to be. In any case, once she moved past her own resistance, we first concentrated on getting Garth's feeds on track. I helped Terry see that he was quite an efficient nurser and that whenever he did linger on her breast, it was just to suckle. She soon became better at hearing the difference between his cries for hunger and his overtired whines—and believe me, they're different. I also suggested that she keep a daily log to chart Garth's feeds, activity time, and naps—and her own time as well (see page 71). Having the structure, seeing the progression of her day in black and white, and knowing what to expect helped Terry become more proficient at interpreting Garth's cries and also enabled her to find time for herself. She felt like a better parent—in fact, she felt better about everything in her life.

After two weeks, she called. "It's only ten-thirty in the morning, Tracy—and I'm up and dressed and ready to go out and do my errands," she said proudly. "You know, the funny thing is, even though I was so worried about being spontaneous, my life was totally unpredictable. Now I can actually find the time to *be* spontaneous!"

Trisha and Jason. Both consultants who worked at home, Trisha and Jason fell near the 1 end of the Wing It/Plan It continuum. They were a sweet couple, in their mid-thirties, but even at our initial consultation, as I sat with them in their living room, I felt compelled to close the doors to their respective offices so as to block the view of stale doughnuts, old coffee cups, and papers spilling hither and thither. Clearly, in this household chaos ruled. Dirty laundry lay on chairs everywhere, and the floor was similarly strewn with socks and sweaters and assorted articles of daily life. In the kitchen, cabinets were open and dirty dishes lined the sink. None of this seemed to bother Trisha or Jason.

Unlike some couples who go into denial, Jason and Trisha, then in her ninth month, knew that once their daughter arrived, everything was going to be different. I helped them understand what concrete and specific alterations in their lifestyle they would have to make once their baby arrived. Not only would their bundle of joy require sacred spots of her own where she could eat, play, and sleep without becoming overstimulated, but also Trisha and Jason would have to respect her need for constancy.

Elizabeth was born on a Saturday and arrived home the next day. I had given them a list of items that they would need to have on hand. To their credit, they bought most of them. They were a little less efficient about setting up the baby's nursery and having all the packages open and everything they needed within easy reach. Despite those few glitches, Jason and Trisha were unbelievably good (to my surprise, I have to admit) at maintaining the E.A.S.Y. routine. It helped that Elizabeth was a Textbook baby. By the time she was two weeks old, her parents had no trouble keeping her on track; by the seventh week, she could go five or six hours at night without waking up.

Make no mistake, though: Trisha and Jason are still fundamentally Trisha and Jason. But at least they got off to a good start. Their house is a little more orderly, but for the most part it continues to look like a war zone. Still, little Elizabeth is thriving because her parents have created a safe, comfortable environment for her *and* set a pace that she can follow. Likewise, Terry is still Terry, kind of torn between her love for Garth and missing her career. I suspect that as much as she promised herself she wouldn't go back to work, she may reevaluate that decision. If she does, with E.A.S.Y. in place, she and Garth will make a smooth transition. And Hannah is still Hannah. She's no longer setting a timer, but her house is immaculate; Miriam hasn't started walking yet, but for now, it's hard to tell a baby lives there. But at least Hannah speaks her daughter's language.

How E.A.S.Y. Is Your Baby?

Naturally, how well a baby does also depends on the baby. My first child, Sara, was a Spirited baby, extremely demanding and high-maintenance, up every hour. She was sharp as a tack, mind you, and the minute her eyes were open, she wanted me to do things with her. She'd exhaust me. The only way we both coped was with a consistent structure. We had a bedtime ritual I never wavered from. When I did, she'd get off track and all hell would break loose. Then along came her younger sister, Sophie, who was an Angel baby right from the start. Accustomed to Sara's shenanigans, I was constantly amazed by my new baby's enduring calm. Truth be told, many a morning I'd find myself leaning over Sophie's crib to see if she was still breathing. And there she was, wide awake and babbling contentedly to her toys. I barely had to think about instituting a routine with that one!

What can you expect from *your* child? There's no way of knowing for sure. But I am certain of one thing: I have never encountered a baby who doesn't thrive on E.A.S.Y. nor a household that isn't improved by a structured routine. If you have an Angel baby or a Textbook baby, his inner clock will probably get him off to a good start without your doing much. But the other types of babies may need a bit more help. Here's what you might expect from your baby.

Angel. Not surprisingly, a baby with a mild, amenable disposition easily adapts to a structured day. Emily was such a baby. We put her on E.A.S.Y. as soon as she got home from the hospital, and that first night in her crib, she slept from 11 P.M. to 5 A.M. and continued to do so until three weeks of age—at which point she slept from 11 to 7. Her mum was the envy of all of her friends. In my experience, this is typical—on a structured routine many Angel babies sleep through the night by three weeks.

Textbook. Here is also a baby you can mold easily, because he's so predictable. Once you initiate a routine, he'll follow it without much diversion. Tommy woke regularly for his feeds and slept happily from 10 P.M. to 4 A.M., and by six weeks, he was sleeping until 6 A.M. I find that Textbook babies usually make it through the night by the time they're seven or eight weeks old.

Touchy. This is our most fragile baby, and she loves the predictability of a routine. The more consistent you are, the better you'll understand each other and the sooner she'll sleep through the night—usually by eight to ten weeks if her cues are read correctly. But watch out if they aren't. Unless a Touchy baby is on a structured routine, it's hard to gauge her cries—and that will only make her more irritable. With Iris, almost anything can throw her off, from an unscheduled visitor to a dog barking outside. Her mum has to pay close attention to Iris's cues. If she fails to notice a hungry or tired sign (see page 200) and waits too long to feed Iris or put her in her crib, this Touchy baby melts down in minutes, and then it's hard to calm her down.

Spirited. This baby, who has a mind of his own, may seem to *resist* your schedule. Or just when you think you have him on a good routine, *he* decides it's not working for him. You then have to take a day and watch his cues. See what he's asking you and then get him back on track. Spirited babies show you what works for them and what doesn't. Bart, for example, suddenly started falling asleep on his mum's breast every time she tried to feed him. Then she'd have trouble waking him—this after he had followed E.A.S.Y. for four weeks. I suggested to Pam that she take a day to listen and observe her son carefully. What she saw clearly was that Bart was sleeping for shorter periods during the day; when he woke, he really hadn't had his quota of nap time. She also realized that she was intervening a little too quickly when he started to wake up, instead of listening to his cues. When she waited awhile instead of rushing in, she found he would put himself back to sleep for a little longer and then was more alert for his feeds. Thus she got him back on track. It takes a Spirited baby about twelve weeks to start sleeping through the night. They act as though they don't want to stay asleep for fear of missing something. They also often have a hard time winding down.

Grumpy. Here is a baby who may not like *any* kind of routine, because he's disagreeable about most things. But if you can get him on track and be consistent about it, he'll be a lot happier. This type of baby is very intense, but you're less likely on E.A.S.Y. to have problems with bathing, dressing, and even feeding, because at least your ornery little one will know what to expect—and will probably also be more content. A Grumpy often gets diagnosed as having colic when in actual fact all he needs is structure and perseverance. Stuart was such a baby. He didn't like to amuse himself, didn't like to be changed, and was grumpy on the breast—and he would show it. Stuart's natural rhythm worked for him but not for his mum, because she didn't particularly appreciate getting up in the middle of the night for no apparent reason. She introduced the E.A.S.Y. method, and now that his day was more predictable, he began sleeping longer periods at night and, in fact, became quite a bit more agreeable during the day. Grumpy babies often sleep through the night by six weeks. In fact, they seem happiest when they're tucked in bed, away from the bustle of the household.

Let me remind you, as I did when I first introduced these "types" in Chapter 1: Your baby may exhibit the characteristics of more than one type. In any case, you mustn't view these descriptions as if they're written in stone. However, I've found that some babies follow the E.A.S.Y. routine more easily than others. And some, like my Sara, *need* a structured routine more than others, too.

But How Do I Learn What My Baby Needs?

Okay, so now you understand yourself and you have an idea of what to expect from your baby. That's a start, but Westminster Abbey wasn't built in a day. The first few weeks on a structured routine may be rocky. It takes time and patience. And it takes the perseverance to stick with your plan. Here are some other tips to remember:

Write it all down. One of the tools I give parents, which is particularly helpful to wingers, is my E.A.S.Y. log. It helps them keep track of both where they are in the process and what the baby and Mum are doing. It's especially important to keep a log during the first six weeks of your baby's life. Remember to chart your own recovery as well. As I will explain in greater detail in Chapter 7, it's as crucial for Mum to rest during those first six weeks as it is for her to learn how to care for her infant.

Over a few days to a week's time you'll see exactly what your baby is doing. You might notice a growth spurt, for example, because he takes more food. Or you might notice that he's hanging on the breast longer. If he is suddenly spending fifty minutes or an hour on your breast where he used to finish a feed in thirty minutes, is he really feeding, or is he just lollygagging, using your breast to go to sleep? You'll know the answer only if you take the time to actively observe him—that's how mums and dads begin to learn the language of infancy and the habits of their particular baby. (More on this, pages 73–99.)

Your E.A.S.Y. Log									
DATE									
Eat						Activity		Sleep	You
AT WHAT TIME?	HOW MUCH (OUNCES)?	ON RIGHT BREAST (MINUTES)?	ON LEFT BREAST (MINUTES)?	B O W E L M O V E M E N T S	U R I N A T I O N	WHAT AND HOW LONG?	BATH (A.M. OR P.M.?)	HOW LONG?	REST? ERRANDS? INSIGHTS? COMMENTS?

This is only a sample log, designed primarily for mums. As you read Chapters 4 through 6, which go into greater detail about feeds, bowel movements, urination, activities, and other aspects of your baby's day, you'll find additional guidelines to gauge your baby's progress. Also, you can adapt this log in any way that suits your particular situation. For example, if you and your partner are sharing parenting fifty-fifty, you might want to indicate who does what. Or if your baby was premature

or came home from the hospital with a particular problem (see pages 261–285), you might need to add another
column indicating any special care that's needed. The
important thing to remember is *consistency*—the log
simply helps you keep track.

Get to know your baby as a person. The challenge for
you is to get to know your baby as the unique and special individual that she is. If your baby is named Rachel,
don't think of her as "the baby"—rather, think of her as
a person named Rachel. You know the order in which
Rachel's day should proceed—feeds, activities, naps. But
you also have to get Rachel's input. That may mean a
few days of experimenting, holding back to really watch
what she's doing.

> **TIP:** *Remember that your baby is not really "yours," but
> a separate person—a gift that you've been given to take
> care of.*

Take it easy . . . literally. E.A.S.Y.—the acronym—is also
meant to be a reminder that babies respond to sweet,
simple, slow movements. That's their natural rhythm,
and we need to be respectful of it. Instead of trying to
get your baby to respond to your pace, slow yourself
down to hers. That way, you'll be able to look and listen, instead of rushing in. Besides being good for her, it's
good for you to "entrain" to, or match the rhythm of,
her less stressful tempo. That's why I suggest taking
three deep breaths before you even pick up your baby. In
the next chapter, I'll explain more about slowing down
and paying close, careful attention.

CHAPTER THREE
S.L.O.W. Down (and Appreciate Your Baby's Language)

> We think that a mother who can read her baby's cues, who can understand what the baby is trying to communicate to her, is most likely to be providing the kind of child-rearing environment that will enrich development and facilitate cognition later on.
>
> —Dr. Barry Lester
> ("The Crying Game,"
> *Brown Alumni Magazine*)

Infants: Strangers in a Strange Land

I try to help parents step into their baby's booties by explaining that a newborn is like a visitor from a foreign country. I tell them to imagine themselves traveling in a strange but fascinating land. The landscape and scenery may be beautiful, the people warm and friendly—you can see it in their eyes, tell from their smiling faces. But getting what you need can be quite frustrating. You walk into a restaurant and ask, "Where is the bathroom?" and are shown to a table, where a plate of pasta is shoved under your nose. Or the reverse happens—you're looking for a good meal, and the waiter leads you to the loo!

From the moment newborns come into the world, that's how *they* feel. No matter how smartly their rooms are decorated or how warm and well-intentioned their parents are, infants are bombarded by unfamiliar sensations that they don't understand. Babies' only form of communication—their language—is their crying and body movements.

It's also important to remember that babies grow in *their* time, not ours. With the exception of the Textbook baby, most infants' development doesn't proceed on a precise timetable. Parents need to just stand back and watch their infants bloom—support them, but don't rush in and rescue them every time something seems wrong.

Putting On the Brakes

When I'm asked to help parents figure out why their baby is fussing or crying, I know Mum and Dad are anxious and want me to *do* something immediately. Much to their surprise, however, I say, "Stop. Let's try to figure out what he's saying to us!" I first hang back a bit in order to watch the little one's movements—the flail-

---

S.L.O.W.

Whenever your baby fusses or cries, try this simple strategy, which takes only a few seconds.

Stop. Remember that crying is your baby's language.

Listen. What does this particular cry mean?

Observe. What is your baby doing? What else is going on?

What's Up? Based on what you hear and see, evaluate and respond.

ing arms and legs, the little tongue curling and darting in and out of his tiny mouth, the back arching. Each gesture means something. I pay close attention to the kind of cries and sounds he's making. Pitch, intensity, and frequency are all parts of baby language.

I also absorb the surroundings. I imagine what it's like to *be* that baby. Besides paying attention to his overall appearance, his sounds and gestures, I look around the room, feel the temperature, and listen to the noises of the household. I observe how his mum and dad look— nervous, tired, or angry—and I listen to what they're saying. I might ask a few questions as well, such as:

"When did you last feed him?"

"Do you usually walk him around before he goes to sleep?"

"Does he often pull his legs up to his chest like that?"

Then I wait. I mean, you wouldn't barge into an adult conversation without knowing exactly what was being said, would you? You would stand back a minute, to figure out whether it's even appropriate to interrupt. But too often with babies, grown-ups tend to jump in headfirst. They coo, rock, pull off a diaper, tickle, cajole, or shake; they might speak a bit too loud or too fast. They think they're responding, but they're not; they're just plowing ahead. And sometimes, because they're acting out of their own discomfort as opposed to responding to the infant's needs, they inadvertently increase their baby's distress.

Over the years, I've learned the value of evaluating before rushing in; hanging back has become almost second nature to me. But I recognize that new parents, who aren't used to the sound of crying and who have their own performance anxiety around babies, often have a harder time of it. Which is why I've come up with another handy acronym for helping parents and other adult caretakers put on the brakes: S.L.O.W. The word itself is a reminder not to rush in, and each letter helps you remember what to do.

Stop. Stand back and wait a heartbeat; you don't have to swoop down and pick up your baby the moment she cries. Take three deep breaths to center yourself and improve your own perception. It will also help you clear your mind of other people's voices and advice, which often make it hard for you to be objective.

Listen. Crying is your baby's language. This moment of hesitation is not to suggest that you should let your baby cry. Rather, listen to what he's saying to you.

Observe. What is his body language telling you? What's going on in the environment? What was happening right before your baby "said" something?

What's Up? If you now put it all together—what you've heard and seen, as well as where your baby is in the daily routine—you will be able to figure out what she is trying to say to you.

Why Stop?

When your baby cries, your natural inclination may be to rescue. You may believe that your infant is in distress; worse, you may think that crying is bad. The *S* in S.L.O.W. reminds you to curb those feelings and, instead, hold back for a moment. Let me explain three important reasons I urge you to stop yourself.

1. Your baby needs to develop his or her "voice." All parents want their children to be expressive—that is, to be able to ask for what they need and to talk about their feelings. Unfortunately, many mums and dads wait until a child begins to develop *verbal* language to start teaching this all-important skill. However, the roots of expression are laid in early infancy, when babies first start to "converse" with us through their coos and cries.

Bearing this in mind, consider what happens when in response to every cry a mum always lifts her little one to her breast or puts a pacifier in his mouth. It not only takes away the baby's voice—essentially "dumbing" him up (which is why we Brits call pacifiers *dummies*)—but unwittingly trains him to *not* ask for help. After all, each different cry is a request from your baby that says, "Meet my need." Now, I doubt you cram a sock into your partner's mouth when he says, "I'm tired." Essentially, though, that's what we do to a baby if we just shove something in his mouth rather than holding back a sec and listening to what he's saying.

The worst part of this is that by rushing in, a parent unwittingly trains her infant *not* to have a voice. When parents don't stop to really listen and learn how to distinguish different cries, those cries, which numerous studies on crying have proven *are* differentiated at birth, in time actually *become* indistinguishable. In other words, when a baby is not responded to at all or if every cry is "answered" with food, Baby learns that it doesn't matter how she cries—it always results in the same outcome. Eventually, she gives up and all her cries *will* sound the same.

2. You need to foster your baby's self-soothing skills. We all know the importance in adulthood of self-soothing. When we feel a bit low, we take a hot bath, go for a mas-

sage, read a book, or take a brisk walk. Everyone's
method of relaxation is different, but knowing what
helps you calm down or settle into sleep is an important
coping skill. We also see evidence of this skill in children
at various ages. A three-year-old might suck his thumb
or clutch a favorite stuffed animal when he's had too
much of the world; a teen might hole up in his room and
listen to music.

Well, what about babies? Obviously, they can't take a
walk or turn on the telly to relax, but they're born with
built-in self-soothing equipment—their cries and the
sucking reflex—and we need to help them learn how to
use it. Infants under the age of three months may not be
able to find their fingers yet, but they certainly can cry.
Among other purposes, crying is a way of blocking out
external stimulation, which is why babies cry when
they're overtired. Actually, we still do this as adults.
Haven't you ever said, "I'm so fed up I could scream"?
What you really want to do is close your eyes, put your
hands over your ears, open your mouth, and wail,
thereby blocking out everything else.

Now, I'm not advocating that we let infants cry themselves to sleep—far from it. I think that's both unrespon-
sive and cruel. But we can use their "tired" cries as cues;
we can darken their rooms, shield them from light and
sound. Moreover, sometimes an infant will cry for a few
seconds—I call it the "phantom baby" cry (see page
210)—and then put himself back to sleep. He has essentially soothed himself. If we rush in, then he quickly
loses that ability.

3. You need to learn your baby's language. S.L.O.W. is a
tool that helps you get to know your baby and understand what she needs. By holding back, waiting to really
distinguish the cry and the body language that goes with

The Proven Benefits of Tuning In

Professor of psychiatry and human behavior Barry Lester, at Brown University's Infant Development Center, has been studying infant crying for over twenty years. In addition to classifying types of cries, Dr. Lester has done studies in which he asks mothers to identify their one-month-old's cries. A match is scored when the mother's perception agrees with the researchers' classification. Babies whose mums scored more matches had higher mental scores at eighteen months of age than babies whose mothers made fewer matches, and they had learned two and a half times as many words.

it, you can meet your baby's needs more appropriately than you would if you just shoved a breast in her mouth or kept rocking her without really understanding her need.

I must once again stress, though, that stopping for a few seconds to go through this mental evaluation process does *not* mean letting your baby cry it out. You're just taking a moment to learn her language. You *do* meet her need, and you *don't* let her get too frustrated. In fact, with this method, you become so good at reading your infant, you spot distress before it has a chance to spin out of control. In short, stopping to look and listen and then to carefully evaluate empowers you and makes you a better parent (also see "The Proven Benefits of Tuning In," above).

A Primer on Listening

It will take a little practice to distinguish your baby's different types of cries, but remember that the *L* in S.L.O.W.—listening—involves also paying attention to the broader picture to find clues of meaning. For the purpose of this discussion, I assume you're now following the E.A.S.Y. routine. Given that premise, here are some tips that will help you listen more intently:

Consider the time of day. At what point in the day did your baby start to fuss or cry? Had she just eaten? Had she been up playing? Sleeping? Might her diaper be wet or dirty? Might she be overstimulated? In your mind, play back what happened earlier or even yesterday. Did your baby do something new, like roll over for the first time or start to crawl? (Sometimes a growth spurt or other type of developmental leap affects a baby's appetite, sleep patterns, or disposition; see page 129.)

Consider the context. What else had been happening in the household? Had the dog been barking? Had anyone been using the vacuum or any other loud appliances? Was there a great deal of noise outside? Any of these things might have upset or startled your baby. Was anyone cooking, and if so, were very pungent smells emanating from the kitchen? Was there any other strong-smelling scent in the air, like a room freshener or aerosol spray? Babies are very sensitive to odors. Also consider the temperature in the room. Was there a draft? Was your baby over- or underdressed? If you had him out of the house longer than usual, was he subjected to unfamiliar sights, sounds, or smells or to strange people?

Consider yourself. Babies absorb an adult's emotions, particularly their mum's. If you're feeling more anxious or tired or angry than usual, this could affect your baby. Or perhaps you had an upsetting phone call or were yelling at someone. If you then nursed your baby, he most assuredly would feel the difference in your demeanor.

Remember, too, that when an infant cries, most of us are anything but objective. It's really not much different from when we see an adult in distress and project onto that person what we *think* he's feeling, based on our own experiences. One person might see a photograph of a woman clutching her stomach and say, "Oh, she's in pain," while another, examining the same photo, might say, "She just got good news—she's pregnant." We project when we hear babies cry, too. We think we know what they're feeling, and if the connotation is negative, we may tense up and worry about what to do next. Infants pick up on our insecurity—and our anger. One mum knew she was overwrought when she found herself "rocking the baby's bassinet just a little too hard."

Be realistic. It's okay *not* to know how to do something; it's okay to wonder how to proceed. It's also okay to get angry. Having misgivings and emotions only makes you a normal parent. What's not okay is to project your anxiety or rage onto your baby. I always tell mums, "A baby never died of crying. Even if it means letting your baby cry a few seconds longer, step out of the room and take those extra few minutes to calm yourself first."

> **TIP:** *To calm a baby, you must be calm yourself. Take three deep breaths. Feel your own emotion, try to understand its source, and, most important, let whatever anxiety or anger you feel drop away.*

Crying Baby = Bad Mother? No, Ducky, It Doesn't!

Janice, a thirty-one-year-old nursery school teacher in Los Angeles with whom I worked, had a devil of a time with S.L.O.W. because she couldn't get past the first letter. Whenever little Eric cried, Janice felt she had to rescue him. Typically, she'd try to feed him or pop a pacifier in his mouth. Over and over, I told Janice the same thing: "Wait a bit, luv, so you understand what he's saying to you." But it was as if she couldn't stop herself. Finally, one day, on her own, Janice realized what was going on, and she shared her insight with me.

"When Eric was two weeks old, I had a conversation with my mother, who had gone back to Chicago by then. She'd come to see him when he was first born, with my dad and sister, but they all left after Eric's *bris*. A few days later, while we were talking on the phone, Mother heard Eric crying in the background. 'What's wrong with him?' she asked in this really condescending manner. 'What are you *doing* to him?' "

Despite her extensive experience with other people's children, Janice was already feeling shaky about her ability to mother her own child, but it was her mum's veiled insinuation that pushed her over the edge. Following that phone call, Janice was convinced she must be doing *something* wrong. Adding insult to injury, at the end of the conversation her mother had added, "*You* never cried as a baby. I was an excellent mother."

There it was, one of the greatest and most damaging misconceptions I hear: *Crying baby equals bad parenting.* Janice had that message imprinted in her brain; who could blame her for trying to rescue Eric? It didn't help that Janice's sister had an Angel baby who rarely cried. Eric, a Touchy baby, was far more sensitive: Every little bit of stimulation shook his world. But Janice couldn't see her situation clearly, because anxiety was clouding her view.

Once we talked it through, however, Janice's perspective began to change. First of all, she remembered that her mother had had round-the-clock child care when she and her siblings were young. Perhaps time had dulled Mum's memory, or perhaps the household help had always whisked any crying children out of her sight. Regardless, the fact is that *every* baby cries, unless there's something wrong (see sidebar on page 84). In truth, a moderate amount of crying is actually good for infants: Tears contain an antiseptic that prevents eye infections. Eric's crying was an indication that he was simply trying to make his needs known.

Granted, when Eric let out a wail, it wasn't easy for Janice to quell the voice in her head that screamed, "Bad mother! Bad mother!" But knowing the source of her anxiety helped Janice think her actions through instead of immediately trying to silence her son. Self-reflection helped her separate her son from the maelstrom of emotions she was experiencing. It also helped her see him more clearly as the sweet, sensitive little boy he was—a far cry from her sister's little angel, but just as wonderful and lovable a gift.

Swapping stories with other first-time mums in my newborn group also helped Janice, because she saw that she wasn't alone. Indeed, I meet many parents who initially have trouble with S.L.O.W. because they can barely get past the first letter—they can't stop themselves. Or if they do, they have trouble listening and observing without letting their own emotions overwhelm them.

Why It's Sometimes Hard to Listen

There are a number of reasons why parents sometimes find it hard to listen to a crying baby and to be objective about what they hear. Perhaps one or more of the following rings true for you. If so, at first you might have

---

Crying Danger Signals

Crying is normal and healthy. But you should call your doctor if
- A typically content baby cries for two hours or more
- Excessive crying is accompanied by
    Fever
    Vomiting
    Diarrhea
    Convulsions
    Limpness
    Pale or blue skin
    Unusual bruising or rash
- Your child *never* cries, or if his cry is extremely weak and sounds more like that of a kitten than a baby

---

trouble with the *L* in S.L.O.W. Take heart, luv: Being aware is often all it takes to change your perspective.

You have someone else's voice in your head. It may be your parents (as was the case with Janice), or your friends, or a particular baby-care expert whom you saw or heard in the media. We also bring a lifetime of past interactions to the experience of parenting, which in turn shapes our views of what a "good parent" is supposed to do or not do (to refresh your memory of what *I* think a good parent is, reread the box on page 12). This includes how you were handled as a child, how your friends deal with their babies, what you've seen on TV and in the movies, and what you've read in books. We all hear others in our heads. The thing is, we don't have to listen.

> **TIP:** *Become aware of the "shoulds" you harbor and know that you don't have to obey them. They might be right for someone else's baby, someone else's family, but not for you.*

By the way, the voice in your head also might be telling you, "Do it *just the opposite* of the way so-and-so does it," but that's just as limiting. After all, hardly anyone is a totally bad parent. Trying *not* to be like a particular person turns him or her into a cardboard stereotype. Let's say your mother was more strict than you want to be with your own children. She also might have been incredibly organized or creative. Why throw the baby out with the bathwater?

> **TIP:** *The true joy of parenting comes when we are empowered and can follow our own inner voice of guidance. Keep your eyes open, become informed; consider all options, all styles of parenting. Then make decisions about what's right for you and your family.*

You attribute adult emotions and intentions to your crying baby. The most common question parents ask when a baby cries is, "Is she sad?" Or they will say to me, "It's as if he cries to disrupt our dinner." For an adult, crying signals an outpouring of emotion, usually overwhelming sadness, joy, and sometimes rage. Even though adult crying often has a negative connotation, it's normal and healthy to have a good cry every now and then. In fact, in our lifetime, each of us produces close to thirty buckets of tears! The reasons *we* cry, though, are different from the reasons normal infants cry. There is no sadness. They're not crying to manipulate others. They don't want to get back at you or purposely ruin your day or evening. They're just babies—and they're pretty simple at that. They've had neither the exposure nor the experiences that we've had. Crying is their way of telling you, "I need to go to sleep," or "I'm hungry," or "I've had enough," or "I'm a little chilly."

You project your own motives or problems onto your baby. Yvonne, whose baby fusses before falling asleep,

TIP: *If you find yourself projecting adult emotions or intentions onto your baby, think of your little one as you would a barking puppy or a mewing kitten. You wouldn't assume that either of them was suffering, would you? You'd just think they were "talking" to you. Do the same with your baby.*

A Healthy Baby's Cries

What They Can Mean	What They Don't Mean
I'm hungry.	I'm angry at you.
I'm tired.	I'm sad.
I'm overstimulated.	I'm lonely.
I need a change of scene.	I'm bored.
My tummy hurts.	I want to get back at you.
I'm uncomfortable.	I want to disrupt your life.
I'm too hot.	I feel abandoned.
I'm too cold.	I'm scared of the dark.
I've had enough.	I hate my crib.
I need a cuddle or a pat.	I'd rather be someone else's baby!

can't tolerate even the little baby noises coming through the walkie-talkie in the nursery, so she rushes in. "Oh, poor Adam," she sighs. "Are you lonely in here all by yourself? Are you scared?" The problem is not little Adam, it's Yvonne. "Oh, poor Adam" is really "Oh, poor me." Her husband travels a great deal, and she's never been very good at being on her own. In another household, Donald worries excessively every time three-week-old Timothy cries. "Does he have a fever?" he asks. "Is he pulling his legs up like that because he's in pain?" As if that isn't bad enough, Donald then takes the next leap: "Oh, no. He's probably going to have colitis just like I do."

Personal hang-ups can weaken one's powers of observation. The remedy is to know your own Achilles' heel and, through this awareness, stop yourself from imagining your worst nightmare whenever your child cries. Do you have trouble being on your own? You might think your child is crying because he's lonely. Are you a hypochondriac? To you, every cry might seem to be a sign of illness. Are you prone to angry outbursts? You could think that your child is angry, too. Do you have low self-esteem? In your eyes, your child's cries might indicate that she feels bad about herself, too. Do you feel guilty about going back to work? When you come home and your baby starts crying, you might think she has missed you. (See the chart on pages 98–99 to find out the reasons babies really cry.)

> *TIP: Always take a moment to ask yourself, "Am I really tuning in to what my baby needs, or am I reacting to my own emotions?"*

You have a low level of tolerance for the sound of crying. This may be because of the voices in your head. That was certainly the case with Janice. But let's face it, a crying baby's pitch can grate. I don't hear a baby's crying as a negative—perhaps because I have been around infants most of my adult life—but most parents, at least initially, do put a negative spin on crying. I see this phenomenon every time I play my three-minute "crying baby" tape for the parents-to-be who attend pregnancy classes. First they laugh nervously. Then they begin to squirm and shift in their chairs. By the end of the tape it's obvious from the look on at least half the faces in the room—often, the fathers'—that they are uncomfortable, if not visibly shaken. At that point, I always ask, "For how long was that baby crying?" No one has ever estimated less than six minutes. In other words, whenever a baby cries, to most people it *feels* twice as long.

Moreover, some parents actually have a lower threshold for noise than others. Their response starts out as solely physical, but then the mind gets into the act, too. The sound of crying pierces the adult silence, and the new parent instantly thinks, "Oh, my God! I don't know what to do." Crying-intolerant dads often want me to "do something about it." But mothers, too, will describe their day as "going downhill" if their baby has had a cranky morning.

Leslie, whose son is two, admits to me, "It's so much easier now that Ethan can actually ask me for things." I remember Leslie as a new mum. She couldn't tolerate her baby's crying, not just because of the noise; his tears also broke her heart, because she was convinced that she had somehow caused his misery. It took me three weeks of living with Leslie to convince her that crying was Ethan's voice.

By the way, it's not just mums who try to silence babies with a breast. Every time newborn Scott cried for more than a few seconds, Brett, a father with whom I recently worked, insisted that his wife nurse their baby. Not only did Brett have a low physical threshold for noise, he also couldn't handle his own anxiety or his wife's. Though they were both high-powered executives, their new baby had leveled their confidence. Additionally, both believed, deep down inside, that Scott's crying was a bad thing.

> **TIP:** *If you are particularly sensitive to noise, you might need to work on acceptance: This is your life right now. You have a baby, and babies cry. It won't last forever. The faster you learn his language, the less he'll cry, but he will still cry. In the meantime, don't put a negative spin on it. Also, get yourself a pair of earplugs or wear your Walkman; neither will prevent you from hearing your baby, but they will mute the sound a bit. As a friend in England observed, "I'd much rather listen to Mozart than to the sound of crying."*

You're embarrassed by your baby's crying. This all-too-common feeling, I must say, seems to afflict women more than men. I saw it happen in a dentist's waiting room where I sat for approximately twenty-five minutes. Across from me was a mum with an infant who appeared to be three or four months old. I observed how the mum first handed him one toy and, then, when he got bored with that, out came another. He started to fuss, so she tried a third toy. I could see that the baby's attention span was dwindling fast. I also saw the mum starting to dread what was happening. Her face bore a look that said, "Oh, no! I know what's next." And she was right. Her little boy started to melt down, and his fussing quickly turned into the distinctive wail of an overtired baby. At that point, Mum looked around the room, ashamed. "I'm so sorry," she announced to everyone in the waiting room.

I felt so bad for her that I walked over and introduced myself. "No need to apologize, luv," I offered. "Your little one is just talking. He's telling you, 'Mum, I am just a little baby, and I've reached my limit of attention. I need a nap!' "

TIP: *When out of the house, it's a good idea to take a stroller or bassinet with you so that you have a handy and safe place for a tired baby to sleep.*

The following also bears repeating, so I'm directing my publisher to print it in bold letters for all mums to see (make signs like this and hang them all over the house, in your car and office, and slip one into your wallet, too):

A CRYING BABY DOES *NOT*
EQUAL A BAD PARENT

Also remember that you and your child are two separate
people—don't take his or her crying personally. It has nothing
to do with you.

You had a difficult delivery. Remember Chloe and Seth
whom you met in Chapter 2? Chloe was in labor for
twenty hours, because Isabella was stuck in the birth
canal. Five months later, Chloe was still feeling sorry for
her baby—or so she thought. What was really happening was that she had transferred her own disappointment onto Isabella. In her mind, she had imagined her
home delivery going off without a hitch. I've observed
this lingering sadness and regret in other mothers as
well. Instead of focusing on the new baby, they get stuck
feeling sorry for themselves, because reality didn't live
up to their expectations. They tend to replay the delivery
in their mind. They feel guilty, especially if the baby had
a problem—and they feel helpless. But because they're
not aware of what's really going on in their psyches,
they can't get past it.

> **TIP:** *If more than two months has passed since your de-
> livery and you find yourself going over the event repeat-
> edly in your mind or telling the story to anyone who's
> willing to listen, try to think or talk about it in a new
> way. Instead of focusing on the "poor baby," admit your
> own disappointment.*

When I meet a mum who I know hasn't finished pro-
cessing her delivery, I suggest that even a chat with a
close relative or a good friend can be enough to help her
change her perspective. As I said to Chloe, trying to val-

idate her experience but at the same time urging her to let go of the drama, "I hear how difficult it was for you. You can't fix it or change it, though. So now you have to move on."

Sharpening Your Powers of Observation: A Head-to-Toe Guide

Along with the sound of a baby's crying come gestures, facial expressions, and body postures. "Reading" your baby involves almost all your sensory organs— your ears, your eyes, your fingers, your nose—as well as your mind, which helps you put it all together. In order to help parents with the O in S.L.O.W., which enables them to interpret their baby's body language, I've taken a mental inventory of the many babies I've known and cared for. Aside from what their cries sound like, I asked myself what they *looked* like when they were hungry, tired, distressed, hot, cold, or wet. I imagined my tiny wards on videotape with the sound off, which forced me to zoom in on what their faces and bodies looked like.

Below is a head-to-toe view of what I saw in my imaginary video. Note that this body language is "spoken" by infants until they're five or six months old, at which point they begin to have more control over their bodies— for example, they may suck a finger to self-soothe. Still, the communication basically stays the same even after this age. Besides, if you start now, by then you'll know *your* infant and, most likely, will understand the dialect of his particular body.

Body Language	Translation
Head	
⇨ Moves from side to side	⇨ Tired
⇨ Turns away from object	⇨ Needs a change of scenery
⇨ Turns to side and cranes neck back (mouth agape)	⇨ Hungry
⇨ If in an upright position, nods, like a person falling asleep on a subway	⇨ Tired
Eyes	
⇨ Red, bloodshot	⇨ Tired
⇨ Slowly close and spring open; slowly close again and spring open again—and again	⇨ Tired
⇨ "Seven-mile stare"—eyes wide, and unblinking, as if they're propped open with toothpicks	⇨ Overtired; overstimulated
Mouth/Lips/Tongue	
⇨ Yawn	⇨ Tired
⇨ Lips pursed	⇨ Hungry
⇨ The appearance of a scream but no sound comes out; finally, a gasp precedes an audible wail	⇨ Has gas or other pain
⇨ Bottom lip quivers	⇨ Cold
⇨ Sucks tongue	⇨ Self-soothing, sometimes mistaken for hunger
⇨ Curls tongue at the sides	⇨ Hungry—the classic "rooting" gesture
⇨ Curls tongue upward, like a little lizard; not accompanied by sucking	⇨ Has gas or other pain
Face	
⇨ Grimacing, often scrunched up, like chewed toffee; if lying down, may also start to pant, roll her eyes, and make an expression that resembles a smile	⇨ Has gas or other pain; or is having a bowel movement
⇨ Red; veins at temples may stand out	⇨ Left to cry too long, caused by holding breath; blood vessels expand

Body Language	Translation
Hands/Arms	
⇨ Hands brought up to mouth, trying to suck them	⇨ Hungry, if baby hasn't eaten in 2¹/₂ to 3 hours; otherwise, needs to suckle
⇨ Playing with fingers	⇨ Needs a change of scenery
⇨ Flailing and very uncoordinated, may claw at skin	⇨ Overtired; or has gas
⇨ Arms shaking, slight tremor	⇨ Has gas or other pain
Torso	
⇨ Arches back, looking for breast or bottle	⇨ Hunger
⇨ Squirms, moving bottom from side to side	⇨ Wet diaper or cold; could also be gas
⇨ Goes rigid	⇨ Has gas or other pain
⇨ Shivers	⇨ Cold
Skin	
⇨ Clammy, sweaty	⇨ Overheated; or has been left to cry too long, which also causes body to expel heat and energy
⇨ Bluish extremities	⇨ Cold, or has gas or other pain and has been left to cry too long; as body expels heat and energy, blood is drained from extremeties
⇨ Tiny goose pimples	⇨ Cold
Legs	
⇨ Strong, uncoordinated kicking	⇨ Tired
⇨ Pulled up to chest	⇨ Has gas or other abdominal pain

What's Up?

In order for you to proceed to the *W* in S.L.O.W., which directs you to put it all together and figure out what's up, refer to the chart on pages 98–99, which will help you evaluate the sounds and movements your baby makes. Every infant is unique, of course, but there are a number of universal signs that usually tell us what a baby needs.

If you pay attention, you'll begin to comprehend your baby's language.

To be sure, one of the most gratifying aspects of my work is seeing *parents* grow, not just their babies. Acquiring these skills is harder for some mums and dads than it is for others. Most parents I've worked with learn to decode "baby talk" within two weeks, although some take up to a month.

Shelly. Shelly came to me because she was sure her daughter had colic. But as Shelly and I talked, the real problem came out—and it wasn't colic. Shelly was most assuredly the "fastest draw in the West," as I playfully called her. As soon as Maggie made the slightest little noise, a boob was out. Shelly picked her up and bam—a breast was in her tiny mouth.

"I can't let her cry—I get too angry," Shelly admitted, "and I'd rather put a breast in her mouth than get mad at her." I could also hear Shelly's guilt. "I must be doing something wrong. Maybe my breast milk isn't good." This lethal cocktail of bad feelings made it difficult for Shelly to even pause, much less stop, listen, and observe.

To get her to see what was happening, I first asked Shelly to keep a log (see page 71). That way, she had to keep track of exactly when Maggie ate, played, and slept. I only needed to look at two days' worth to know what the problem was. Maggie was literally eating every twenty-five to forty-five minutes. Her so-called colic was from too much lactose, which meant her problem would magically disappear if she was on E.A.S.Y. and thus feeding at proper intervals.

"Your baby will lose her ability to tell you what she wants if you don't learn to tune in to what her different cries mean," I explained. "They'll all start to merge into one big 'pay attention!' cry."

At first, I had to coach Shelly, helping her identify Maggie's different cries. After a few sessions, Mum was thrilled. She was able to distinguish between at least two of them: hunger, which was a steady *waa, waa, waa* rhythm, and overtired, which consisted of short cough-like bursts in the back of Maggie's throat, accompanied by squirming and an arched back. If Shelly didn't catch Maggie at that point and help her to get to sleep, that fussing turned into all-out wails.

As I noted earlier, your own emotional turmoil can get in the way, as it did with Shelly. She's gotten better at using the S.L.O.W. technique, and I suspect her skills will continue to improve. Most important, her awareness now helps her see little Maggie as a separate being with feelings and needs of her own.

Marcy. Marcy, clearly one of my star pupils, became a crusader once she learned how to tune in to her little one. She called initially because her breasts were sore and painful, and her son seemed to be an erratic eater.

"Dylan only cries when he's hungry," she insisted when we first met. When she explained that he got "hungry" almost every hour, I knew that she wasn't yet able to distinguish Dylan's cries. Straightaway, I helped Marcy see that she needed to put her three-week-old son on a routine, which would help give his day a pre-dictable structure and, not so incidentally, hers as well. Then I spent an afternoon with her. At one point, Dylan started making little coughlike cries.

"He's hungry," Marcy announced. She was right; her boy nursed nicely, but after a few minutes he started to fall asleep.

"Wake him gently," I coaxed. She looked at me as if I had suggested torturing him. I instructed her to stroke his cheek (more tricks on page 133 for waking your sleepy baby during feeds). Dylan started sucking again. He stayed on his mum's breast for a full fifteen minutes and had a good burp afterward. Then I laid him down on a blanket and propped some brightly colored toys within view. He was quite content for about fifteen minutes, at which point he started fussing. He wasn't quite crying— it was more like complaining.

"See?" said Marcy. "He must be hungry again."

"No, luv," I explained, "he's just getting tired."

And so we put him to bed. (I won't go into further details here, because I talk about putting babies to sleep in Chapter 6.) Suffice it to say that within two days, Dylan was on E.A.S.Y., eating every three hours. Just as important, Marcy was a new woman. She told me, "I feel like I've learned a foreign language that's composed of sounds and movement." She even started advising other mothers. "Your baby doesn't just cry because he's hungry," she told a mother in our newborn group. "You have to hang back a moment and wait to see what he's saying."

Keeping Yourself at Baby Speed

Yes, this all takes practice, but you'll be amazed at how differently you'll react to your infant once you keep this handy method in mind. S.L.O.W. will also change your perspective. It will enable you to see your child as the separate person she is and remind you to listen to her unique voice. It only takes a few seconds, mind you, to employ this strategy, but in those few seconds you will be the best parent your baby could ever hope to have.

When you figure out what your baby is saying and get ready to respond, the acronym S.L.O.W. should also serve as a reminder: *Move slowly and gently in your baby's presence.*

To make this point, I often do this demonstration in my new-parent classes: I ask everyone to lie on the floor. Without saying a word, I walk over to someone, take hold of his or her legs, and roughly pick them up and thrust them over the person's head. Everyone bursts out laughing, of course, but then I explain my motives. "That's what it feels like to a baby!"

Let us never assume that it's okay to approach a baby without introducing ourselves or do something without warning, and then explaining, what we're doing. It's simply not respectful. So when your little one cries, and you know it's because he's uncomfortable in his diaper and wants a change, tell him what you're about to do, talk him through it, and when you're finished, say, "I hope that made you feel better."

In the next four chapters, I will go into greater detail about feeding, diapering, bathing, playing, and sleep. But no matter what you're doing with or for your little one, take it slow.

Cause	Listen	Observe	Other Ways to Evaluate/ Comments
Tired or overtired	Starts as cranky, irregular-frequency fussing, but if not stopped quickly, it escalates to an overtired cry: first, three short wails followed by a hard cry, then two short breaths and a longer, even louder cry. Usually they cry and cry—and if left alone, will eventually fall asleep.	Blinks, yawns. If not put to bed, physical signs can include back arching, legs kicking, and arms flailing; may grab own ears or cheeks and scratch face (a reflex); if you're holding him, squirms and tries to turn into your body. If he continues to cry, his face will become bright red.	Of all cries, the most often misinterpreted for hunger. Therefore, pay close attention to *when* it occurs. It may come after playtime, or after someone has been cooing at Baby. Squirming is often mistaken for colic.
Overstimulated	Long, hard cry, similar to overtired.	Arms and legs flail; turns head away from light; will turn away from anyone trying to play with him.	Usually comes when Baby has had enough playing and adult keeps trying to amuse him.
Needs a change of scenery	Cranky fussing that starts with noises of annoyance rather than outright cries.	Turns away from object placed before her; plays with fingers.	If it gets worse when you change Baby's position, then she might be tired and needs a nap.
Pain/gas	Unmistakable shrill, high-pitched scream that comes without warning; may hold breath between wails and then start again.	Whole body tenses and becomes rigid, which perpetuates cycle, because then gas can't pass; pulls knees upward to chest, face is scrunched in an expression of pain, tongue wiggles upward, like a little lizard.	All newborns swallow air, which can cause gas. Throughout the day you'll hear a tiny squeaky, wincing sound in the back of the throat—that's air swallowing. Gas also can be caused by irregular feeding patterns (see page 299).

Anger—see "Overstimulated" and "Tired." Babies aren't really "angry"—that's adult projection. They're just not being read correctly.

Cause	Listen	Observe	Other Ways to Evaluate/ Comments
Hunger	Slight coughlike sound in the back of the throat; then out comes the first cry. It's short to begin with then more steady: *waa, waa, waa* rhythm.	Baby starts to subtly lick her lips and then "root"— tongue starts coming out and turns head to side; pulls fist toward mouth.	The best way to discern hunger is to look at when Baby last ate. If she's on E.A.S.Y., it removes some of the guesswork. (Everything you want to know about eating is in Chapter 4.)
Too cold	Full-out crying with bottom lip quivering.	Tiny goose bumps on skin; may shiver; cold extremeties (hands, feet, and nose); skin can sometimes have bluish tinge.	Can happen with a newborn after a bath or when you're changing or dressing her.
Too hot	Fussy whine that sounds more like panting, low at first, about five minutes; if left alone, will eventually launch into a cry.	Feels hot and sweaty; flushed; pants instead of breathing regularly; may see red blotchiness on Baby's face and upper torso.	Different from fever in that cry is similar to a pain cry; skin is dry, not clammy. (Take your baby's temperature to be sure.)
"Where'd you go? I need a cuddle."	Cooing sounds suddenly turn into little short *waas* that sound like a kitten; crying disappears the minute Baby is picked up.	Looks around, trying to find you.	If you catch this straightaway, you may not need to pick Baby up. A pat on the back and soft words of reassurance work better because they foster independence.
Overfeeding	Fussing, even crying, after meal.	Spits up frequently.	This often occurs when sleepiness and overstimulation are mistaken for hunger.
Bowel movement	Grunts or cries while feeding.	Squirms and bears down; stops nursing; has bowel movement.	May be mistaken for hunger; Mum often thinks she's "doing something wrong."

CHAPTER FOUR

The *E*—Whose Mouth Is It Anyway?

> When a nurse tells you that your baby is hungry, it goes to your most vulnerable spot. Thank God I read and took classes.
> —Mother of a three-week-old

> Food comes first, then morals.
> —Bertolt Brecht

Mothers' Dilemma

Eating is the main source of human survival. We adults have a wide variety of choices, but whatever diet we choose, *someone* always has an opinion about it. For example, I could probably find a hundred people who support a vegetarian diet but oppose high-protein foods. I'm sure I'd have no trouble coming up with another hundred who swear by a high-protein diet. Who's right? Ultimately, it doesn't matter. Despite what various experts tell us, *we* have to make the choice about our own diets.

Unfortunately, mothers-to-be face a similar quandary when deciding how to feed their babies. Given the current controversy over breast milk versus formula, the choice is compounded by huge propaganda campaigns. Obviously, in books about breastfeeding or on websites sponsored by LaLeche League International or by the U.S. Public Health Service, both of which vigorously support a culture of breastfeeding, the material is slanted toward giving your baby human milk. But you're just as likely to find the opposite bias on a website sponsored by a formula manufacturer. Let's face it: If you purchase a manual for a Cuisinart, it's highly unlikely that you'll find information in it about using a whisk.

So as a new mum, what are you to do? Try to maintain a balanced view and, in the end, decide what's right for *you*. Take all opinions into account, but be cautious about whom and what you consult; know what a particular resource is trying to "sell." As for friends, listen to their experiences, but pay less attention to the horror stories. Admittedly, there are instances in which a breastfed baby is malnourished, just as there are cases of tainted formula. But those examples are far from the norm.

In this chapter, to help you become clearer about your choice, I provide empowering information—without the rocket science or statistical numwhack that conventional breastfeeding books tend to bombard you with. I urge you to use this knowledge and the commonsense tips I offer, but most of all, rely on your own instincts.

Right Decision/Wrong Reason?

What saddens me greatly is that many mums, confused about what's "best" or "right," sometimes make a decision for all the wrong reasons. Time and again I'm called in as a lactation educator after a baby is born, and what I discover is that the mum has pressured herself into a breastfeeding regimen, either because her spouse or someone in the family has pushed her, because she's afraid of losing face with her friends, or because she has read or heard something that convinced her that there really is no other choice.

Lara, for example, called my office because she had gotten off to a bad start. Little Jason wasn't latching on properly, and whenever Lara tried to nurse him, he cried. Her postpartum period was particularly bad, because she had had a C-section. Not only did she have sore breasts, she had pain from the incision. Meanwhile, her husband, Duane, felt clueless, helpless, and overwhelmed—not a good thing for a man to feel.

Of course, everyone around the couple had an opinion. Friends who dropped by would give their advice about breastfeeding. One friend was particularly taxing. You know the type: If you had a headache after giving birth, she tells you *she* had a migraine; if you had a C-section, *she* had a D-section; if your nipples hurt from breastfeeding, *hers* became infected. Some comfort to Lara from *that* one.

Meanwhile, there was Lara's mum, a rather stern woman, telling the youngest of her three daughters to "get over it"—after all, Lara wasn't the first person to nurse a baby. An older sister was equally unsympathetic, insisting that she had had no problem getting *her* babies to latch on. Lara's dad was nowhere in sight, but her mother announced to all who cared to listen that Father was so upset that his daughter was in pain that he couldn't bring himself to come back to the hospital a second time.

After a few minutes of observing these interactions, I politely asked everyone to leave and urged Lara to tell me how *she* felt.

"I can't do this, Tracy," she said, huge tears rolling down her cheeks. Breastfeeding was "too hard," Lara confessed. During pregnancy, she had imagined herself with a baby gently suckling at her breast, love for her newborn oozing out of every pore. The reality wasn't even close to Lara's madonna-and-child fantasy. Now she felt both guilty and scared.

"That's okay," I told her. "Yes, it is overwhelming. Yes, it is a responsibility. But you're going to get through this with my help."

Lara smiled weakly. To reassure her even more, I told her that everyone goes through some version of what she was experiencing. Like Lara, many women don't realize that breastfeeding is a *learned* skill; it takes preparation and practice. And not everyone can or should do it.

Deciding How to Feed Your Baby

- Explore the differences between formula-feeding and breastfeeding.
- Consider logistics and your own lifestyle.
- Know yourself—your level of patience, your comfort with the idea of nursing in public, your feelings about your breasts and nipples, and any preconceived notions of motherhood that might affect your view.
- Remember that you can change your mind and that you can always decide to do *both* (see page 137).

Making the Choice

First of all, breastfeeding *is* harder than most prospective mothers imagine. Second, it's not for everyone. As I told Lara, "This is about meeting not just your baby's needs, but also your needs. When people place pressure on a mother who doesn't want to breastfeed or hasn't really taken the time and given thought to the pros and cons, you're not going to have a happy camper.

The point is, we *do have choices*. One can make a good case for either formula-feeding or breastfeeding. It depends on the individual. Moreover, the choice is not simply a physiological one; it's an emotional decision. I urge women to understand both what's involved and what's at stake—for the baby and for herself. I recommend seeking out a class where you can actually *see* breastfeeding. Find a breastfeeding mum and listen to her take on the matter. Ask your pediatrician, contact a midwife or birthing center, or look in the yellow pages under "lactation consultants" or "lactation educators."

Remember, too, that pediatricians usually have a predisposition toward one feeding regimen or another. Therefore, while you're exploring your options, it's best to interview several pediatricians but not necessarily choose one until you've made your final decision about feeding. In Los Angeles, for example, I know several doctors who frown on formula-feeding; some won't even take new mothers unless they breastfeed. A mother who opts to formula-feed would feel quite uncomfortable with such a practitioner. On the other hand, if you want to nurse your baby and happen to choose a pediatrician who knows very little about breastfeeding, you wouldn't be well served there, either.

Many books on baby care list the advantages and disadvantages of formula and breast, but I've tried to get at this issue another way. This is a highly charged decision, one that seems to defy a rational approach. Therefore, I'm going to list the points one must consider and give you my thoughts about each regimen.

Mother/child bonding. Breastfeeding advocates go on about "bonding" as a reason for women to breastfeed. I grant you that women feel a special closeness when a baby suckles, but mums who formula-feed also feel close to their infants. Besides, I don't think that's what cements the relationship between mother and child.

True closeness comes when you get to know who your baby is.

Baby's health. Many studies trumpet the benefits of breast milk (when Mum is healthy and well nourished). In fact, human milk consists mostly of microphages, cells that kill bacteria, fungi, and viruses, as well as other nutrients. Breastfeeding advocates typically list a whole range of particular illnesses that mother's milk can prevent, including ear infections, strep throat, gastrointestinal problems, and upper respiratory diseases. While I agree that human milk is undoubtedly good for babies, we mustn't go overboard. The often-quoted research findings represent *statistical probabilities;* breastfed babies sometimes contract those diseases, too. Moreover, there are significant differences in the composition of breast milk from hour to hour, month to month, and woman to woman. Also, formula today is more refined and chock-full of nutrients than ever. While it may not offer an infant natural immunity, formula definitely provides babies with the Recommended Dietary Allowances (RDAs) of nutrients they need to thrive. (Also see the "Feeding Fashions" sidebar on page 108.)

Mother's postpartum recovery. After delivery, breastfeeding offers several benefits to Mum. The hormone that's released—oxytocin—speeds delivery of the placenta and constricts uterine blood vessels, which minimizes blood loss. As the mother continues to nurse, repeated release of this hormone causes the uterus to return more quickly to its prepregnancy size. Another plus for Mum is quicker weight loss after delivery; the internal production of milk burns calories. This is offset, however, by the fact that a nursing mum needs to *keep on* an extra five to ten pounds of weight to ensure that the baby is getting proper nutrition. With formula, there are no such concerns. No matter how a mum feeds, her breasts may be sore and sensitive. A formula-feeder has to go through a sometimes painful period as the milk in her breasts dries up, but a breastfeeding mum might have other breast problems (see pages 128–129).

Mother's long-term health. Studies suggest, but do not prove, that breastfeeding might offer women protection against premenopausal breast cancer, osteoporosis, and ovarian cancer.

Mother's body image. After the baby arrives, women often say, "I want my body back." It's not just a matter of losing weight. It's more about body image. Breastfeeding feels to some women as if they have to "give up" their bodies. Also, breastfeeding does change the look of most women's breasts even more than pregnancy does. When you breastfeed, certain *irreversible* physiological changes take place that enable the breasts to more efficiently manufacture milk: The ducts start to fill with milk, and when the baby latches on, the lactiferous sinuses pulsate and tell your brain to maintain a steady supply (see the sidebar "How Your Breasts Produce Milk," on page 117). Some mums with flat nipples will even end up with "T-shirt nipples" after nursing. Though her breasts will change again once the woman stops nursing, they'll never go back to what they were before. Small-breasted women who breastfeed longer than a year can become flat as pancakes; large-breasted women may experience sagging. Therefore, if a woman is concerned about her body image, it might *not* be best for her to breastfeed. She's likely to hear that she's "selfish" for making such a decision, but who are we to make her feel guilty and wrong?

Another factor is the emotional as well as physical comfort with the idea of putting one's breast into a baby's mouth. Sometimes women don't like to touch or even hold their own breasts, or they don't like it when their nipples are stimulated. If a woman has such discomfort, there's a good chance that she'll have trouble with breastfeeding.

Difficulty. Although breastfeeding, by definition, is "natural," the technique is nonetheless a learned skill—more difficult, at least initially, than feeding a baby formula through a bottle. It's important for mothers to practice the art of breastfeeding, even before the baby arrives (see page 116).

Convenience. We hear much about the convenience of breastfeeding. In part, it's true, especially in the middle of the night—when Junior cries, Mum just whips out a breast. And if Mum breastfeeds exclusively, there will be no bottles or nipples to sterilize. However, most women also pump breast milk, which means they have to take the time to express their milk, and they have to deal with bottles as well. Also, while breastfeeding may be convenient on one's own turf, many women find it difficult to find time and space for pumping at work. Finally, breast milk is always the right temperature. But here's something you may not know: *Formula doesn't need to be warmed* (babies don't seem to show a preference), so at least in the premixed version, it's almost as convenient as breast milk. Both require storage precautions as well (see page 122 about storing breast milk, 134 about storing formula).

Cost. On average during the first year, your baby will require an estimated 14,500 ounces of food—39.7 ounces per day (less, of course, as a newborn). Breastfeeding is definitely the less costly alternative, because breast milk is free. Even if you factor in the cost of a breastfeeding consultant, classes, various accessories, and rental of a breast pump for a year, the monthly toll is around $65, half the average monthly outlay if you buy formula. You can buy most formulas in powder (meant to be mixed with water), concentrate (which requires an equal part of water), or the ready-to-feed version—which is understandably the most expensive, often costing $200 or more a month. (I'm not including the cost of bottles and nipples in this equation, because many breastfeeding mums buy bottles as well.)

Feeding Fashions

Today, breastfeeding is all the rage. That doesn't mean formula is "bad." In the postwar decades, in fact, the majority believed that formula was best for babies, and only a third of all mothers nursed their babies. Currently, around 60 percent of mums breastfeed—although fewer than half of them are still nursing six months later. Who knows? As this book is being written, scientists are experimenting with the notion of genetically altering cows to produce human breast milk. If that happens, perhaps in the future everyone will tout cow's milk.

In fact, a 1999 article in the *Journal of Nutrition* suggests "that it may ultimately be possible to design formulas better able to meet the needs of individual infants than the milk available from the mother's breast."

Your partner's role. Some fathers feel left out when a mum breastfeeds, but this must be a woman's choice. In fact, most mums—regardless of how they feed their babies—*want* their partners to be involved, and they should be. Involvement is more a matter of motivation and interest than feeding method. A partner can participate whether Mum decides to give the baby formula *or* breast milk, as long as she's willing to pump her milk. With either feeding regimen, a father's help translates into a much-needed breather for Mum.

A WORD TO DAD: You may want your wife to breastfeed because your mother or sister did, or because you think it's best. Or you may not want her to. Either way, your wife is an individual; she has choices in life, and this is one of them. She doesn't love you any the less if she wants to breastfeed; she's not a bad mum if she doesn't. I'm not saying you both shouldn't discuss your concerns, but ultimately, this is her decision to make.

Contraindications for baby. Based on the results of metabolic screening, which is routinely done on newborns to test for a number of different diseases, your pediatrician may advise against breastfeeding. In fact, in some cases very specific lactose-free formulas are indicated. Likewise, if a baby has a high degree of jaundice (caused by an excess of bilirubin, a yellowish substance usually broken down by the liver), some hospitals will insist on formula (see page 138). As for allergies to formula, I think Americans tend to be overly concerned about this. A mum will tell me that her baby got a rash or gas from a particular formula, but breastfed babies develop these problems, too.

Contraindications for the mother. Some mothers can't breastfeed, either because they've had surgery on their breasts (see sidebar page 110), because they have an infection, such as HIV, or because they're taking a drug that taints their milk, such as lithium or any major tranquilizer. Although research indicates that physical factors such as breast size and nipple shape are irrelevant, some mothers *will* have more problems than others establishing a good flow and getting the baby to latch on. Most of these problems can be handled (see pages 128–129), but some mums won't have the patience to hang in there.

The proverbial bottom line is that while it *is* good for a baby to have some breast milk, especially during the first month, if that's not the mother's choice or if for some reason the mother *can't* breastfeed, formula-feeding is a perfectly acceptable alternative—for some, the preferable alternative. A woman may feel she doesn't have the time to breastfeed, or the notion of nursing her baby simply doesn't appeal to her. Particularly when it's not her first child, she may fear that the sight of her nursing might somehow upset the family's equilibrium—perhaps her older children will feel jealous.

In any case, when a woman doesn't want to breastfeed, we need to support her and we need to stop heaping on the guilt. We also have to stop using the word *commitment* only in connection with breastfeeding. *Any* kind of feeding regimen takes commitment.

If You Have Had Breast Surgery . . .

- If it was reconstruction or reduction, find out whether the surgeon cut through the nipple or behind the breastbone. Even if the lactiferous duct was severed, your baby can still suckle if you use a supplemental nursing system, whereby the baby sucks simultaneously on both the nipple and a feeding tube.
- Seek out a lactation consultant, who can help you determine whether the baby is latched on correctly and, if necessary, show you how to work with a supplemental feeding system.
- Have your baby weighed every week for at least six weeks to make sure he or she is gaining weight at the proper rate.

Feeding Happily Ever After

Getting started right is half the battle (for specifics about the first feeds, see page 117 if you're breastfeeding, page 132 if you're formula-feeding). It's important to set aside a special place in your home—your baby's nursery or some quiet spot away from the hubbub of the household—and reserve that space solely for feeds. Take your time. Respect your baby's right to have a peaceful meal. Don't be on the telephone or having a chat across the fence with Nelly with Baby in hand, a bottle or breast in his mouth. Feeding is an interactive process; *you* must pay attention, too. It's how you get to know your baby. And it's how your baby gets to know you. Also, as your baby gets older, he or she will be more susceptible to visual and auditory distractions, which can disrupt his meal.

Mums often ask, "Is it all right to talk to the baby while I'm feeding her?" Absolutely, but in a quiet, gentle way. Think of it as conversation over a candlelit dinner. Use very low tones, nothing abrupt, and be encouraging: "C'mon, have a little more—you need to

> **TIP:** *When your baby dozes off during a feed, to jumpstart his sucking reflex try any of these strategies: With your thumb, gently rub in a circular motion the palm of his hand; rub his back or underarm; or "walk" your fingers up and down his spine—a technique I call "walking the plank." Never put a wet washcloth on a baby's forehead to keep him awake or tickle his feet, as some suggest. That's like me coming under the table and saying, "You haven't eaten all your chicken, so let me just tickle your feet to get you going again." If none of these strategies works, I would leave the baby for half an hour and just let him sleep. If your baby constantly falls asleep while feeding and it's difficult to rouse him, ask your pediatrician's advice.*

eat a bit more." I often make sweet goo-goo noises or stroke a baby's head. Not only are these ways of engaging with an infant, but they're also part and parcel of keeping her awake. If a baby closes her eyes and stops sucking for a moment, I'll say, "Are you in there?" or "C'mon now, no sleeping on the job—after all, this is your *only* job!"

As I spelled out quite clearly in Chapter 2, no matter which feeding regimen a mum chooses, I am *never* an advocate of on-demand feeding. Besides ending up with a demanding baby, what often happens is that parents, not yet attuned to the different sounds their baby makes, always think that crying equals hunger. That's why we have a lot of overfed infants—a problem that is often mistaken as "colic" (see page 300). In contrast, if you keep your baby on an E.A.S.Y. routine, you feed every two and a half to three hours on the breast, or every three to four hours on formula, and you know that the cries in between are for other reasons.

Eating Profiles

Temperament influences the way a baby eats. Predictably, **Angel** and **Textbook** babies are usually good feeders, but so are **Spirited** babies.

Touchy babies often get frustrated, especially if they're breastfed. These infants don't allow for much flexibility. If you start to feed a Touchy baby in one position, he needs to feed that way all the time. You also can't talk loud while you're feeding him, change your position, or move to another room.

Grumpy babies are impatient. If you are breastfeeding, they don't like to wait for the letdown. They sometimes tug on Mum's breast. They're often fine with a bottle, as long as it has a free-flowing nipple (more about nipples on page 135).

In the sections that follow, I go into the various particulars of breastfeeding (pages 116–132), formula-feeding (pages 132–136), and combining the two (pages 137–142). But first, here are some issues that crop up no matter how your baby is fed.

Feeding positions. Whether you feed by breast or bottle, you should nestle your baby comfortably in the crook of your arm, pretty much level with your breast (even if you're bottle-feeding), so that his head is elevated slightly, his body is in a straight line, and he doesn't have to strain his neck in order to attach to your breast or take his bottle. His inner arm is tucked down, next to him or around your side. Take care not to tilt him so that his head is lower than his body, as that will make it difficult for him to swallow. If you're bottle-feeding, your baby should be lying on his back; if breastfeeding, he should be turned slightly toward you, his face onto your nipple.

Hiccups. All babies get hiccups, sometimes after feeding, sometimes after a nap. They're thought to be caused by a full tummy or eating fast, which is exactly what happens to adults who bolt down their food. The diaphragm gets out of rhythm. There is not much you can do—except bear in mind that hiccups go as quickly as they start.

Burping. Whether they are breastfed or bottle-fed, all babies swallow air. You can often hear it—a little wincing sound or a gulp. The air collects as a little bubble in your baby's tummy, sometimes making her feel full before her stomach actually is, which is why you need to burp her. I like to burp babies before we give the breast or bottle, because babies swallow air even when they're lying down, and then burp them again when they're finished. Or if a baby stops in the middle of a feed and starts fussing, that often means she has a little air. In that case, a midfeed burp would be appropriate.

There are two ways to burp a baby. One is to sit your baby upright on your lap and gently rub her back while resting her chin on your hand. The other way, which I personally prefer, is to hold the baby upright with her arms relaxed and flopped over your shoulder. Her legs should be straight down, creating a direct route for the air to move up and out. Gently rub in an upward motion on the left-hand side at the level of her tummy. (If you pat her any lower, you're patting the kidneys.) With some babies a rub is all you need; others need gentle patting as well.

If you have been patting and rubbing for five minutes and there is no burp, you can pretty much assume that your baby doesn't have any air bubbles in his tummy. If you lay him down and he starts to squirm, gently pick him up—and out will come a luscious burp. Sometimes an air bubble travels beyond the tummy, entering the intestines instead. That can cause a great deal of discomfort. You'll know this because your baby will pull his legs to his tummy, start crying, and tense his entire body. Sometimes you will also hear him pass gas, at which point his body will then relax. (For other tips about gas, see page 302.)

Intake and weight gain. No matter how they feed, new mums often worry, "Is my baby eating enough?" Formula-feeding mums can *see* what their infants ingest. Some breastfeeding mothers actually feel the tingling or pinched sensation that sometimes accompanies the let-down reflex, so at least they know they're producing. But if a woman doesn't have such sensitivity—and many don't—I always tell her, "You can see your baby sucking, but also listen for the sound of her swallowing."

Breastfeeding mums who worry can also take a "yield," as I suggest in the sidebar on page 121. In any case, if your baby is content after she eats, it's a sign that she's getting a proper feed.

I also remind parents, "What goes in must come out." Your newborn will have six to nine wet diapers in a twenty-four-hour period. The urine will be pale yellow to almost clear in color. He will also have two to five bowel movements, which will vary from yellow to tan with a mustardlike consistency.

> **TIP:** *If you use disposable diapers, they will absorb the urine so well that it's hard to tell when your baby pees or what color it is. During the first ten days especially, place a tissue in your baby's diaper to determine if he is urinating and how often.*

Finally, the best indicator of intake is weight gain, although normal newborns lose up to 10 percent of their birth weight in the first few days. In utero, they were constantly being fed by the placenta. Now they have to learn to feed independently, and getting started takes a bit of time. However, most full-term babies, if provided with adequate fluids and calories, return to their birth weight by the time they're seven to ten days old. Some infants take longer, but if your baby has not gained back this weight by two weeks, a visit to your pediatrician is in order. Infants who aren't back to birth weight by three weeks are clinically considered "failure-to-thrive" babies.

> **TIP:** *Babies under six pounds can't afford to lose 10 percent of their weight. In such cases, supplement with formula until the breast milk comes in.*

The normal range of weight gain is between four and seven ounces a week. But before you go obsessing about your baby's weight gain, bear in mind that breastfed infants tend to be leaner and gain weight slightly more slowly than their bottle-fed counterparts. Some anxious mothers buy scales or rent them. Personally, as long as you visit your pediatrician regularly, I think it's sufficient to weigh a baby once a week during the first month, once a month thereafter. If you have a scale, though, remember that weight fluctuates day to day, so don't weigh your baby more often than every four to five days.

Breastfeeding Basics

There are entire books devoted to breastfeeding; if you have already made the decision to nurse your baby, I'll just bet that by now you have *several* of them on your bookshelf. As when you learn any skill, the keys are patience and practice. Read, attend a lactation class, or join a breastfeeding support group. In addition to understanding how your body produces milk (see sidebar on next page), here's what *I* consider most important.

Practice while you're pregnant. The major (and often only) cause of breastfeeding problems is improper latch-on. I prevent this in mums I work with, because I meet with them four to six weeks before their due date. I explain to them how their breasts work and show them how to place two little round elastoplasts (you Yanks call them Band-Aids) on their breasts, one inch above and one inch below the nipple, which is precisely where they'll be holding their breasts when nursing. This gets them used to placing their fingers properly. Try it yourself—and practice.

How Your Breasts Produce Milk

Immediately after your baby is born, your brain secretes *prolactin,* a hormone that initiates and maintains milk production. Prolactin and the hormone *oxytocin* are released each time your baby sucks on your breast. The *areola,* or darkened area around the nipple, is rough enough for a good latch-on, soft enough to allow the baby to compress easily. As your baby sucks, the *lactiferous sinuses*—ridges inside the areola—send a signal to your brain: "Produce milk!" When your baby suckles, the lactiferous sinuses pulsate, activating the *lactiferous ducts,* passages that connect the nipple with the *alveoli,* the small sacs inside your breast where milk is stored. This gentle squeezing acts like a pump, pulling the milk down from the alveoli into the lactiferous ducts and finally to the nipple, which acts like a funnel, dispensing the milk into your baby's mouth.

Remember that babies do not manually suck milk from the nipple; milk is produced through the stimulation the baby's sucking provides. The more stimulation, the more milk. Therefore, correct positioning and correct latch-on are vital to success. Get these two right and breastfeeding *will* seem "natural." If the baby is not positioned right and correctly latched on, however, the lactiferous sinuses cannot send a message to the brain, and neither of the hormones needed for breastfeeding will be released. Consequently, no milk will be discharged, and both Mum and Baby will suffer.

> **TIP:** *For a proper latch-on, your baby's lips should be flanged around the nipple and areola. As for correct positioning, extend his neck slightly, so that his nose and chin touch your breast. This will help keep his nose clear without your having to hold your breast. If you're large-breasted, put a sock under your breast to keep it up.*

Do the first feed as close to your baby's birth as you can. The first feed is important—but not for the reason you may think. Your baby isn't necessarily hungry. However,

Breastfeeding: The First Four Days

When babies are six pounds or more at birth, I usually give their mums a chart like this to guide them through the first few feeds.

	Left Breast	**Right Breast**
First day: feed all day, whenever baby wants	5 minutes	5 minutes
Second day: feed every 2 hours	10 minutes	10 minutes
Third day: feed every 2½ hours	15 minutes	15 minutes
Fourth day: begin single-side feeding and your E.A.S.Y. routine	40 minutes maximum, every 2½ hours, switching breasts each feed	

the first feed establishes a blueprint in his memory of how to latch on correctly. If at all possible, have a nurse, a lactation consultant, a good friend, or your mum (if she breastfed) come into the delivery room to help you with that first latch-on. When a mum has had a vaginal delivery, I try to get the baby latched on right there and then, in the delivery room. The longer you delay, the harder it can be. In that first hour or two, your baby is most alert. Over the next two or three days, he goes into a sort of shock—the after-effect of his trip through the birth canal—and his eating and sleeping patterns probably will be irregular. Hence, when a woman has had a C-section, and the first feed doesn't happen for a good three hours or more after birth, Mum and Baby are both groggy. In such cases, it usually takes more time and patience for a proper latch-on. (I don't advise parents to wake their babies for feeds at this time, except in cases of low birth weight—under five and a half pounds.)

For the first two or three days, you'll produce colostrum—the "power bar" component of breast milk.

What's in Breast Milk?

If you left a bottle of breast milk out for an hour, it would separate into three parts. From top to bottom, you would see a progressively thicker liquid, which is also what your milk is like as it's delivered to your baby:

Quencher (first five to ten minutes): This is more like skim milk—I think of it as the soup course, because it satisfies Baby's thirst. It's rich in oxytocin, the same hormone released during lovemaking, which affects both mother and child. Mum gets really relaxed, similar to the feeling after an orgasm, and baby gets sleepy. This part of breast milk also has the highest concentration of lactose.

Foremilk (starts five to eight minutes into the feed): More like the consistency of regular milk, foremilk has a high protein content, which is good for bones and brain development.

Hind milk (starts fifteen or eighteen minutes into the feed): This is thick and creamy, and it's where all the goody-goody fat is—the "dessert" that helps your baby put on weight.

It's thick and yellow, more like honey than milk, and it's packed full of protein. During this time, when your breast milk is almost pure colostrum, you'll nurse fifteen minutes on one side, fifteen on the other. When you begin to produce breast milk, however, you'll switch to single-side feeding (see page 118).

Know your own breast milk and how your breasts produce it. Taste it. That way, if it has been stored, you'll know whether or not it has soured. Pay attention to the feeling when your breasts are full. As milk flows from them, the sensation is usually a tingling or a rushing feeling. Some mums have a fast letdown, as the milk ejection reflex is known, which means that their milk flow is quite rapid. Their babies sometimes tend to sputter and choke in the first few minutes of a feed. To stop fast letdown, put a finger on the nipple, as if you're stopping a flow of blood from a cut. Don't be alarmed if you can't feel your letdown; sensitivity varies from woman to woman. When mothers have a slow milk ejection reflex, their babies appear frustrated and may pop on and off the breast to try to stimulate the flow. Slow letdown may be a sign of tension; try to relax more, perhaps by listening to a meditation tape before a feed. If that doesn't work, "prime" your breasts with a hand pump until you see the milk flow, and then put the baby on your breast. It can take three minutes for this to happen, but it saves the baby from becoming frustrated.

Don't switch sides. Many nurses, doctors, and lactation experts in this country tell women to switch sides after ten minutes, thereby giving your baby a chance to suckle both breasts at every feeding. One look at the sidebar on

---

The Cabbage Myth

Nursing mothers are often told to stay away from cabbage, chocolate, garlic, and other strong foods lest they "get into" her breast milk. Nonsense! A normal, varied diet has no effect on breast milk. I am reminded of the mothers in India, whose spicy diets would upset most *adult* Americans' stomachs. But neither they nor their infants are bothered.

Babies don't get gas from cabbage or the like. They get it from swallowing too much air, from being burped incorrectly, or because they have immature digestive systems.

Occasionally a baby may be sensitive to something in the mother's diet—typically the proteins found in cow's milk, soy, wheat, fish, corn, eggs, and nuts. If you believe your baby is reacting to something in your diet, eliminate that food for two or three weeks and then try it again.

Remember that exercise affects your breast milk, too. When you exercise, your muscles produce lactic acid, which can give your baby a tummyache. Therefore, always wait one hour before breastfeeding.

---

page 119, which defines the three components of breast milk, tells you why this isn't good for your baby.

Particularly in the first weeks of your baby's life, we want to make sure she reaches the hind milk. If you switch sides after the first ten minutes, at best your baby is only starting to get foremilk and never gets to the hind milk. Even worse, this switching eventually sends a message to your body that it's not necessary to produce hind milk.

If, instead, you keep the baby on your breast for an entire feed, she gets equal portions of all three types of milk—a balanced diet. Moreover, your body will get used to the regimen. If you think about it, this is how mums of twins *have to* feed. In the middle of nursing, wouldn't it be silly for them to suddenly switch sides? In truth, it's just as unproductive for the mum of a single infant to do that.

But How Much?

Unless you pump and weigh your milk (see tip below), it's hard to know the amount your baby's getting. Although I *don't* advise watching the clock, many mums ask the approximate time it takes a baby to nurse. As babies grow, they become more efficient eaters and take less time. Below is an estimate, followed by the approximate amounts consumed at each feed:

4–8 weeks: Up to 40 minutes (2–5 oz.)
8–12 weeks: Up to 30 minutes (4–6 oz.)
3–6 months: Up to 20 minutes (5–8 oz.)

> **TIP:** If you're worried about your supply of breast milk, for two or three days do what I call a "yield"—a concept taken from my farming roots. Once a day, fifteen minutes before a feed, pump your breasts and measure what you are yielding. Taking into account that a baby can extract at least one ounce more by physically sucking at your breast, you have a good idea of what you're producing.

Storing Breast Milk

I once visited a mum who was utterly distraught because the three-quarters of a gallon of pumped breast milk she had in her freezer had defrosted during a power outage. Dumbfounded, I asked her, "Darling, are you trying to set a new world record? Why did you store this much milk in the first place?" Certainly, pumping and storing breast milk is an excellent idea, but don't go overboard. Here are some points to remember:

- Freshly expressed breast milk should be placed in the refrigerator immediately and stored for no longer than seventy-two hours.
- You can freeze breast milk up to six months, but by then your baby's needs are different. A month-old baby's nutritional requirements are different from a three- or six-month-old baby's. The miracle of breast milk is that the composition changes as your baby grows. Hence, to ensure that the calories in the frozen milk meet your baby's needs, store no more than twelve four-ounce bags and rotate them every four weeks. Use the oldest milk first.
- Breast milk can be stored in sterilized bottles or specially designed plastic bags meant to hold it (chemicals from ordinary plastic bags can leach into the milk). Either way, it always should be labeled with the date and time. Store milk in two- and four-ounce containers to avoid waste.
- Remember that breast milk is human fluid. Always wash your hands, and keep handling to a minimum. If possible, pump directly into freezer bags.
- Thaw breast milk by placing the sealed container in a bowl of warm water for around thirty minutes. Never use a microwave; it will change the composition of your milk by breaking down the protein. Shake the container to blend any fat that may have separated and risen during thawing. Feed thawed milk immediately or store it in the refrigerator for no longer than twenty-four hours. You can combine fresh breast milk with thawed, but never refreeze.

TIP: After every feed, use a safety pin to mark the breast you'll use next. You also might feel a fullness in the breast that hasn't been emptied.

When I work with a mum from the first day, she single-side feeds by the third or fourth day. Often, though, I get desperate calls from mothers who have been told by their pediatricians or lactation educators to switch sides. Typically, their babies are anywhere from two to eight weeks old.

For example, Maria, whose son was three weeks old, told me, "My baby is eating every hour to every hour and a half at the most. I can't handle it." Maria's pediatrician wasn't concerned: Justin was gaining weight slowly, but he was, at least, gaining. That Justin ate *every* hour didn't bother the doctor—*he* wasn't doing the feeding! I told Maria about single-sided feeding. Because Maria's body was already accustomed to switching sides, we had to gradually change Justin's routine. I had Maria start each feed by putting Justin on one side for only five minutes, and then the remainder of the feed was concentrated on the second side. By continuing this for three days, at every feeding, it took the pressure off the breast that wasn't going to be used and prevented engorgement (see page 128). Equally important, it sent a message to Maria's brain: "We won't be needing that other breast just now." The milk in the unused breast was reabsorbed into Maria's system, where it was stored for Justin's next feed, three hours later. By the fourth day, Maria was able to single-side feed.

Don't watch the clock. Breastfeeding is never about time or ounces. It's about becoming aware of yourself and your baby. Breastfed babies usually eat a bit more frequently because breast milk gets digested more quickly than formula. So if you have a two- or three-month-old infant nursing for forty minutes, within three hours his system has digested the entire amount. (See the sidebar on page 121 for guidelines about how long it might take for your baby to feed.)

> **TIP:** *After breastfeeding, always wipe off your nipples with a clean washcloth. The residue of milk can be a breeding ground for bacteria and cause thrush on your breast and in your baby's mouth. Never use soap, because it dries out your nipples.*

Stand up for your right to breastfeed the way you want. Hardly anyone in this country will tell you not to switch sides. However you decide to feed your baby, stick with it.

> **A TIP FOR PARTNERS AND FRIENDS:** *When your mate (or a good friend) first begins to breastfeed, learn what she learns and continue to be a keen observer. Make sure that your baby is latched on correctly. However, don't be too vigilant. Even though you may be well-intentioned, don't, in the name of "coaching," offer a running commentary: "Attagirl, you got it. . . . Oh, no, he slipped off the breast. . . . There he goes again. . . . Yes, he's got it, he's sucking like a little champ. . . . Oops, he's off again. . . . Just hold him up a little. . . . Yeah, that's it, that's it. . . . Oh, no, he's off again!" Put yourself in her shoes. Mum needs loving support, not a sportscaster calling the plays. It's hard enough for a woman to learn the art of breastfeeding without feeling judged.*

Find a mentor. Breastfeeding technique was once passed down from mother to daughter. But because of the popularity of formula from the late forties through the late sixties, an entire generation of potential breastfeeders decided to bottle-feed. As a result, many young mothers today can't ask their own mothers for help, because Mum was a formula-feeder. Even sadder, young women are often given conflicting information. In the hospital, for example, a nurse on one shift tells her to position the baby this way; a nurse on the next says something different. Such chaos can not only affect a mother's milk supply, it also can put her into a state of emotional turmoil, and that, more than anything, can affect her ability to nurse. Because of this confusion, I set up breastfeeding support groups for my mums. There's no one better to help you over the initial hurdles than another woman who's recently been through it. If there's no one to turn to, find a lactation consultant in your area who can arm you with preventive measures and be on call should any problems develop.

> **TIP:** *Pick your mentor wisely—someone who has patience, a sense of humor, and good feelings about breastfeeding. Take negative input or far-fetched stories with a grain of salt. This brings to mind poor Gretchen, who told me she didn't want to breastfeed "because my friend's baby swallowed her nipple."*

Keep a breastfeeding diary. Once you get past the first few days and begin single-side feeding, I always suggest keeping track of when your baby feeds, for how long, on which breast, and other pertinent details. On page 127, I've reprinted the sheet I give out to my mums. Feel free to adapt it to suit your needs. You'll see that I filled in examples on the first two lines.

A Pump Primer

Pumping breast milk is not meant to replace breastfeeding, but rather to complement and enhance the experience. Pumping allows you to empty your breasts so that your baby can have your breast milk even when you're not around to give it to her. It can also prevent problems such as engorgement (see page 128). Make sure a lactation educator shows you how to use the pump properly.

What type? If your baby is premature, you'll need a strong industrial type. If you plan to be away from your baby only occasionally, a hand or foot pump will do. In any case, learn to hand-express in case of power failures.

Buy or rent? Buy if you're returning to work and plan to breastfeed for a year; rent if you plan to breastfeed for less than six months. Rented pumps are always serviced and, therefore, can be shared, as long as each person purchases new attachments. Pumps you buy are best used by one person.

What to look for? Buy or rent a pump in which the motor can be regulated for speed and strength. Stay away from those that require you to manually adjust the pump cycle by placing your finger over a hose—they're unsafe.

When? Generally, it takes an hour after a feed for your milk to replenish itself. To increase your supply, for two days pump ten minutes after the baby has fed. On returning to work, if you can't pump at the time you'd normally feed, at least pump at the same time every day—for example, fifteen minutes at lunchtime.

Where? Don't pump in the bathroom at work; it's unsanitary. Close the door to your office or find some other quiet place. One of my mums told me that on her job they had a "pump room," which was kept scrupulously clean for breastfeeding mothers.

Observe my forty-day rule. Some women get the hang of breastfeeding within a few days; some take longer. If you're one of the latter, please don't start panicking.

Time of Day	Which breast?	Duration of feed	Do You hear swallowing?	Number of wet diapers since last feed	Number and color of stools since last feed	Supplement: water/ formula?	Amount of milk pumped	Other
6 A.M.	❑L ❑R	35 min.	❑Y ❑N	1	1 yellow very soft	none	1 oz. @ 7:15 A.M.	Seemed a little fussy after eating
8:15 A.M.	❑L ❑R	30 min.	❑Y ❑N	1	0	none	1.5 oz. @ 8:30 A.M.	Had to wake him during the feed
	❑L ❑R		❑Y ❑N					
	❑L ❑R		❑Y ❑N					
	❑L ❑R		❑Y ❑N					
	❑L ❑R		❑Y ❑N					
	❑L ❑R		❑Y ❑N					
	❑L ❑R		❑Y ❑N					
	❑L ❑R		❑Y ❑N					
	❑L ❑R		❑Y ❑N					

Give yourself forty days of not expecting too much. Of course, everyone (Dad included) wants breastfeeding to go smoothly immediately, so after two or three days, you or your partner might become impatient and concerned. But to really get comfortable and to breastfeed correctly, it often takes longer. What's so special about forty days? That's about six weeks, which is usually how the postpartum period is defined (more about that in Chapter 7). For some women, it will take that long to get into breastfeeding. Even with a proper latch-on, you may experience a problem in your breasts (see chart on page 128), or your baby may not catch on at once. Give both of you a break and allow time for trial and error.

Breastfeeding Troubleshooting Guide

Problem	Symptoms	What to Do
Engorgement: Breasts become filled with fluid. Sometimes it's milk, but more often it's the surplus fluid—blood, lymph fluid, and water—that settles in the extremities, especially after a C-section.	Breasts are hard, hot, swollen; may be accompanied by flulike symptoms—fever, chills, night sweats; can also make it difficult for baby to latch on, thereby causing sore nipples.	Wrap breasts in a hot, wet cloth diaper; do overarm exercise (ball-throwing motion), five sets every two hours, just before you feed, and rotate your arms and ankles. Consult physician if the condition is not lessened within twenty-four hours.
Blocked Milk Duct: Milk congeals in lactiferous duct and becomes the consistency of cottage cheese.	Localized lump in breast, painful to the touch.	If untreated, this can lead to mastitis (see below). Apply heat and rub your breasts in a small circular motion around the lump, stroking toward the nipple. Imagine yourself trying to knead a curd of cottage cheese in order to turn it into milk. (You won't actually see the milk come out of your breast.)
Pain in nipples	Nipples may be cracked, sore, tender, and/or red; chronic cases evidence blisters, burning, bleeding, and pain throughout and between feedings.	A normal condition for the first few days of nursing, which will disappear once your baby begins rhythmic sucking. If the discomfort persists, your baby is not latched on correctly. Seek the help of a lactation consultant.
Oxytocin overload	Mum gets sleepy during breastfeeding because of the production of "love hormone"—the same hormone released during orgasm.	No real prevention, but it might be a good idea to try to get more rest between feedings.

Problem	Symptoms	What to Do
Headache	Occurs during or immediately after feeding, the result of your pituitary gland releasing oxytocin and prolactin.	Seek medical advice if it persists.
Rash	All over the body, like hives.	An allergic reaction to oxytocin. Antihistamines are usually recommended, but talk to your doctor first.
Yeast infection	Breasts are sore, or you feel a burning sensation in them; your baby may also have a diaper rash with red spots.	Call your doctor. You might both need medication to take care of the infection; your baby will need cream or ointment for his bottom, but don't use it on your breasts—it can clog your glands.
Mastitis: Inflammation of the mammary gland.	Uneven bright red line across the breasts; breasts are hot; flulike symptoms as well.	Immediately consult a physician.

TIP: Throughout the day, the calories you ingest are for your baby, as well as for your own body. That's why it's so important to sustain your intake of food while breast-feeding—no crash diets. Maintain a healthy, well-balanced diet, high in protein and complex carbohydrates. Also, because your baby is taking fluid from your body, too, be sure to drink sixteen glasses of water per day—twice the recommended amount.

Breastfeeding Dilemmas: Hunger, a Need to Suckle, or a Growth Spurt?

It's important to remember that newborns have a physical need to suckle approximately sixteen hours out of every twenty-four. Breastfeeding mums, in particular, sometimes confuse this need to suck with the "rooting" a baby does when she's actually hungry (see page 99). For example, Dale, who was breastfeeding, described this unmistakable pattern when she called for my advice: "Troy is hungry all the time, it seems. So when he cries, I put him on my breast, he sucks for around three minutes, and then he falls asleep. I keep trying to wake him, because I'm afraid he's not getting enough to eat." Here was a baby that weighed nine pounds at three weeks, so I knew Troy couldn't be malnourished. Rather, Dale kept mistaking her baby's sucking reflex for hunger, even though he had eaten an hour earlier. When he then fell asleep on her breast, she'd poke and stroke him but wouldn't get him to take more than a few swallows of milk. She then would disengage Troy from her breast. The trouble was that twenty or thirty minutes had passed by then, and he'd already been through one cycle of sleep (see page 210). When she then took him off her breast, probably just as he was coming into REM sleep, he'd wake up. Disturbed, he'd then want to suckle again *to soothe himself, not because he was suddenly hungry.* So Mum would sit down, and the cycle would begin again.

The problem here—and it's a common one—was that Dale unwittingly trained Troy to be a "snacker." And now she was fighting a losing battle. Think about it: That's why you don't give your toddler a cookie between meals. If a child munches all day, he can't eat a proper meal, can he? Neither can babies who are fed every hour or hour and a half. This problem doesn't happen as often with bottle-feeding, because Mum can actually *see* how many ounces her baby is taking. However, with either feeding method, when a baby is on a good three-hour routine, you'll know he's getting a proper meal, and you probably won't even have to wake him during feeds, because he's getting proper rest, too.

Use Your Common Sense

Though I recommend a structured feeding routine, I'm not saying that if a baby lets forth a hunger cry after two hours, you don't feed him. In fact, during a growth spurt, he or she may need to eat a bit more often. What I am saying is that your baby will eat better and his intestines will work better if he gets proper meals at regular intervals.

Nor am I saying that if once in a while your baby needs an extra cuddle or a feed because he's growing so fast, you ought to withhold it. What I am saying is that I hate to see infants upset because their mums and dads don't start as they mean to go on. It's *parents* who get a baby into bad habits; it's not the little one's fault. So, if you use common sense now, you can prevent traumatizing your baby later. (More about breaking bad habits in Chapter 9.)

Now let's take another situation that can confuse a breastfeeding mum—growth spurts. Say your baby has been feeding regularly every two and a half to three hours and suddenly seems extra hungry—almost as if she wants to eat all day long. She is probably on a growth spurt—a period of a day or two during which an infant needs more food than usual. Growth spurts usually happen around every three to four weeks. If you pay attention, you'll see that these all-day hunger binges only last around forty-eight hours, and then you're back on E.A.S.Y. Street.

Whatever you do, don't confuse a growth spurt with your milk supply lessening or drying up altogether. In fact, your baby is growing, her needs have changed, and her wanting to suckle more is nature's way of sending a message to your body: "Produce more!" Miraculously, in a healthy mum, the body will manufacture whatever

Baby needs to ingest. With formula-feeding, if your baby was on a three-hour feed cycle and suddenly seemed hungrier, you'd simply give him more food. That's all a breastfeeding mum has to do, too. Also, with single-side feeding, when your infant empties one breast (which usually happens by the time he's twelve pounds), you simply switch to the other side, thereby giving him all the milk he needs.

If your baby seems extra hungry *only at night*, it's probably *not* a growth spurt. Rather, it's a sign that she's not getting enough calories and you need to adjust your E.A.S.Y. routine to accommodate your baby's need for more calories. This may be a good time to "cluster-feed" (see page 208).

> **TIP:** *In the morning, after a good night's rest, your breast milk is richest in fat. If your baby seems extra hungry at night, pump early in the day and save that fat-rich milk for a nighttime feed. This will give your baby the extra calories she needs, give you and hubby an evening break, and, most important, silence that ever-annoying voice that says, "Am I producing enough milk to sustain my baby?"*

Formula-Feeding Basics

It doesn't matter what your reasons are; if you've read, researched, and come to the conclusion that you want to put your baby on formula, that's fine. *Stand up for your right to give your baby formula.* Bernice, who read literally everything she could get her hands on, including complex medical reports, told me, "If I were a lesser person, Tracy, I would have been thrown into guilt. Because of the information I got about formula—stuff that even the nurses didn't know—they had to respect my decision. But I feel sorry for women who aren't quite this

Breastfeeding Bugaboos

What Happens	Why	What to Do
"My baby often squirms halfway through his feed."	In infants under four months, this could mean that she needs to have a bowel movement. She can't poop and suck at the same time.	Take her off the breast, lay her on your lap, allow her to poop, and then resume nursing.
"My baby often falls asleep when I'm trying to feed him."	Your baby may be getting a heavy dose of oxytocin (see the sidebar on page 119). Or he might be snacking and really isn't hungry.	To wake a sleeping baby, see the tip on page 111. But also ask yourself: "Is my baby on a structured routine?" This is the best way to determine whether he's really hungry. If he's eating every hour, he may be snacking instead of getting a good bellyful of food. Put him on E.A.S.Y.
"My baby bobs on and off my breast."	It could be impatience with a slow letdown. If it's accompanied by her pulling her legs up, it could be gas. Or she might not be hungry.	If this happens repeatedly, you probably have a slow letdown reflex. "Prime" yourself by pumping first (see page 120). If it's gas, try the remedies on page 302. If none of these works, she's probably not interested in nursing. Take her off your breast.
"My baby seems to 'forget' how to latch on."	All babies, especially boys, at times "forget"—they lose focus. It also can mean that a baby is overhungry.	Put your pinky into your baby's mouth for a few seconds, to give him a focus and a reminder of how to suck. Then pop him back on the breast. If he's overhungry and you know you have slow letdown, prime your breasts before latching him on.

strong." Your best defense against the formula critics—although you shouldn't need one—is facts.

To choose a formula, read the ingredients. There are lots of different types of formulas out there, all of which have been carefully tested and approved by the U. S. Food and Drug Administration (FDA). Basically, formula is made with either cow's milk or soy. Personally, I prefer cow-based formulas to soy-based, although both are fortified with vitamins, iron, and other nutrients. The difference is that the butterfat you'd get in cow-milk formula is replaced by vegetable oil in soy formula. Although soy-based formulas have neither animal protein nor lactose, which are allegedly linked to colic and certain allergies, I advise trying a hypoallergenic cow-based formula first. There is no hard-and-fast proof that soy prevents these problems. Besides, there are nutrients in cow's-milk formulas that aren't in soy. As for the concern about rashes and gas caused by formula, remember that these problems erupt in breastfed babies as well. Such symptoms are usually *not* an adverse reaction, although more blatant symptoms, such as projectile vomiting or diarrhea, might be.

Storing Formula

Formula, which comes in powdered form, concentrate, or, for even greater convenience, ready-mixed in cans, is dated by the manufacturer. Cans can be kept *unopened* until the last-use date. Once in bottles, however, no matter which form you use, formula only keeps twenty-four hours. Most manufacturers do *not* recommend freezing. As with breast milk, never use a microwave; though it doesn't change the composition of formula, it heats the liquid unevenly and can scald your baby. Never reuse a bottle that your baby hasn't finished. To avoid waste, prepare only two- and four-ounce bottles until your newborn has demonstrated a bigger capacity.

Pick nipples that most closely resemble your own. There are many different types of nipples on the market—flat, long, short, bulbous—with bottles to match. I always recommend a Haberman feeder for a newborn, a bottle with a special valve in the end, which allows infants to get milk only when they suck hard, just as they have to with breastfeeding. Although some nipples regulate the flow more than others, with all but the Haberman, the formula just falls into the bottle, and gravity, not Baby, determines the flow (see also the box "The Myth of Nipple Confusion," page 137). As a rule, I suggest using a Haberman until the baby is three or four weeks old, even though it costs a bit more than other feeding systems. Switch to a slow-flow nipple for the second month, a second-stage nipple for the third month, and a regular-flow nipple from the fourth month until weaning. Besides considering flow, if you're planning to both breast- and bottle-feed your baby, it's important to find a nipple that closely matches your own. For example, if you have flat nipples, try the Nuk; if your nipples are firm and erect, the Playtex, Avent, or Munchkin might be best.

How Much Formula?

With formula-feeding, the composition never changes, as it does with mother's milk, but the baby—understandably—needs to eat more.

Birth to 3 weeks: 3 ounces every 3 hours

3–6 weeks: 4 ounces every 3 hours

6–12 weeks: 4 to 6 ounces (usually plateauing at 6 ounces by 3 months) every 4 hours

3–6 months: Increases to 8 ounces every 4 hours

I recently visited Irene, a breastfeeding mum who was planning to go back to work. She had an array of eight different feeding systems, all of which her little Dora had rejected. "She gags or rolls them round her mouth," Irene lamented, "and every feed is a nightmare." That was a lot of nightmares, I thought, considering she had to feed her baby on average eight times a day. So I said, "Let me take a good look at your breast, and then we'll go shopping." Which is what we did. We found a nipple that most closely resembled Irene's. Over the next few days, Dora still gave her a bit of a hard time, but it was certainly easier to get her accustomed to a nipple that resembled Mum's than it was with the other eight.

When shopping for bottles and nipples, also look for combinations that have a universal screw top, so that you can interchange if necessary. I've seen a few systems that are very pleasing to the eye and come with all sorts of fantastic promises—"just like mother's breast," "natural tilt," "prevents gas." Take the advertising with a grain of salt, and see which works best for *your* baby.

Be gentle when you first feed. The first time you put a nipple into your baby's mouth, stroke her lips with the nipple of the bottle and wait until she responds by opening her mouth. Then gently slide the nipple in as she latches on. *Never* force a bottle into your baby's mouth.

Don't compare your feeding regimen to a breastfeeding mother's. Formula is digested more slowly than human milk, which means that formula-fed babies can often go four hours between feeds, instead of three.

The Third Alternative: Breast *and* Bottle

My even-handedness about breast milk and formula aside, I always tell parents that even a little bit of breast milk is better than none. Some mums are shocked to hear this, especially those who've consulted doctors or organizations that advocate breastfeeding and believe that feeding is an all-or-nothing proposition.

"Can I really do both?" they ask. "Is it possible to nurse my baby *and* give her a bottle?" My answer is always "Of course you can." I also explain that by "both" I mean that a baby can be given breast milk and formula, or given only breast milk, but by bottle as well as by breast.

The Myth of Nipple Confusion

A lot has been made of "nipple confusion" as a reason for not feeding babies with both breast and bottle. I believe that's a myth. What can confuse a baby is flow, and that can be easily remedied. An infant on the breast uses different tongue muscles than a bottle-fed one. Also, a breastfeeder can regulate the amount of milk he takes in by changing the way he sucks, but with a bottle, there's a constant flow controlled by gravity, not the baby. If a baby chokes on a bottle, it's best to use a Haberman feeder, which allows a baby to get milk only when he sucks hard.

Granted, some mums are certain about their preferences right from the beginning. Bernice, who did a tremendous amount of research while pregnant, was 100 percent certain about her decision to give Evan formula—so sure that she asked her obstetrician to give her a hormone injection to immediately dry up her milk supply. Margaret, on the other hand, was equally decisive about breastfeeding. But what about the in-between mums? Some, because of a limited milk supply during the first few days, *have* to supplement with formula.

Other women *choose* to feed with both bottle and breast right from the beginning because they don't want to limit their own lives. A third group starts with one regimen and later has a change of mind. Of these, most mums breastfeed first and then add formula; but, believe it or not, it sometimes goes the other way round, too.

If an infant is under three weeks old, it's relatively easy to get him to take a bottle if he's been on the breast, or vice versa, and for him to continue to do both. After three weeks, though, the change can be very hard on mother and child (see box on page 142). Therefore, if you're at all ambivalent about giving your baby only the breast, remember that window and act sooner rather than later.

Let's look at some cases in which mums opted for the best of both worlds.

Carrie: needed a supplemental feeding. Especially if Mum has had a C-section, she may not be able to produce the milk her infant needs in the first few days of life. A morphine drip, typically given postdelivery, shuts the body down, although the mother may not realize that her milk is not flowing. This is what happens in tragic cases where a baby nurses on his mother's breast and, in the ensuing weeks, suffers from severe dehydration or even dies from malnutrition. He was sucking, but unbeknownst to Mum, nothing was coming out. This is also why it's so critical to check an infant's urine and stool output and to weigh your baby once a week (see page 115).

Unfortunately, many mums are unaware of the fact that it can take up to a week for their milk to come down. Hence, no matter how well positioned or firmly latched on a baby is, if Mum isn't producing, Baby is not going to thrive. In the hospital, when the nurse comes in and informs a mother that she needs to give her infant glucose water or supplemental feedings of formula, she may resist: "No formula for *my* baby!" She's heard that supplemental feeding will "ruin" her breast milk. The truth is, ducky, if you're not producing enough milk, you don't have a choice.

Even when formula is introduced, I tell my mothers to put the baby on the breast anyway, because the sucking helps activate Mum's lactiferous sinuses, which a breast pump cannot do. Whereas Baby's suckling sends a message to your brain to produce milk, a mechanical pump only empties the alveoli, where the milk is stored. Hence, you give formula but you also continue pumping every two hours, to get your flow going. Carrie, for instance, who had twin lads via C-section, had no milk for the first three days. Because the babies' blood sugar levels were low, we gave them formula straightaway. Carrie still put the babies on her breast—for twenty minutes every two hours—but we also topped the boys off with one ounce of formula.

After the feeding, Mum pumped, and she also pumped an hour after that. On the fourth day, Carrie's milk started to come in, and instead of one ounce of formula, the babies were given only half an ounce. Make no mistake: This is exhausting for the mother. No wonder on the eve of the third day of pumping, Carrie literally threw the breast pump across the room. Dad and I stood clear while she had her meltdown, and then life went on. By the fifth day, though, the twins were entirely on breast milk.

Freda: didn't want to breastfeed but wanted her baby to have breast milk. As I mentioned earlier, because of feelings about their bodies, particularly their breasts, some mums reject the idea of breastfeeding, but they are cognizant of the health benefits to Baby. Freda, for example, breastfed her baby only for the first few days, just to get her milk flowing. She then continued to pump until her baby was about a month old, at which point it was clear that her milk was beginning to dry up. I also know of a surrogate mother who pumped her milk and sent it frozen via FedEx to the baby's adoptive mother. In either case, pumping alone could not sustain the production of breast milk for longer than five weeks.

Kathryn: concerned about family harmony. When pregnant with her third child, Kathryn had decided that she would breastfeed the new baby, too, just as she had done with Shannon, age seven, and Erica, five. Steven had no trouble latching on in the hospital, but when Kathryn got home, she was overwhelmed. There simply wasn't enough time in the day to breastfeed Steven, so Mum reluctantly switched to formula. Around two weeks later, she called me as a last resort. She wanted to have the same close feeling with Steven that she had experienced breastfeeding his older sisters, but everyone was telling her it was too late. Besides, she had already seen how disruptive breastfeeding had been to her family life. "What I really want," Kathryn confided, "is to breastfeed two times a day—in the morning when he gets up, and at lunchtime, before the older children get home from school." I explained to Kathryn that breasts are miraculous—if you put the baby on only twice a day, your breasts will make just enough milk for those two feeds. To relactate—get her breast milk back—Kathryn, in effect, "primed the pump" by putting Steven to her breast twice a day *and* using a breast pump six times a day. At first, even though Steven suckled at her breast, Kathryn had to top him off with formula. By the fifth day, he seemed more content after feedings, and by using the pump, she could see that her milk had indeed come back. In Kathryn's case, once her milk came back in, she no longer needed to pump. In the end, Kathryn was getting the intimate contact she craved, but in a way that didn't adversely affect the rest of her family.

Vera: going back to work. If a woman is planning to go back to work, she has to either pump and store her own breast milk or introduce formula. Some women will wait until the week before, adding a bottle of formula once or twice a day, but if a baby hasn't had a bottle, I suggest introducing it three weeks before she's ready to return. Vera, for example, who worked as a secretary in a large industrial complex and couldn't afford to stay at home, opted to breastfeed in the morning, give her baby formula all day, and breastfeed when she came home. Her husband always gave the nighttime bottle.

Similar scenarios unfold when a mother simply wants more time for herself, or when she has to travel. A mum who works at home—say, a painter or a writer—also might want to express her breast milk, simply to allow another caretaker to handle some of the feedings.

> **TIP:** *Fatigue is a working mother's worst enemy, regardless of how she chooses to feed her baby. One of the ways to minimize exhaustion in the first few weeks back is to start on a Thursday rather than a Monday.*

Jan: surgery prevented breastfeeding. With serious illness or surgery, it is often physically impossible for a mother to continue breastfeeding. In such cases, the World Health Organization suggests that you ask other mothers to donate breast milk. But let me tell you, that's a beautiful fantasy—and nothing more. When Jan's baby was only a month old, she was told she had to have surgery and would be away from her baby for at least the three-day hospital stay. I called twenty-six mothers who I knew were breastfeeding, and of all of them, only *one* was willing to donate her milk—and just eight ounces at that. You would have thought I was asking for gold, not breast milk! As it turned out, Jan was able to pump a significant amount of her own milk, but she also gave her baby formula, and believe me, he was none the worse for the experience.

Making the Switch

Within the first three weeks, babies easily switch back and forth from breast to bottle. If you wait, though, you'll probably have a tougher time. A breastfed baby will initially balk at a bottle, because human flesh is all that his mouth knows and expects. He's likely to roll the nipple in his mouth and won't know how to suck or latch on. The reverse would be true as well. If a baby is not used to the feeling of his mother's nipples, he won't instinctively know how to latch on.

Formerly breastfed babies often go on feeding strikes, refusing to eat during the day. When Mum comes home, with all intention of giving the breast for those last few meals before bedtime, Baby has other ideas. Such a little one will wake his mum throughout the night, trying to make up for the meals he's missed. He doesn't know or care that it's night; he's running on empty.

What do you do? For two days, keep presenting bottle and no breast (or vice versa, if you're trying to get a bottle-fed baby on the breast). Remember that babies are always willing to go back to their original feeding mode. Whether your baby is used to breast *or* bottle, once it's in his memory, there's no such thing as his rejecting it.

Beware: This is hard work. Your baby will feel frustrated and cry a lot. He's saying to you, "What the dickens are you trying to put into my mouth?" He might even gulp and sputter as he feeds, particularly if he's making the switch to a bottle, because he doesn't know how to regulate the stream of liquid that pours out of a rubber nipple. Again, Haberman feeders eliminate this flow problem.

To Pacify or Not to Pacify: Every Mother's Question

Pacifiers have been around for centuries—and for good reason. Just about the only part of his body that a newborn can control is his mouth. He suckles in order to have the oral stimulation he needs. In the olden days, mums would use a rag or even put a porcelain stopper in an infant's mouth for oral soothing.

In Praise of Thumb Sucking

Sucking on fingers is an important form of oral stimulation and self-soothing behavior. Even babies in the womb suck their thumbs. Once they emerge, they begin to suck thumbs or other fingers at night, often when no one is around to witness it. The problem is, your own negative association with thumb sucking colors your view. Maybe you were taunted as a child for doing it. Maybe a parent once slapped your hand, called it a "bad habit," or said you (or someone else) were "disgusting" for doing it. I've heard of parents covering a baby's hands with mittens or a foul-tasting potion or even restraining an infant's arms—all to discourage thumb sucking.

The fact is, whether or not you **like** the idea, sucking is what babies **do**, and it's something we should encourage. Be objective. Remember that this is one of the first ways in which your infant gains control over his body and his emotions. When he discovers that he has a thumb and that sucking on it can make him feel better, it gives him a fantastic sense of control and accomplishment. A pacifier may do the same thing, but it's controlled by a big person and can get lost. One's thumb is always on hand—you should pardon the pun—and it can be put in and taken out at your baby's will. I assure you, your baby will give up her thumb **when she's ready**, just as my Sophie did.

Pacifiers needn't be thought of in a negative light. The modern-day controversy has arisen, in part, because of their misuse. When a pacifier is employed improperly, it becomes what I call a prop—something an infant becomes dependent upon for self-soothing. And, as I mentioned earlier, when parents use pacifiers to calm their babies instead of holding back and listening to what their child really needs, they effectively silence him or her.

I like to use a pacifier for the first three months of life to give a baby adequate sucking time, to calm her before sleep or a nap, or when I'm trying to get her to skip a night feed (I explain my methods in Chapter 6, pages 207–209). After that period, however, infants have more control over their hands and will be able to self-soothe using their own fingers or thumbs.

Myths about pacifiers abound. Some believe, for example, that if you give a baby a pacifier, he won't learn how to suck his own thumb. Poppycock! I guarantee that your baby will knock out the pacifier to get to his thumb. My Sophie did exactly that and continued to suck her thumb for the next six years. As she got older, she only sucked her thumb at bedtime—and, may I add, she never got buck teeth!

When purchasing a pacifier, apply the same principle as when buying nipples: Get a shape to which Baby is accustomed. There are some thirty or so different varieties of pacifiers on the market now. With that range of selection, Mum, you can surely find one that matches your own nipples or the type of plastic nipples you use on her bottles.

Wean, Baby, Wean!

Weaning has come to mean two different things. Contrary to a popular misconception, weaning doesn't mean going off breast milk. Rather, it refers to a natural progression common to all mammals: the transition from a liquid diet, be it mother's milk or formula, to solid foods. Often, babies don't need to be "weaned" from the breast at all. As you introduce solids, your baby takes less and less from the breast or bottle, because he's getting nourished in other ways. In fact, some babies will—on their own—begin to give up the breast at around eight months, and Mum simply gives them a sippy cup instead. Other babies are, of course, more tenacious. Trevor, a year old, wasn't interested in stopping, although his mum and dad were more than ready. I told his mum, Eileen, to be firm and to say "No more boobie!" whenever Trevor pulled at her shirt, which he did for a few days. I had warned both parents, "You're going to have a couple of days where he's going to be upset and he'll keep at you. After all, he's been nursing for more than a year and never had a bottle." Within a few days, though, Trevor finally drank willingly from his sippy cup. Another mother, Adrianna, waited for two years before telling her little boy "No more boobie." As is often the case, this was not her baby's doing. Adrianna was reluctant to give up the closeness that breastfeeding engenders. (On pages 308–310, I fill you in with more details of Adrianna's story.)

Most pediatricians suggest waiting until your baby is six months old before starting to introduce solid foods. With the exception of very large babies (seventeen to twenty-two pounds at four months) or infants suffering from esophageal reflux, the baby equivalent of heartburn, I agree. By the sixth month, your baby needs the extra iron found in solid foods, as her store of iron has been depleted by this point. Also, her protrusion reflex, which causes a baby to stick out her tongue when anything (like a nipple or spoon) touches it, has disappeared, so she is better able to swallow mushy solids. Also by six months, head and neck control has developed. Your baby is now able to communicate a lack of interest or tell you she's had enough by leaning back and turning away.

Weaning is quite simple, actually, if you follow these three important guidelines:

• *Start with one solid food.* I prefer pears because they're easy to digest, but if your pediatrician suggests another food, such as rice cereal, by all means follow that. Give the new food twice a day, morning and afternoon, for two weeks before introducing a second solid.

Breast Manners

At around four months, babies' hands start to wander, and they turn their heads and twist their bodies. While nursing, they'll fiddle with your clothing or jewelry, and they'll poke your chin, nose, or eyes if they can reach. As they get older, they can develop other bad habits that, once they begin, are hard to change. So start now to teach your baby what I call "breast manners." In each case, the trick is to be firm but gentle, reminding her of your boundaries. Also, try breastfeeding in a quiet environment, to cut down on distractions.

For fiddling: Hold his hand and gently take it away from your body or whatever he's touching. Say, "Mummy doesn't like that."

For distractions: The worst is when a baby gets distracted and tries to turn her head . . . with Mum's nipple still in her mouth. When that happens, take her *off* the breast and say, "Mummy doesn't like that."

For biting: When a baby's teeth come in, almost every mum gets bitten. It should only happen once, though. Don't be afraid to react appropriately, pulling away and saying, "Ouch, that hurts. Don't bite Mummy." That's usually enough, but if it doesn't stop him, remove him from your breast.

For shirt pulling: Toddlers still nursing sometimes do this when they want to be pacified. Simply say, "Mummy doesn't want her shirt up. Don't pull on it."

• *Always introduce a new food in the morning.* This gives you all day to see if your baby is having an adverse reaction to the food, such as a rash, vomiting, or diarrhea.

• *Never mix foods together.* That way there's no question about allergic reactions to a particular food.

In the chart on the next page, "The First Twelve Weeks," I list the specifics of what foods to introduce and when. By the time a baby is nine months old, I introduce chicken broth, using it to flavor baby cereal, which tastes basically like paste, or to dilute veggies I puree at home. However, I suggest waiting until the baby is one year old before introducing meat, eggs, or whole milk. Of course, your pediatrician should be the last word on this.

Never force or struggle with a baby who doesn't want to eat a particular food. Feeding should be a pleasant experience for the baby and the whole family. As I said at the outset of this chapter, eating is basic to human survival. If we're lucky, the people who care for us will also make us recognize and enjoy the tastes and textures of good food. This appreciation starts in infancy. A love of food is one of the most wonderful gifts you can give your baby. Not so incidentally, a good balanced diet will also give her the energy and strength she needs to get through her day. And as we will see in the next chapter, that's a tall order for a growing baby.

Weaning: The First Twelve Weeks

The following twelve-week schedule is based on weaning a six-month-old child. You will do the morning feed as usual, breast or bottle, and serve "breakfast" two hours later. "Lunch" should be midday and "dinner" late afternoon. Complete breakfast and dinner by finishing off on the breast or bottle. Remember that every baby is different; ask your pediatrician what's right for yours.

Week	Breakfast	Lunch	Dinner	Comments
1 (6 months old)	Pears, 2 teaspoons	Bottle or breast	Pears, 2 teaspoons	
2	Pears, 2 teaspoons	Bottle or breast	Pears, 2 teaspoons	
3	Squash, 2 teaspoons	Bottle or breast	Pears, 2 teaspoons	
4	Sweet potatoes, 2 teaspoons	Squash, 2 teaspoons	Pears, 2 teaspoons	
5 (7 months old)	Oatmeal, 4 teaspoons	Squash, 4 teaspoons	Pears	Increase the amount to meet your growing baby's needs
6	Oatmeal, and pear, 4 teaspoons each	Squash, 8 teaspoons	Oatmeal and sweet potato, 4 teaspoons each	Now you can give more than one food at a meal
7	Peach, 8 teaspoons	Oatmeal and squash, 4 teaspoons each	Oatmeal and pear, 4 teaspoons each	
8 (8 months old)	Banana	From this point on, you can mix and match the above foods, introducing a new food each week as shown at the left, 8 to 12 teaspoons per meal		
9	Carrots			
10	Peas			
11	Green beans	You can continue to mix and match foods, introducing a new food each week as shown, 8 to 12 teaspoons per meal		
12 (9 months old)	Apple			

CHAPTER FIVE
The *A*—Wake Up and Smell the Nappy

> Babies and young children think, observe, and reason. They consider evidence, draw conclusions, do experiments, solve problems, and search for the truth. Of course, they don't do this in the self-conscious way that scientists do. And the problems they try to solve are everyday problems about what people and objects and words are like, rather than arcane problems about stars and atoms. But even the youngest babies know a great deal about the world and actively work to find out more.
>
> —Alison Gopnik, Andrew N. Meltzoff, and Patricia K. Kuhl in *The Scientist in the Crib*

In the Waking Hours

To a newborn, every day is a wonder. From the moment babies emerge from the womb, their growth is exponential, as is their ability to explore and delight in their surroundings. Think about it: When your baby was only a week old, she was seven times as old as she was on the day she was born; by the end of her first month, she was light years ahead of where she was on day one, and so on and so on. We see these changes most during babies' activities, defined here as whatever infants do during their waking hours that engages one or more of their senses. (Eating is clearly an activity, too, one that stimulates a baby's sense of taste, but I've covered that in the last chapter.)

A baby's perception starts to develop in the womb. Scientists speculate, in fact, that babies appear to be able to recognize their mother's voice at birth, because they've heard it, however muted, in utero. Once they enter the world, all five senses continue to sharpen in this order: hearing, touch, sight, smell, and taste. Now, it may not sound like much activity to you to be lying on a changing table getting diapered or dressed, to be given a bath or massage, or to be gazing at a mobile or grabbing for a stuffed animal. But it is through these varied endeavors that babies not only sharpen their senses but also begin to learn who they are and what their world is about.

A lot has been written in recent years about maximizing a child's potential. From the moment they're born, some experts suggest structuring a baby's environment in ways that give him a head start. While it's absolutely true that parents are a child's first teachers, I'm less concerned about giving babies knowledge than I am about inspiring their natural curiosity and civilizing them— that is, helping them understand how the world operates and how to interact with people.

To that end, I encourage parents to think about any activity their baby does as an opportunity to foster security and, at the same time, independence. Those two goals may seem at odds, but they do actually go together. The safer children of any age feel, the more they're likely to venture out and to amuse themselves without need of assistance or outside interference (except if they're in danger). Thus, the *A* in E.A.S.Y. offers this paradox: *Activities help us bond with our babies but also help us give them their first lessons in freedom.*

You need to *do* less for children than you probably realize. That doesn't mean leaving him or her alone, though. It means striking a balance—giving your baby the guidance and support he needs and, at the same time, respecting his natural course of development. The truth is, even without your help, whenever your baby is awake, she is listening, feeling, watching, smelling, or tasting something. Especially in the early months, then, when everything is new (and to some infants, scary), your most important job is to ensure that each experience makes your baby feel comfortable—and safe enough to want to continue to explore and grow. The way to do this is to create what I call a "circle of respect."

Drawing a Circle of Respect

Whether you're lifting your baby out of the crib in the morning, bathing him, or playing peekaboo, it's vital that you remember that he is a separate person, deserving of your undivided attention and respect but also capable of acting on his own. I want you to try to envision yourself drawing a circle around your baby, an imaginary boundary that delineates his personal space. Never enter your baby's circle of respect without asking permission, telling him why you want to come in, and explaining what you're doing. This may sound contrived or silly, but remember that he's not just a baby—he's also *a person*. If you keep in mind the following basic principles, which I'll explain in greater detail and illustrate throughout this chapter, you will easily and naturally maintain a circle of respect during every activity your baby does:

• *Be with your baby.* Make her the undivided object of your attention *at that moment.* This is bonding time, so focus. Don't be on the phone, worrying about getting the laundry done, or ruminating on a report that you have to complete.

• *Delight your baby's senses, but avoid overstimulation.* Our culture encourages excesses and overstimulation—

Your Baby Knows More than You Think

Mostly in the last twenty years or so, thanks in large part to the miracle of videotape, infant researchers have been able to discover just how much babies can process. Where we once thought of infants as "blank slates," we now know that newborns come into the world with keen senses and a rapidly expanding set of abilities that enable them to observe, to think, even to reason. By watching infants' facial expressions, their body language, their eye movements, and their sucking reflexes (babies suck harder when they're excited), scientists have validated amazing infant capabilities. Following are a few scientific findings; you'll find more scattered throughout this chapter.

• Infants can discriminate one image from another. As early as 1964, scientists discovered that babies wouldn't continue to stare for long periods at repeated images, whereas new images captured the infants' attention.

• Babies flirt. They coo, smile, and gesture in rhythm with the intonation of your voice.

• Infants as young as three months old form expectations. In a laboratory situation, after exposure to a series of visual images, infants were able to detect patterns and would move their eyes in anticipation of the next image, indicating that they were expecting it.

• Infants can remember. Memory has been documented in infants as young as five weeks old. In one study, when a group of toddlers who had been tested as infants (from six to forty weeks of age) were brought back to the same laboratory at almost three years old, even though they didn't use words to describe their memories of the earlier experience, all indicated familiarity with the task they were again asked to perform (reaching for objects in the light and in the dark).

and parents unwittingly contribute to the problem, because they don't realize how delicate their baby's senses are or how much infants actually take in (see sidebar opposite). I'm not suggesting that we stop singing to our children, playing music for them, showing them brightly colored objects, or even buying toys for them, but less is more where babies are concerned.

• *Take care to make your baby's environment interesting, pleasant, and safe.* You don't need money for this; you need common sense (see pages 164–176).

• *Foster your baby's independence.* This may sound counter intuitive—how can a baby be independent? Well, luv, I'm not saying you ought to pack his bags just yet. Of course, he can't literally be on his own, but you can begin to help him gain the confidence to venture forth, to explore, and to play independently. Therefore, when your baby is at play, it's always a good idea to observe more than interact.

• *Remember to talk with, not at, your baby.* Having a dialogue implies a two-way process: Whenever your child is involved in an activity, you watch and listen and wait for *his* response. If he tries to involve you, of course, you jump in. If he "asks" for a change of scene, definitely honor his request. Otherwise, let him explore.

• *Engage and inspire, but always let your baby lead.* Never place a baby in a position she can't get into (or out of) on her own. Don't give her toys that are outside of her "learning triangle" (more about this on pages 164–172).

From the time your baby wakes up until you tuck him in for his nighttime sleep, keep the above guidelines in mind. Remember that everyone, including your baby, deserves to have personal space. Below, as I take you through your baby's day, you'll see how each of these principles comes to bear.

Wake Up, Little Susie! Wake Up!

How would you like it if, every morning, your partner came into your bedroom just as you were departing dreamland and yanked off the covers? And suppose he then yelled at you, "C'mon, it's time to get up!" Wouldn't that startle and annoy you? Infants feel the same way if their parents don't take care to start the day off right.

Be gentle, quiet, and considerate when you greet your baby in the morning. I usually walk in singing an English ditty, "Good morning, good morning, we danced the whole night through, good morning!" Choose whatever cheery wake-up song you like, as long as it identifies this time as the morning. Or make one up, as Beverly did, using the familiar tune of "Happy Birthday" but singing "Good morning to you. . . ." After my song, I say, "Hey, Jeremy, did you have a nice sleep? It's so good to see you. You must be hungry." As I bend down, I warn him, "I'm going to pick you up now. . . . Here we go—one, two, three, up we come!" Later in the day, after a nap, I might add, "I'll bet you feel good after your nap. What a big stretch!" Here too, before picking him up, forewarn him, as you did in the morning.

Of course, no matter how *you* greet your baby in the morning, your little love bucket has ideas of his own. Just like grown-ups, babies have different attitudes upon waking. Some get up with a smile already on their faces, while others pout or even cry. Some are immediately ready to greet the day, while others need a bit of encouraging.

Here's a rundown of what you might expect from our various baby types:

Angel. All smiles, cooing and goo-gooing, these babies seem eternally happy to be in their environment. Unless they're particularly hungry or their diaper is soaked through, they're content to play in their crib until someone comes in to get them. In other words, they rarely go past the first wake-up alert (see sidebar on the next page).

Textbook. If you don't catch these babies by Alert 1, they let you know they're up by making little crotchety Alert 2 noises that mean, "Get in here." If you go in, saying, "I'm right here—I didn't go anywhere," they're fine. If you don't show up, they sound Alert 3 loud and clear.

Touchy. These little ones almost always wake up crying. Because they need reassurance, they often sound the three alerts of waking in rapid succession. Unable to tolerate being left in their cribs for more than five minutes, they're likely to have a meltdown if you don't get there by Alert 1 or 2.

Grumpy. Because they don't like to be wet or uncomfortable, these babies also sound the three alerts rather quickly. You can forget about coaxing a morning smile out of them—you could stand on your head or do somersaults, but these little ones still won't crack a smile.

Spirited. These babies, who are very active, high-energy types, often skip the first stage of waking up and immediately sound Alert 2. They fuss and squirm, uttering lit-

tle cough-cough kind of cries, and will end up wailing if
no one shows up at that point.

The Three-Alarm Wake-up System

Some babies wake up and amuse themselves and never get past the
first alert—they're content to hang out in their cribs until someone
comes to get them. Others go through all three alerts quickly, no
matter how fast you react.

Alert 1: A creaking or fussy sound, accompanied by fidgeting. It
means, "Hello? Is anyone there? Why aren't you coming in to get
me?"

Alert 2: A coughlike cry in the back of the throat that stops and
starts. When they stop, they're listening for you. When you don't
come, they mean, "Hey, get in here!"

Alert 3: An all-out cry, with arms and legs flailing. "Come in now!
I'm serious!"

Interestingly, the waking behavior you see in an infant
is often what you continue to get even as he or she grows
up. Remember I told you that my Sophie was so quiet
and mild-tempered that many mornings, I worried she
had stopped breathing? Well, to this day Sophie is a delight in the morning; she wakes easily and bounds out of
bed. Her sister, a Spirited baby who often woke up fussing, still needs a bit of time to come round after a night's
sleep. Unlike Sophie, who immediately gets into conversation in the morning, Sara likes it when I let *her* speak
first, rather than my prattling on about the day to come.

Diapering and Dressing

As I mentioned earlier, I often ask new mums and dads
in my parenting classes to lie on their backs and close

their eyes. Then, without warning, I choose one of the men, pick up his legs, and thrust them overhead. Needless to say, he's quite startled. When the others realize what I've done, they think it's rather funny and we all have a good laugh. But then I explain the reason for my fun and games: That's what it feels like to an infant when you change his diaper without warning or explanation. In effect, you've invaded his circle of respect. If instead I had said, "John, in a moment I'm going to lift your legs up," then not only could John prepare himself for my touch, but he would also know that I am taking his feelings into account. I give infants the same consideration.

Researchers have noted that it takes three seconds for touch to register in your infant's brain. For a baby, then, having her legs yanked upward, her lower body bared, and her bottom wiped is a scary proposition, even more so when cold alcohol is applied to her belly button. Studies also have shown that infants have a keen sense of smell. Even newborns turn their heads away from a foul-smelling alcohol-soaked cotton swab. One-week-old babies can use smell to identify their mothers. Put this all together, and you realize that when her space is invaded, your infant is keenly aware that *something* is happening, although she may not be able to express herself.

The fact is, most babies cry on the changing table because they don't know what's happening to them and/or they don't like it—not one bit. I mean, really, what would you expect, putting a baby in the most vulnerable, exposed position—legs apart? How do *you* feel spread-eagled in the gynecologist's office? I always tell my own doctor, "I need to know exactly what you're doing down there." Babies don't yet have the words to *ask* us to slow down or to respect their boundaries, but their cries amount to the same thing.

Cloth Versus Paper

Although cloth has made a comeback, an overwhelming majority of parents still prefer disposable diapers. It's a matter of choice, but I like cloth diapers because they're cheaper, softer on Baby's bottom, and ecologically conscious.

Also, some babies have an allergic reaction to the absorbent granules in disposable diapers, a condition sometimes confused with diaper rash. The difference is that diaper rash is localized, usually around the anus, whereas with an allergy the rash will span the entire area covered by the diaper, up to the waist.

Another problem with disposable diapers is that they are so absorbent and do such a good job of keeping urine away that only Grumpy babies seem to realize they're wet. When toddlers aren't toilet-trained by three, sometimes it's because paper diapers don't let them know they're wet.

One caution with cloth: You'll need to be vigilant about checking for wetness, which can lead to diaper rash.

When a mum says to me, "Edward hates the changing table," I say, "He doesn't hate the table, luv, he hates what's *happening* on it. You probably need to ease up a bit and talk with him." Moreover, with diapering, as with all activities, you must attend to the task at hand. For Pete's sake, don't have the cordless cradled between your shoulder and ear. Think of it from your baby's perspective. Imagine what you look like leaning over him— let's not even mention that you could plonk him on the head with it. It "says" to your baby, "I'm ignoring you."

When I change a baby's diaper, I try to maintain a steady dialogue. I bend down, putting my face around twelve to fourteen inches from hers—straight on, never at an angle, because babies see better that way—and I talk her through the process: "We're going to change your diaper now. Let's just lay you down here, so I can

undo your pants." I keep talking so as to let her know
what I'm doing. "I'm unsnapping your jammies now.
There we go. Ooh, look at what lovely thighs you have.
Now I'm going to lift your little leggies up. Here we
go. . . . I'm opening your nappy. . . . Oh, I see you have
a little parcel for me in here. . . . I'm going to wipe you
now." With little girls, I take care to wipe from front to
back; with boys, I put a tissue over the penis to avoid a
squirt in the face. If the baby starts to cry, I ask, "Am I
going too fast? I'll slow down."

> **TIP:** *When your baby is naked, rest your hand gently on
> her chest or lay a Beanie Baby or other lightweight
> stuffed animal there. That little bit of extra weight helps
> her feel less exposed and vulnerable.*

I must add that you also might need to go a little
faster on the changing table. I've seen some who take
twenty minutes to change a soiled diaper. That's far too
long. I mean, if you figure that they change the baby before feeding, feed for forty minutes, then do another
change after eating, that's an hour and twenty minutes.
They're affecting the child's activity period, both because of the time spent and, if the baby doesn't like
being changed, because of the stress and exhaustion.

> **TIP:** *For the first three or four weeks, invest in some
> inexpensive nightgowns that tie or snap down the front
> and are open at the bottom, providing easy access for
> diapering. In the beginning, you're bound to have a few
> leaky diapers every now and then. Having a pile of extra
> nighties on hand saves time and worry.*

It may take you a few weeks to get the hang of it, but
you should strive for a five-minute diaper change. The
key is to have everything ready—top of the cream and

wipes open, diaper unfolded and ready to slip under Baby's bottom, your Diaper Genie or wastebasket open and ready for the dirty nappy.

> **TIP:** *When you first lay Baby down for a diaper change, slip a clean diaper under his bottom. Open the soiled diaper but don't remove it until you've cleaned the genital and anal areas. When you're finished, remove the old diaper and the new one will be right where you need it.*

When all the tricks of the trade fail to calm a baby, try changing him in your lap—many babies prefer it, and it saves you the trouble of standing over a changing table.

Too Many Playthings/Too Much Stimulation

Okay, luv. Your baby's had her first feed, she's got a fresh diaper on, and it's time to play. Here's where parents often get confused. They either minimize the importance of Baby's play, not realizing that a great deal of learning is taking place even when a baby stares, or they go completely bonkers and are in their infant's face all the time, cajoling, showing toys, shaking things. Neither extreme is good. Judging from the parents I meet, most err toward the latter—overinvolvement—which is why I regularly get calls like this one from Mae, three-week-old Serena's mum:

"Tracy, what's wrong with Serena?" she pleads. I can hear a baby screaming, and in the background is the voice of Wendell, Serena's beleaguered dad, desperately trying to calm her.

"Well," I say, "tell me what happened *before* she started crying."

"She was just playing," Mae offers innocently.

"Playing what?" Mind you, this is a three-week-old we're talking about, not some toddler.

"We had her in the swing for a while, but then she started fussing, so we took her out and put her in the chair."

"And then?"

A Guide to What Affects Your Baby

Hearing (auditory)	Talking
	Humming
	Singing
	Heartbeat
	Music
Sight (visual)	Black-and-white cards
	Striped material
	Mobile
	Faces
	The environment
Touch (tactile)	Contact with skin, lips, hair
	Cuddling
	Massage
	Water
	Cotton balls/cloth
Smell (olfactory)	Humans
	Cooking odors
	Perfume
	Spices
Taste (gustatory)	Milk
	Other foods
Movement (vestibular)	Rocking
	Carrying
	Swinging
	Riding (stroller, car)

"She didn't like that, either, so we put her on the blanket, and Wendell tried to read to her," she went on. "Now we figure she's tired, but she still won't go to sleep."

What Mae doesn't mention—probably because she thinks it's irrelevant—is that the swing also plays music, the chair vibrates, and the blanket is part of a contraption with a bright red-white-and-black mobile dancing over the baby's head. On top of that, Dad is holding *The Runaway Bunny* near her face.

You think I'm exaggerating? Not really, luv. I've witnessed similar scenes in countless households.

"I suspect your little lass is just overstimulated," I offer gently, pointing out that the poor little thing has been enduring an environment that—from her baby perspective—is like spending a day at Disneyland!

"But she *likes* her toys," they protest.

Never one to argue with a parent, I suggest my cardinal rule: *Put away anything that shakes, rattles, jiggles, wiggles, squeaks, or vibrates.* I tell them to try it for just three days and see if Baby calms down. (Unless something else is wrong, she usually will.)

Sadly, Serena's parents—indeed, most parents nowadays—are victims of our culture. With nearly four million new babies born every year, the furnishings of babyhood have spawned entire industries. Billions of dollars are spent annually convincing us we must create a proper "environment" for our babies, and parents buy into the idea big time. They think that if they're not constantly entertaining their baby, they're somehow failing her, because she's not getting enough "intellectual stimulation." And if, by some miracle, they don't pressure themselves, one of their friends will: "You mean you didn't get Serena the baby bouncer for the doorway?"

Mae and Wendell's friends will ask accusingly, as if their daughter would grow up deprived without one. That's pure codswallop!

Myth: "Get Them Used to Sounds of the Household"

Parents are often told it's a good idea to accustom their babies to loud noises. I ask you, would you like it if I came into your room in the middle of the night while you were sleeping and played loud music? That's not respectful. Should you be any less considerate of your baby?

Of course we should play music and sing to our children. Of course we should show them brightly colored objects and even buy toys for them. But when we do too much and present infants with too many choices, babies become *over*stimulated. It's hard enough on them to be cast out of the cushy comfort of the uterus—some forced to squeeze their way through a narrow birth canal, others literally plucked from the womb—into the harsh fluorescent light of the delivery room. Along the way, they encounter surgical instruments, drugs, and a host of hands that pull, prick, and scrub them, typically within seconds of their arrival. As I pointed out in Chapter 1, each baby is unique, but almost every newborn must endure some sort of tumult. For the more sensitive types, birth itself presents more stimulation than they can handle.

Add to that the normal sights and sounds of your household—TVs, radios, pets, cars driving by, vacuums, lawn mowers, and countless other appliances. Factor in your own voice, imbued with whatever anxiety you harbor, your parents', in-laws', and other visitors' coos and whispers, and wow! That's a lot to handle if you're a less-than-ten-pound mass of nerves and muscles. And now here's Mum or Dad in your face, asking you to *play*. It's enough to make an Angel baby cry.

Playing Within the Learning Triangle

What exactly do I mean by play? Well, it depends on what your baby can *do*. Now, most books will give you age-related criteria about playthings, but I'm against that. It's not that such guidelines aren't helpful; it's good to know what's typical at various ages. In fact, that's how I organize my Mummy-and-me classes—newborns to three months, three to six months, six to nine months, and nine months to one year. It's just that so many mothers and fathers I encounter don't realize that among *normal* children there is tremendous diversity in infants' capabilities and awareness. I see this played out repeatedly in my classes. Invariably, one of the mothers, who has read somewhere that her five month old should be rolling over, becomes alarmed. "Oh, no, Tracy, he must be slow," she'll tell me, because her little boy is just lying there. "How can I help him learn how to roll over?"

I don't believe in exerting any kind of pressure to perform. I always tell parents that their baby is *an individual*. The statistics in books can't possibly take into consideration the idiosyncracies and differences from human to human. Such benchmarks are meant to be used as a *guide* only. Your baby will reach each plateau of development in his or her own time.

Besides, babies are not dogs; you don't "train" them. Respecting your child means allowing her to develop without goading her or panicking if she isn't like your friend's baby or doesn't live up to some book's description. Let her take the lead. Mother Nature has a wonderful, logical plan. If you roll your baby over before she's ready to do it herself, she won't learn how to do it any faster. In fact, she's not rolling over yet because she hasn't developed the physiological capabilities to do so. By trying to push her, you inadvertently make her life more stressful than it ought to be.

Hence, I suggest that parents always stay within their baby's "learning triangle"—that is, present physical and mental tasks the baby can manipulate and get pleasure from *on his own*. For instance, almost every newborn I visit has a stockpile of rattles in his room—silver ones, plastic ones, rattles shaped like Os and duckies and barbells. *No* rattle is appropriate for an infant, because he can't grab yet. His parent ends up shaking the rattle in his face, but the baby is certainly not playing with it. Remember my ground rule: *When your baby has a toy, observe rather than jump in.*

To know what fits inside your child's learning triangle, consider his accomplishments to date—what he can *do*. In other words, instead of looking at age-related guidelines in some book, *look at your baby*. If you stay within his learning triangle, your child will acquire knowledge naturally, at his own pace.

From Day One

It's impossible even for researchers to know the precise moment infant comprehension kicks in, so from the moment your baby arrives, you should

- Explain everything you do to or for your baby
- Talk about your daily activities
- Show family photos and use people's names
- Point out and identify objects ("See the doggie?" "Look, another baby, just like you.")
- Read simple books and look at pictures
- Play music and sing (see the box on page 167 for specific guidelines)

He mostly watches and listens. For approximately the first six to eight weeks, your baby is an auditory and visual creature, but he's becoming progressively more alert and aware of his surroundings. Even though his vision extends only eight to twelve inches, he can see you and may even reward you with a smile or a coo. Take a moment to "answer" him. Researchers have documented that at birth, babies can discriminate human faces and voices from other sights and sounds—and they prefer them. Within a few days, they're able to recognize familiar faces and voices and will choose to look at them rather than gaze at an unfamiliar image.

When your baby is not spending time looking at your face, you may notice that he also has a particular fondness for staring at lines. What's the deal? To him, straight lines appear to be moving, because his retinas are not yet fixed. You don't have to invest in a set of fancy flash cards to amuse him. With a black marker, draw straight lines on a white index card. These give your baby a focal point, which is important because his vision is still blurry and two-dimensional.

If you want to purchase a toy for your newborn, a "womb box," a device placed in the crib that mimics sounds Baby heard in the womb, is something you can buy even before your baby arrives. With newborns, however, I advise keeping only one or two toys in the crib. Rotate them when he stops looking at them. Be aware of the impact of color—primary colors stimulate babies, pastel colors calm them down. At any given time of day, choose colors to have a desired effect—for example, don't put a red-and-black flash card into the crib if your baby is getting ready for a nap.

Music to Grow By

Babies love music, but it, too, must be age-appropriate. At the end of each of my Mummy-and-me classes, I always play music as follows:

Up to three months: I play lullabies only—soft, soothing music, nothing plinky like nursery rhymes. A collection I use, *A Child's Gift of Lullabies,* is available on CD and cassette. If you have a pleasant voice, by all means sing your own lullaby.

Six months: I play only *one* song at the close of class, usually a simple nursery rhyme, like "Eensy Weensy Spider," "The Wheels on the Bus," "Baa Baa Black Sheep," "I'm a Little Teapot."

Nine months: I play three of the above songs, but play them only once.

Twelve months: I add a new song, for a total of four, and play two repetitions of each. Now we can also incorporate gestures.

She gains control over her head and neck. Once your baby is able to turn her head, usually somewhere in the second month, and move it from side to side, perhaps even lift it a bit (usually by the third month), she also has better control over her eyes. You might catch her watching her own hand. In laboratories, it has been shown that even one-month-old babies can imitate facial expressions—if the adult sticks out his tongue, the baby does, too; if he opens his mouth, so does the baby. This is a good time to invest in a clip-on mobile that you can move from crib to playpen. I know that's the first thing most parents buy for their infants, but before two months, a mobile is basically an ornament. Babies like to turn their heads (often to the right), so don't position it directly in her line of sight—nor should it be any farther away than fourteen inches. At this point (around eight weeks), your baby is beginning to see in three dimensions. Her posture has straightened out, and she holds her hands open much of the time. She catches her own hands, mostly by accident. She also can remember and predict more accurately what comes next. In fact, at two months, babies can recognize and remember someone from a previous day. She'll soon wiggle delightedly when she sees you, and begin tracking you as you move across the room.

Whereas straight lines will amuse a newborn or four-week-old infant, by eight weeks pictures of faces will make them smile. Now you can upgrade your home-made flash cards by drawing wavy lines, circles, and simple pictures, like a house or a smiley face, on them. You also can put a mirror in her crib; when she smiles, it smiles back at her. However, remember that although your baby loves to stare at things, when she's had enough, she doesn't yet have the mobility that would en-able her to move away from an object that no longer in-terests her. Be vigilant; if she is making cranky, fussing noises, it means "I've had enough." Come to her rescue before you've got an all-out cry on your hands.

He reaches and grasps. Pretty much anything—including his own body parts—fascinates a baby who can reach and grasp, which happens at around three or four months. And everything goes straight into his mouth. By now your baby can also lift his chin and make gurgling noises. His favorite plaything is you, but this is also a good time for simple, responsive toys, such as rattles and other safe objects that generate noise or feel good to the touch, like a foam hair curler. Infants love to explore and are thrilled when they can cause a reaction. Just watch your little one when he shakes a rattle; his eyes go wide. Babies comprehend cause and effect now, so any-thing that makes a noise gives them a feeling of accom-plishment. He's so much more responsive than he was just a short while ago—you'll be delighted by his constant cooing—and it just gets better and better from now on. He also knows how to get your attention when he's had enough. He'll drop a toy, make a coughlike noise in the back of his throat, or let forth a cranky little cry.

She can roll. The ability to roll over onto one side, which happens anywhere from the end of the third month to the fifth month, is the beginning of a baby's mobility. Before you know it, your baby will be rolling both ways, and the fun continues. She will still love toys that make a noise, but you can also give her everyday household items, like a spoon. These simple objects will be the source of endless delight. Watch her with a plastic plate and you will see her turn it this way and that, push it away, and grab it again. She is a little scientist, continuing to explore. She also will love to play with little shapes, cubes or balls or triangles. Believe it or not, by mouthing them, she's figuring out what they are and can sense their differences. We know, from research, that very young infants can identify shapes with their mouths. Even at one month, babies in the laboratory have been shown to match visual displays to tactile sensations. When given a bumpy nipple or a smooth one and shown pictures of both a bumpy and a smooth object, they look longer at the object that is the same shape as the one they've been sucking.

He can sit up. Babies can't sit up until they've grown into their heads, usually around six months old; before that, they're top-heavy. When babies can sit up by themselves, they begin to develop depth perception. After all, the world from a sitting position looks far different from the way it appears when a baby is prone. Now he also is able to transfer objects from one hand to the other; he can point and gesture as well. His curiosity will propel him to move toward things, but physically he's not quite there yet. *Let him explore on his own.* He has control over his head, arms, and torso at this point but not his legs. So he may lean forward and lunge for something he wants, but end up on his chest because he's still a bit top-heavy. His arms and legs will flail in the air, like he's flying. Parents often jump in the minute a baby utters a fussy noise and, instead of waiting and watching, they give the baby the toy he's after. I say stop! Don't hand him that toy right away. Stand back; offer your encouragement instead. It inspires confidence to say, "Good job. You're nearly there." Use your judgment, though; you're not coaching him for the Olympics. You're just giving him a bit of parental encouragement. After he's tried to reach it, you *can* hand him the toy.

Give him simple playthings that reinforce an action, like a clown or a jack-in-the-box that pops up when he pushes the right button or lever. Toys such as this are best because babies love to see that they can make things happen. You might be tempted to buy lots of playthings at this point. Restrain yourself; remember that less is more, and that many of the things you'll want to buy your baby *won't* amuse him. In fact, I chuckle when I hear parents whose children are at this stage say, "My baby doesn't like this toy." They don't realize it's not a matter of like or dislike—the baby simply doesn't understand the toy. He doesn't know how to make it *do* something for him.

She can move. When your baby really starts to crawl, usually between eight and ten months, it's time to child-proof your house if you haven't already (see the box on page 174), so that you can create ample opportunities for her to explore. Your little one might even be starting to pull herself up at this point. Some babies first crawl backward or go round in circles, because their legs are ready to crawl but their body hasn't grown long or strong enough to accommodate the weight of their heads. What's more, curiosity and physical development go hand in hand. Before this, your baby didn't have the cognitive skills to process complicated thought patterns— for example, to think, "I want that toy across the room, so I have to do this to get there." Now all of that is beginning to happen.

Once she is able to set her focus on various goals, your crawling baby will become as busy as a little bee. She'll no longer be content to sit in your lap. She still will love cuddling, but first she's got to explore and work off some of her natural energy. She'll find new ways to make noise—and to make trouble. The best playthings are toys that encourage her to put things in and take things out. Of course, she will initially be more proficient at *undoing*—she'll take everything out but rarely put anything back. Eventually, by around ten months to a year, she'll gain the dexterity to put things together and even to clean up her toys from the floor and put them in the toy box. She probably will be able to pick up small objects, too, because her fine motor skills are developing, which enables her to master a pincerlike grasp, using her thumb and index finger. She also likes rolling toys, ones that she can pull toward her. And

TIP: *Make sure everything your baby plays with is washable, is sturdy, and has no sharp edges or strings that can come loose and be swallowed. An object is too small to play with if it can fit inside a cardboard toilet paper roll; it could get stuck in Baby's throat or pushed into an ear or nose.*

she might also start to develop an attachment for a particular toy, like a stuffed animal or a lovey blanket.

Now when you play nursery rhymes, you can add movements, which your baby can imitate. Songs and rhythms teach children about language and coordination. At this point, a favorite game will be peekaboo, which teaches your baby object permanence. This is important, because once your baby learns the concept, he also will understand that if *you* go into the next room, you don't disappear, either. You can reinforce this by saying, "I'll be right back." Use a variety of household items as playthings, and be creative. A spoon and a plate or pot are great for banging. A colander makes a wonderful peekaboo shield.

As your baby expands her physical and mental repertoire, remember that she is an individual. She won't do exactly what your sister's baby did at the same age. Maybe she'll do more, or maybe she'll do it differently. She, like any human being, will have her own idiosyncracies, her own likes and dislikes. Watch her; learn who she is from what she does, rather than trying to make her into what you want her to be. As long as she's safe, supported, and loved, she will blossom into an amazing and unique little being. She will be in constant motion, learn new skills every day, and never fail to surprise you.

To Childproof or Not?

Childproofing is an important and somewhat complicated issue. You want your baby to be safe from dangers, such as poisoning, burning, scalding, drowning, cutting herself, or falling down the stairs. And you also want to protect your home from the potential damage that a curious baby can cause. The question is, How far must you go? A veritable industry has sprung up out of parents' concerns. A mum recently told me that she spent $4,000 childproofing her home—the alleged babyproofer came into the woman's house and installed locks on virtually every cabinet, including some that her son wouldn't be able to reach for another eight to ten years! He also had talked the woman into putting up gates in places no baby could possibly reach. I prefer a much simpler and less costly approach (see the box on page 174). For example, a suitable play space can be nothing more than a three-by-three area, cordoned off with pillows or bumpers.

What is more, if you remove *too* much from your home, you deprive your baby of the opportunity to explore. You also eliminate teaching moments in which he learns right from wrong. Let me explain with a story from my own life.

When my girls were young, I childproofed my house by removing dangerous chemicals, blocking doorways to areas I didn't want explored, and taking other such precautions. At the same time, though, I also taught the girls that they had to respect *my* possessions. We had a little arrangement of Capodimonte figurines on a low shelf in our living room. Once Sara began to crawl, she became curious about everything. One day I noticed that the figurines had caught her eye. So instead of waiting for her to grab one, I showed it to her, saying, "This is Mummy's. You can hold it now, while I'm here with you. But it's not a toy."

Sara, like most babies, tested me a few times. She'd make a beeline for the figurines, but just as she was about to reach for one, I'd say in a light but firm tone, "Uh-uh. No touching. That's Mummy's—it's not a toy." If she persisted, I'd sharpen my delivery to a curt "No!" Within three days, she barely noticed those little fig-

Childproofing Basics

The trick is to look at your home from the eyes (and height) of a child. Get down on all fours and crawl around! Following are the dangers you'll want to prevent.

- **Poisoning.** Remove all cleaning fluids and other dangerous substances from under the kitchen and bathroom sinks and store them in high cabinets. Even if you install clips to lock cupboard doors, can you risk a strong or clever toddler breaking in? Purchase a first-aid kit. If you believe your baby has ingested any poisonous substance, call your physician or 911 before doing anything.
- **Airborne pollutants.** Have your home checked for radon, a naturally emitted radioactive gas. Install smoke and carbon monoxide detectors—and check the batteries regularly. Quit smoking cigarettes, and don't allow anyone else to smoke in your home or car.
- **Strangling.** Keep drape and blind cords, as well as electric wires, out of reach by using pegs or masking tape to secure them above baby level.
- **Electric shock.** Cover all outlets, and make sure every lamp socket in your house has a light bulb in it.
- **Drowning.** Never leave your baby unattended in the tub. Install a cover lock on the toilet, too. Baby is still top-heavy and can fall into the bowl and drown.
- **Burns and scalding.** Install stove knob guards. Secure a cover over the bath tap, either with a plastic guard (available in most hardware stores) or by wrapping a towel around it, which prevents Baby both from touching a hot faucet and from sustaining a serious injury if she hits her head. Set your water heater to 120 degrees to avoid scalding.
- **Falling and stair accidents.** Once your baby becomes active, if you still use a changing table, keep a hand and two eyes on him at all times. Install gates at the top and bottom of the stairs, but don't let yourself become complacent. Always be right next to him when your baby is beginning to learn how to climb stairs. He'll be an ace at going up, but he won't know how to get down.
- **Crib accidents.** The U. S. Consumer Product Safety Commission requires slats in a crib to be 2⅜ inches apart. Don't use a crib manufactured prior to 1991, when that regulation was passed, or an antique crib in which the slats are wider apart. Crib bumpers, an American invention, were a shock to me when I first came here. I usually tell parents to put them away, because active babies can roll under them and get stuck or, worse, suffocate.

urines. I followed the same procedure with her little sister, Sophie.

Cut to a few years later, and enter my friend's little boy, who had come to play with Sophie. In his own house every low shelf was bare, because his mummy had removed virtually all her possessions from reach. Needless to say, he was ready to have a field day with my figurines. I tried the same approach with him that I had used with Sara, but there was no stopping this little boy. Finally, I said, "No!" rather sharply. His mum looked at me in horror. "We don't say no to George, Tracy."

"Well, ducky," I said, "maybe it's time you started. I can't very well let him come round here to destroy things my girls know enough not to touch. Besides, this isn't George's fault—it's yours, because you haven't taught him what's his and what's yours."

The lesson of this cautionary tale is quite simple: If you remove all objects from your child's reach, she never learns to respect the beautiful and fragile things in your own home, and she certainly won't know how to behave in someone else's home. Moreover, *you* won't be offended, as George's mum was, when another parent informs your child that something or someplace in the house is, indeed, off-limits to children.

I always suggest that you set aside a baby-safe area. When your baby asks to look at something, let her. Let her feel it, manipulate it—but always in your presence. Interestingly, kids tire of adult things, because our knickknacks usually don't *do* anything except sit on a shelf. Once your baby is allowed to handle an object, there's a good chance she'll quickly become bored. Her eye will catch something else, and off she'll go.

Bear in mind, too, that your little one is bound to think that the slot in your VCR is a lovely letter box. She'll see it as a wonderful place to put her fingers, her

> **TIP:** *It only takes a few days to teach a child not to touch something, but you will probably have to repeat the process in different areas of the house, with various objects. During this teaching phase, you might not wish to take the risk I took. Therefore, replace your most valuable and treasured ornaments with inexpensive doodads.*

crackers, or anything else she can stuff inside. Instead of worrying, cover it. It also may pay to invest in a miniature version of something you own that your child seems to find fascinating. For instance, most babies love to play with knobs and buttons. Invest in a toy that looks like a TV remote control or a radio—anything she can manipulate. After all, she's not interested in wrecking the house or ruining your equipment; she just wants to imitate what she sees you doing.

Winding Down

After a hard day's work of eating, sleeping, and playing, your baby deserves a little rest and relaxation in the form of a bath. In fact, once a baby is two or three weeks old, you might notice that he's fussier than usual in the evenings. As he becomes progressively more active and absorbs more of his surroundings, he needs to calm down from the stimulation of his day. His bath can be the *A* that comes after the five or six o'clock feed, around fifteen minutes after his last burp. Of course, you could give your infant a bath in the morning, or at any other point during the day, but to me, the ideal time is before bed, because it's the best way to wind down. It's also one of the most special parent-child experiences, often Dad's favorite chore.

With the exception of Touchy babies, who hate baths

for the first three months, and Grumpy babies, who only tolerate them, most babies love baths—*if* you go slow and follow my step-by-step instructions in "Bathing 101" (see page 179).

Sponging Pointers

- Have everything you need—washcloths, warm water, alcohol, cotton balls, ointment, and towel—close at hand and ready to use.
- Keep baby warmly wrapped. Going from head to toe, wash one part of her body at a time; pat dry, and move on.
- Use a small washcloth to clean the groin area; always wipe away from the genitals toward the anus.
- To clean the eyes, use a cotton ball, one ball per eye, sweeping outward from the corner closest to the nose.
- To clean the cord stump, use a cotton swab dipped in alcohol. Go right to the base. Babies sometimes cry, although it doesn't hurt; it just feels cold.
- If your baby boy has been circumcised, keep the incision moist and protected against urine by covering it with a Vaseline-smeared piece of gauze or cotton. Don't put any water on your baby's penis until it is healed.

Your baby's first bath will come at around fourteen days, time enough for the umbilical cord to fall off and, with boys, for the circumcision to heal. Before that, you will give your baby sponge baths (see sidebar on this page, "Sponging Pointers"). In either case, take care to see the experience *from your baby's perspective*. It should be a fun, interactive time, lasting at least fifteen or twenty minutes. As with dressing and diapering, be respectful. Remember how vulnerable your baby feels, and use your common sense. Try always to take the gentlest route.

For example, when you're dressing your baby after a bath, don't try to yank a onesie (T-shirt) over his head and then attempt to force his arms into the sleeves. Babies' heads are very heavy—two-thirds of their body weight until approximately eight months of age. When you try to dress them in clothes that pull on over the head, their noggins usually flop all over the place. Also, when you try to coax a baby to slip into the sleeves of a shirt by pulling on *her arm,* she will resist. Because she's used to being in a fetal position, she'll instinctively pull back, wanting her arms close to her body. Instead, bunch up the cloth at the baby's wrist and tug on *the sleeve,* not on the baby.

To avoid the struggle altogether, I urge parents not to buy shirts that go over a baby's head. (If you already have some of these, see the sidebar on this page.) Buy shirts with snaps up the front, one-piece outfits with snaps down the body or with Velcro closures on the shoulder. Always go for ease and convenience rather than style.

The T-Shirt Dilemma

I don't recommend them, but if you've already bought shirts for your baby that go over her head, here's the best way to avoid a battle.

- Lie her down on her back.
- Scrunch the material up and stretch the neck wide. Go from under your baby's chin, quickly over her face, and to the back of her head.
- Push your own fingers through the armholes first and then grab hold of your baby's hand. Pull it through the armhole, like you're threading a needle.

If your baby cries at bath time and you've taken care to follow the steps outlined below, which will make the experience safe, slow, and enjoyable, it's probably a matter of your baby's sensitivities and temperament rather than anything you've done. If Baby seems chronically distressed at bath time, it's best to wait a few days and then try again. If he is still upset, which may be the case if you have a Touchy baby, you may have to continue to sponge-bathe for the first month or two—and there's nothing wrong with that. You've got to read your baby. If he's telling you, "I don't like what you're doing—I can't tolerate it," you must wait a spell.

Bathing 101: My Ten-Step Guide

Below is the bathing procedure that I teach to my clients. Each step is important. Before you even begin, have everything on hand (see sidebar below), so that there's a minimum of fumbling when you take your slippery baby out of the water. By the way, I know that some people say you can bathe a baby in the kitchen sink, but I prefer the bathroom—it's where bathing ought to take place.

As you read the steps, remember that you also have to maintain a dialogue with your baby throughout. Keep talking. Listen and watch for his response, and continue to tell him what you're doing.

Bath Essentials

✓ Flat-bottomed plastic tub (I like to prop it on a bath stand rather than the floor, because that's easier on one's back, and because the stands usually have drawers and a shelf to keep everything in easy reach)
✓ Pitcher of warm, clean water
✓ Liquid baby wash
✓ Two washcloths
✓ Hooded or oversized towel
✓ Clothes and fresh diaper ready on the changing table

---

1. *Set the mood.* Make sure the room is warm (72–75 degrees Fahrenheit). Put on music—any kind of gentle pop music (it's to help you relax as well).

2. Fill the tub two-thirds full. Put a capful of baby wash directly into the water. The temperature should be around 100 degrees Fahrenheit, slightly warmer than body temperature. Test the water on the inside of your wrist, never your hand; the water should feel warm, not hot, because Baby's skin is more sensitive than yours.

3. Pick up your baby. Place the palm of your right hand on your baby's chest, and scissor your fingers so that three fingers go under his left armpit and your thumb and index finger rest on his chest. (Reverse that if you're a lefty.) Slide your left hand behind his neck and shoulders and gently bend his body forward, transferring the weight of his body onto your right hand. Now place your left hand under his bum and lift. With him slumped over your right hand, he's now in a sitting position, bent forward slightly and perched on your left hand.

Never lower a baby into the tub on his or her back. It's disorienting to an infant, somewhat like going backward off a diving board.

---

4. Put him in the tub. Slowly lower your baby into the tub in that sitting position, his feet first and then his bum. Then transfer your left hand to the back of his head and neck to support him. Very slowly ease him back into the water. Now your right hand is free. Use it to put a wet washcloth on his chest to keep him warm.

5. Don't use soap directly on Baby's skin. Remember that you've put some baby wash in the water. With your fingers, wipe his neck and groin area. Lift his legs a bit so you can get to his bottom. Then take a little pitcher and pour the water over his body to rinse the soapy water off. He hasn't been playing in the sandbox, luv, so he's not really dirty. His bath at this point is more for establishing a routine than for cleanliness.

6. Use a washcloth around his head to wash his hair. Very often babies haven't got much hair. Even if they do, they don't need a shampoo and set. Take the open washcloth and wipe it around his scalp. Pour fresh water to rinse, taking care not to get water in Baby's eyes.

Never leave a baby unattended in a bathtub. If by chance you've forgotten the baby wash, just rinse him or her with clear water this time, and remember to have everything ready for the next bath.

---

7. Don't get water in his ears. Make sure the hand that's supporting his back doesn't dip too low in the water.

8. Get ready to end the bath. With your free hand, grab the hooded towel (or an oversized towel without a hood). Put the hood (or the corner of the oversized towel) between your teeth and tuck the ends under your armpits.

9. Take the baby out. Carefully shift your baby into the sitting position you used at the beginning of the bath. Most of his weight should be on your right hand, which, with fingers scissored, is supporting his chest. Lift him up, his back toward you, and place his head in the center of your chest a little under where the hood, or the corner of the big towel, is. Wrap the ends of the towel around his body and flop the hood or towel corner over his head.

10. Take him to the changing table to get dressed. Do it exactly the same way for the first three months. There's security in repetition. In time, depending on your baby's nature, instead of getting him into his jammies straight-away, you can add a massage to this time of relaxation.

The Medium Is the Massage

The earliest research on infant massage focused on pre-mature babies, demonstrating that controlled stimula-tion could speed the development of the brain and nervous system, improve circulation, tone muscles, and reduce stress and irritability. The next logical conclusion was that normal babies would benefit, too. Indeed, mas-sage has emerged as a wonderful way to support infant health and growth. The research notwithstanding, I've seen firsthand that it teaches babies to appreciate the power of touch. Babies who've been massaged seem to feel more comfortable with their own bodies as they grow into toddlerhood. I give a class in infant massage at my store in California, and it's one of my most popu-lar offerings. After all, it's a chance for parents to get to know their infant's body, to help the baby relax, and for parent and child to feel utterly connected and in tune.

Consider as well how an infant's senses develop. After hearing, which begins in the womb, the next sense to de-velop is touch. At birth, a baby experiences a change in both temperature and tactile stimulation. His cries tell us, "Hey, I'm feeling that." In fact, sensations precede the development of emotions—a baby feels hot, cold, pain, hunger before he knows what they actually mean.

Although I've seen some mums start even earlier, three months old is an optimal time to begin giving your baby massages. Start slowly and pick a time when you're not rushed or preoccupied, so that you're 100 percent in-volved in the process. You can't speed through the process or do it halfheartedly. And don't expect your baby to lie there for fifteen minutes the first time you try it. Rather, start with a three-minute rub and build up to progressively longer sessions. I love to combine massage with the evening bath, because it's so relaxing for both the adult and the baby. But anytime that *you* have time is the right time.

Naturally, some infants take to massage better than others. Angel, Textbook, and Spirited babies are relatively fast adapters. With Touchy and Grumpy babies, though, we need to start more slowly, because these types of babies take longer to get used to the stimulation. In time, massage can raise their stimulation threshold, allowing their tolerance to build gradually. A Touchy baby finds relief from his sensitive nature, and a Grumpy baby will learn to relax. Massage can even reduce the tension in a colicky baby—tension that would otherwise increase her discomfort.

One of my greatest massage success stories was Timothy, a Touchy baby who was so sensitive it was hard to even diaper him. He cried when his mum or I tried to put him in the tub, so much so that he was nearly six weeks old before he had a proper bath. Timothy's disposition was really upsetting to Lana, his mum. His dad, Gregory, asked if there was any way he could take over some of the burden. He was already giving Tim a bottle of Mum's milk at eleven every night, but during the day, he was out of the house. I suggested that he take a shot at giving his sensitive little boy a bath. I often enlist fathers in this way. It gives them a chance to really get to know their babies and, just as important, to connect with their own nurturing side.

Gregory started slowly with the bath and eventually was able to get Timothy into a tub. Then I added another assignment: massage. Gregory watched carefully as I followed the steps I outline below. We proceeded very cautiously, letting Timothy get used to first my and then his dad's touch.

Massage Essentials

You can use either the floor or a changing table; choose a position that's comfortable for you, too. You'll also need

✓ Pillow

✓ Waterproof pad

✓ Two fluffy bath towels

✓ Baby oil, vegetable oil, or specially formulated baby massage oil (never use a scented aromatherapy oil, which is too strong for baby's skin and too pungent for his sense of smell)

Timothy is nearly one now, and he's still a sensitive little boy, but he has come a long way. His increasing ability to withstand stimulation is, at least in part, a direct result of the nightly bath and massage his dad still gives him. Of course, Tim would have had the same benefits if his mum massaged him, but after a day with her Touchy baby, Lana needed the evening break to help herself recharge. Besides, children need to have these kind of bonding moments with their fathers. It gives them a different kind of self-confidence when they share such intimate time. So while Lana experienced the closeness that breastfeeding engenders, Gregory was able to foster a similar attachment through cuddling and skin-to-skin contact.

Massage 101: Ten Steps to a More Relaxed Baby

As I did with bathing, I offer you the ten-step process I teach. Make sure you have everything on hand that you need—see "Massage Essentials" on page 184. Remember to go slow, to tell your baby *before* you touch her what you're going to do, and to explain each step along the way. If at any time your infant seems uncomfortable (you don't have to wait for a cry; her squirming will tell you), that's the time to stop the massage. Don't expect your baby to lie there for a full-body massage the first time you try this. You'll have to build tolerance a few minutes at a time. Start with a few movements, lasting only two or three minutes. Over several weeks, or longer, work up to fifteen or twenty minutes.

1. Make sure the environment is conducive. The room should be warm, around 75 degrees, with no drafts. Put on soft music. Your "massage table" will consist of a waterproof pad placed on top of a pillow; over that, lay a fluffy bath towel.

2. Prepare for the experience. Ask yourself, "Can I really be in the here and now with my baby, or is there another better time for me to do this?" If you're certain that you can give fully of yourself, wash your hands and take a few deep, centering breaths to relax. Then prepare your baby. Lay her down. Talk to her. Explain, "We're going to give your little body a massage." As you're explaining what you're about to do, put a small amount of oil (a teaspoon or two) into your hands and briskly rub your palms together to warm the oil.

3. Ask permission to begin. You will begin at your baby's feet and work your way up to his head. Before you even touch your baby, though, explain, "I'm going to pick up your little foot now. I'm just going to stroke the bottom of it."

4. *Legs and feet first*. On her feet, use a thumb-over-thumb movement—one thumb rubs the foot upward, taking turns with the other thumb, which moves in the same direction. Gently stroke the sole of her foot, heel toward toe. Press in all over the bottom of the foot. Squeeze each toe delicately. You can say the nursery rhyme "This little piggy . . ." while you're doing each toe. Massage over the top of the foot toward the ankle. Make small circles around the ankle. As you go up the leg, gently do the "rope twist": Wrap your hands loosely around your baby's legs. As you move your top hand toward the left, move your bottom hand toward the right, in effect gently "twisting" his skin and muscles and thereby increasing the circulation in his legs. Do this all the way up each leg. Then slip your hands under your baby's bottom and massage both buttocks, stroking the legs down to the feet.

5. *Stomach next*. Put your hands on the baby's tummy and make gentle sweeping motions outward. Using both thumbs, gently massage from the belly button toward the outside. "Walk" your fingers from the stomach to the chest.

6. *Chest*. Say "I love you" and make a "sun-and-moon" motion by using both of your index fingers to trace a circle—the "sun"—that starts at the top of your baby's chest and ends around his belly button. Now take your right hand and go back up, tracing a "moon" (a backward C) up to the top of his chest; then do the same with your left hand (a forward C). Repeat this a few times. Then do a heart-shape movement—with all your fingers on the chest, at the center of his breastbone, gently trace a heart, ending at his belly button.

7. Arms and hands. Massage under the arm. Do the rope-twist movement, then do open-hand massage on both arms. Roll each finger and repeat the "This little piggy" rhyme, this time with the fingers. On the top of the hand, make small circles around the wrist.

8. Face. Take care to be extra gentle around the face. Massage the forehead and eyebrows, and use your thumbs around the eye area. Go down the bridge of your baby's nose, back and forth across the cheek, from her ears toward her upper and lower lips and back. Make small circles around the jaw and behind her ears. Rub her earlobes and under her chin. Now gently turn her over.

9. Head and back. Make circles on the back of your baby's head and shoulders. Using a back-and-forth motion, stroke her up and down. Make small circles along the back muscles, which are parallel to the spinal column. Allow your hands to travel the full length of her body, from the top of her back all the way down to her bottom and then to her ankles.

10. End the massage. "We're all done now, darling. Don't you feel good?"

If you follow the above steps every time, your baby will look forward to the experience. Again, remember to respect your baby's sensitivities. *Never* continue with a massage if he cries; let a few weeks go by and try again, this time for an even shorter period. I can only assure you that if you can acclimate your baby to the joy of touch, she will not only benefit in the long run, it will also be easier for her to get to sleep—the subject of our next chapter.

CHAPTER SIX

The *S*—To Sleep, Perchance to Cry

> I had hardly had a new baby for two weeks when it hit me that I was never again going to be rested. Well, maybe not never. I had some wisp of hope that perhaps when the kid went off to college, I'd get a full night's sleep again. I could sure as hell see it wasn't going to be during his infancy.
> —Sandi Kahn Shelton in *Sleeping Through the Night and Other Lies*

Good Sleep, Good Baby

In their earliest days, babies sleep more than they do any other single thing—some as much as twenty-three hours a day during the first week! And that, as Martha Stewart would say, is a good thing. Of course, sleep is important to all humans, but to babies it means everything. When an infant sleeps, his brain is busy manufacturing new brain cells, which are needed for mental, physical, and emotional development. Indeed, babies who are well rested are just like we are after a good sleep or a refreshing nap: alert, focused, and at ease. They feed well, they play well, they have lots of stamina, and they interact well with the people in their environment.

In contrast, a baby who doesn't sleep well won't have the neurological resources she needs to function efficiently. She's likely to become cranky and uncoordinated. She won't attend well to her mum's breast or to a bottle. She won't have the energy she needs to explore her world. And, worst of all, being overtired will actually ruin her sleep. That's because bad sleep habits are self-perpetuating. Some babies get so overtired that they can't physically wind down or drop off. They finally fall asleep only when they are totally exhausted. It's painful to see an infant so wired and upset that she literally has to scream herself to sleep in order to block out the world. What's even worse is that when she finally does sleep, it's fitful and abbreviated, sometimes no more than twenty minutes, so she's cranky practically all the time.

Now, that all might seem pretty obvious. But what a good many people don't realize is that *babies need parents' direction* to establish proper sleep habits. In fact, the reason so-called sleep problems are common is because so many parents don't realize that *they*, not their babies, must control bedtime.

What makes the situation even worse is the pressure. Virtually the first question anyone asks the parent of a very young baby is "Does she sleep through the night yet?" If the baby is older than four months, the question might change slightly ("Is she a good sleeper?"), but the bottom line for the poor parent, who often has had little sleep himself, is the same: guilt and tension. One mum, writing on a parenting website, admitted that because so many friends had asked if her child woke up in the middle of the night and how often, she finally stayed up all night to observe her baby's sleep pattern.

This is a peculiarly American phenomenon. I've never seen a culture with quite such an abundance of myths and fads related to babies' sleep habits. In this chapter, therefore, I want to share with you my ideas about sleep, many of which might contradict what you have read or heard from others. I'll help you learn how to spot fatigue before it turns into overtiredness, and what to do if you have missed that precious window of opportunity. I'll teach you how to help your baby get to sleep, and ways of stopping sleep difficulties before they become entrenched and ongoing problems.

Forgoing the Fads: Sensible Sleep

Everyone has an opinion about the best way to get a baby to sleep and what to do when you can't. I won't go into the fads of previous decades, but as I write this book in the year 2000, two distinctly different schools of thought are capturing parents' (and media) attention. In one are those who favor a practice alternately known as co-sleeping, shared sleeping, the family bed, or the Sears method, after Dr. William Sears, the California pediatrician who popularized the idea of allowing babies to sleep in their parents' bed until they *ask* for a bed of their own. The rationale behind this is that children need to develop positive associations with bedtime (I couldn't agree more) and that the best way to ensure this is to hold, cuddle, rock, and massage until Baby falls asleep (I couldn't agree less). Sears, by far the most vocal proponent of the method, told a journalist in a 1998 *Child* magazine article, "Why would a parent want to put her child in a box with bars in a dark room all by herself?"

Others who share the family bed philosophy often cite parenting practices in cultures such as Bali, where infants are not allowed to touch the ground until they're three months old. (Of course, *we* are not in Bali.) The LaLeche League suggests that if Baby's having a rough day, Mum should stay in bed with her, giving her the extra contact and nurturing she needs. It's all in the service of "bonding" and "security," so these folks see nothing wrong with Mum and Dad giving up all their time, their privacy, or their own need for sleep. And, to make this practice work, Pat Yearian, a family-bed advocate who is quoted in *The Womanly Art of Breastfeeding*, suggests that disgruntled parents change *their* perspective: "If you can adjust your mental attitude to one of greater acceptance [that your baby *will* keep waking you], you will find yourself able to enjoy those quiet moments in the night with your infant who needs to be held and nursed, or with your toddler who just needs to be with someone."

At the other extreme is the delayed-response approach, which is more often called "Ferberizing," after Dr. Richard Ferber, the director of the Center for Pediatric Sleep Disorders at Boston's Children's Hospital. His theory holds that bad sleep habits are learned and therefore can be unlearned (I couldn't agree more). To that end, he recommends that parents put babies into their own cribs while they're still awake and teach them how to fall asleep on their own (a point I also agree with). However, when a baby cries instead of drifting off to sleep, in effect saying, "Come get me out of here," Ferber suggests letting him cry it out for ever-lengthening periods—five minutes the first night, ten the next, fifteen, and so on (which is where Dr. Ferber and I part company). Dr. Ferber is quoted in *Child* as explaining, "When a youngster wants to play with something dangerous, we say no and set limits that he may balk at. . . . Teaching him that you have rules at night is the same thing. It's in his best interest to get a good night's sleep."

Obviously both schools of thought have certain merits; the experts that champion them are highly educated and well credentialed. Understandably, the issues each approach raises are often and hotly debated in the press. For example, in the fall of 1999 when the U.S. Consumer Product Safety Commission cautioned parents about co-sleeping, saying that it carried a high risk of suffocation or strangulation "to sleep with your baby or put the baby down to sleep in an adult bed," Peggy O'Mare, editor of *Mothering* magazine, denounced the warning with an impassioned article entitled, "Get out of My Bedroom!" Among other points, she questioned just who these sixty-four parents were who allegedly rolled over on their babies. Were they drunk? Drugged? Likewise, when the press or a parenting expert criticizes the delayed-response strategy as being insensitive to babies' needs, if not downright cruel, an equally zealous legion of parents comes forth insisting that the method saved their health and their marriage—and, by the way, their baby now sleeps through the night.

Perhaps you're already a member of one of these camps or the other. If one of these practices works for you, for your baby, for your lifestyle, then by all means stick with it. The trouble is, the people who call upon me for help often have tried both. A typical scenario is that one of the parents is initially attracted to the family-bed idea and "sells" the concept to his or her partner. After all, it's a romantic notion, in many ways harkening back to simpler times. Sleep-with-your-baby has the same ring to it as back-to-the-earth. It also makes the prospect of middle-of-the-night feeds sound easier. Gung ho at first, the couple decides to not buy a crib. But then, a few months or even further down the line, the honeymoon ends. Mum and Dad, taking care *not* to roll over on the baby, are losing sleep because they're so vigilant, or because they've become ultrasensitive to every little baby noise Junior utters in the middle of the night.

The baby may wake up as frequently as every two

hours, counting on someone to pay attention. Some little ones just want a pat or nuzzle to get back to sleep; others think it's playtime. The parents may end up taking shifts—one night in the bed, one night in the guest room to catch up on lost sleep. But if both of them aren't 100 percent behind the idea to begin with, the skeptical one is bound to begin to feel resentful. Typically, this is when the idea of Ferberizing seems most tempting.

So Mum and Dad purchase a crib and decide it's time for Baby to have a bed of her own. Now, think of what such a monumental change is like from her point of view: "Here's Mum and Dad, welcoming me for several months in their bed, cuddling up, cooing at me, doing basically whatever it takes to keep me happy, and then bam! The next day, I'm banished, put in a room down the hall, a setting so strange I feel lost. I don't think 'jail' and I'm not afraid of the dark, because that's not in my baby mind to know, but I do think, 'Where'd everyone go? Where are those warm bodies that usually lie next to me?' So I cry, because that's my way of asking, 'Where are you?' And I cry and I cry and I cry, and no one comes. Finally, they do. They pat me, tell me to be a good girl, and go back to sleep. But no one has taught me yet how to go to sleep on my own. I'm just a baby!"

My point is that extreme practices don't work for many people, certainly not for the babies I'm called on to help. Therefore I prefer, right from the beginning, to take a middle-of-the-road, commonsense approach, which I call sensible sleep.

What Is Sensible Sleep?

Sensible sleep is an antiextremist point of view. You will see that my philosophy incorporates certain aspects of both schools of thought, but I believe that the cry-it-out theory doesn't take Baby into consideration and the family bed gives parents short shrift. Sensible sleep, by contrast, is a whole-family approach that respects *everyone's* needs. In my view, babies need to learn how to fall asleep on their own; they need to feel safe and secure in their own cribs. But they also need us to comfort them when they're distressed. The first set of goals won't be met unless we also bear in mind the second. At the same time, parents need to have adequate rest, moments for themselves and each other, and a life that isn't all-baby-all-the-time. But they also need to devote time, energy, and focus to their babies. These two sets of goals are not contradictory. To achieve them, bear in mind the points below, which are the underpinnings of sensible sleep. Throughout the chapter, as I explain how to deal with the *S* in E.A.S.Y., you'll see how each principle translates into a practical reality.

Start as you mean to go on. If you're initially attracted to the notion of shared sleeping, think it through. Is this how you want it to be three months from now? Six months? Longer? Remember that everything you do *teaches* your baby. Therefore, when you put him to bed by cuddling him on your chest or rocking him for forty minutes, in effect you're instructing him. You're saying, "This is how you get to sleep." Once you go down that road, then you'd better be prepared to cuddle and rock him for a long, long time.

Independence is not neglect. When I say to the mother or father of a day-old infant, "We want to help her become independent," they sometimes look at me. "Independent? She's only a few hours old, Tracy." So I ask, "Well, *when* would you start?" That's a question no one can answer, not even the scientists, because we don't know the precise moment when an infant begins to truly comprehend the world or develop the skills she needs to cope with her environment. Therefore I say, start now. Fostering independence, however, doesn't mean letting her cry it out. It means meeting her needs, including picking her up when she cries, because, after all, she's trying to *tell* you something. But it also means putting her down as soon as the need is met.

Observe without intervention. You may recall this directive when I talked about playing with your baby. The same holds true for sleeping. Babies go through a predictable cycle each time they fall asleep (see page 197). Parents need to understand this so that they don't rush in. Rather than interrupting a baby's natural flow, we need to step back and let the baby fall asleep on his own.

Don't make your baby dependent on props. A prop is any device or intervention that when withdrawn will cause an infant distress. We can't expect babies to learn how to fall asleep on their own if we train them to believe that Dad's chest, a thirty-minute carry, or a breast in the mouth will always be there to soothe them. As I said in Chapter 4, I'm all for pacifiers (see page 143 and, in this chapter, page 203), but not when they're used to dummy a child up. For one thing, it's not respectful to thrust a pacifier or a boob in Baby's mouth to silence her. Furthermore, when we do such things or when we carry, rock, or endlessly cuddle an infant in the name of getting her to sleep, we actually make her dependent on props, take away her opportunity to develop self-soothing strategies, and prevent her from learning how to fall asleep on her own.

By the way, a prop is different from a transitional object, like a stuffed animal or a blanket, that *your baby adopts* and becomes attached to. Most babies don't do this until they're seven or eight months old—before that, "attachments" are usually parent-driven. Of course, if your child is comforted by a favorite cuddly toy, allow her to have it. But I'm against anything *you* give to quiet her down. Instead, let her discover her own means of calming herself.

Develop bedtime and nap time rituals. Bedtimes and nap times must be done the same way each time. As I've stressed throughout, babies are creatures of habit. They like to know what's coming next, and research has proven that even very young infants who have been conditioned to expect a particular stimulus are able to predict when it's coming.

Sleep Types

Although there is a predictable three-stage process to falling asleep (opposite), it's important to know how *your* baby drifts off. If the cycle is not interrupted by an adult's intervention, **Angel** and **Textbook** babies will fall asleep easily and independently.

With a **Touchy** baby, who is prone to meltdowns, you have to be ultraobservant; if you miss this baby's window, he gets keyed up and it's very hard for him to wind down.

A **Spirited** baby tends to fidget a lot; you may have to block out her visual stimulation. She sometimes gets a wild, wide-eyed look when she's tired, as if there are little matchsticks propping her eyelids open.

A **Grumpy** baby may fuss a little, but he's usually happy to have his nap.

(See also the general discussion of baby types on pages 66–70.)

Know how your particular baby goes to sleep. One major shortcoming of any "recipe" for putting a child to sleep is that nothing works for everyone. Therefore, although I offer many guidelines for parents, among them the predictable three stages of sleep infants pass through (see sidebar on this page) before finally falling off, I always advise getting to know *your* baby.

The best way is to actually keep a sleep diary. Starting in the morning, write down wake-up time and keep track of every nap during the day. Note when he goes to bed and when he wakes in the middle of the night. Do this for four days, which is a long enough period to give you an indication of your baby's sleep patterns, even if his nap times seem erratic.

The Three Stages of Sleep

Babies pass through these stages every time they fall asleep. The entire process usually takes around twenty minutes:

Stage 1: The Window. Your baby can't *say* "I'm tired," but he will *show* you by yawning and exhibiting other signs of fatigue (see the box on page 200). By the third yawn, get him to bed. If you don't, he'll start to cry rather than pass into the next stage.

Stage 2: The Zone. At this point, your baby has a fixed, focused gaze—or, as I call it, the "seven-mile stare"—that lasts for three or four minutes. His eyes are open, but he's not really seeing—he's off somewhere in the stratosphere.

Stage 3: Letting Go. Now your baby resembles a person nodding off on a train: He closes his eyes and his head drops forward or to the side. Just as he seems to be falling asleep, his eyes open suddenly and his head whips backward, jolting his whole body. He'll then close his eyes again and repeat the process anywhere from three to five times more until he finally enters dreamland.

Marcy, for example, was sure she couldn't chart eight-month-old Dylan's daytime sleeping habits: "He never naps at the same time, Tracy." But after four days of recordkeeping, Marcy saw that although the times varied a bit, Dylan always had a short nap between nine and ten in the morning, had another forty-minute sleep between twelve-thirty and two, and got very cranky around five, at which point he'd fall off for about twenty minutes. Knowing this about Dylan helped Marcy plan her own day and, just as important, helped her understand her little boy's moods. She was able to go with Dylan's natural biorhythms to structure his day so that he was sure to get proper rest. Whenever he got fussy, she was able to move into action more quickly, because she knew when he was ready for a nap.

The Yellow Brick Road to Dreamland

Remember in *The Wizard of Oz,* Dorothy followed the yellow brick road in order to find someone who would show her the way home? What she found at the end, after a series of mishaps and scary moments, was her own inner wisdom. Essentially, I help parents do pretty much the same thing by reminding them that good sleep habits begin with them. Sleep is a learned process that is initiated and reinforced by parents. Hence, they have to *teach* their babies how to get to sleep. And this is what the road to sensible sleep entails.

Pave the way for sleep. Because babies thrive on predictability and learn from repetition, we must always do and say the same things before naps or bedtime, so that in their baby minds they think, "Oh, this means I'm going to sleep." Do the same rituals in the same order. Say, "Okay, luv, we're going nighty-night" or "It's beddy-bye time." As you take her to her room, be quiet and low-key. Always check to see if she needs a change of nappy, as you want her to be comfortable. Go to the blinds or curtains and draw them shut. I usually say, "Good-bye, Mr. Sunshine. I'll see you after my nap."

If it's bedtime and dark out, I say, "Good night, Mr. Moonpenny." I don't believe in having babies sleep in the living room or kitchen; that's simply not respectful. Would you like your bed in the middle of a department store, with people moving about you? No, and neither does your baby.

Look for the signs along the road. Like us, babies yawn when they start to get tired. The reason humans yawn is that as the body becomes fatigued, it doesn't work as efficiently; the normal supply of oxygen brought in by the lungs, heart, and blood system diminishes a bit. Yawning is the body's way of gulping down extra oxygen (fake a yawn, and you'll see that it forces you to inhale deeply). I tell parents to try to act on their baby's first yawn—if not the first, at least by the third. If you miss the signs (see the box on the next page), certain types of infants, such as Touchy babies, quickly go into a meltdown.

> **TIP:** *Stress the benefits of rest in setting the mood. Don't present sleep as a punishment or struggle. If a child has been told "You're going for a nap" or "You have to rest now," in a tone that really says "You're banished to Siberia," he or she grows up to become someone who thinks that naps are bad or that sleep means missing out on the fun.*

Wind down as you near the destination. Adults like to read a book or watch the telly before bed to help them switch gears from the activity of the day. Babies need the same thing. Before bedtime, a bath and, if she's three months or older, a massage will help prepare her for sleep. Even at nap time, I always play a soothing lullaby. For about five minutes, I sit in a rocking chair or on the floor to give Baby an extra snuggle. You also can tell her a story if you like, or just whisper sweet nothings into

Sleepytime Signs

Just like grown-ups, infants yawn and become less able to focus when they're tired. As they get older, their changing bodies find new ways to tell you they're ready for sleep.

When they gain control over their heads: As they become sleepier, they turn their face away from objects or people, as if trying to shut out the world. If carried, they bury their face into your chest. They make involuntary movements, flailing their arms and legs.

When they gain control of their limbs: Tired babies may rub their eyes, pull at their ears, or scratch at their faces.

When they begin to gain mobility: Babies who are getting tired become visibly less coordinated and lose interest in toys. If held, they'll arch their backs and lean backward. In their cribs, they can inch their way into a corner and may wedge their heads there. Or they'll roll one way and get stuck because they can't roll back.

When they can crawl and/or walk: Coordination goes first when older babies are tired. If trying to pull themselves up, they'll fall; if walking, they'll stumble or bump into things. They have full control of their own bodies, so they'll often cling to the adult who is trying to put them down. They can stand up in their cribs but often don't know how to get back down—unless they fall, which frequently happens.

---

her ear. The purpose of this, however, is to calm your baby, not to make her fall asleep. Therefore, I stop the cuddle if I see the seven-mile stare—Stage 2—or if her eyes are starting to close, which means she's already starting Stage 3. (It's never too early to begin bedtime stories, but I don't generally introduce books until around six months, when babies are better able to focus and sit up.)

TIP: *Don't invite guests to your house when you're putting your baby to bed. That's not fair. Your baby wants to be part of the action. He sees your company and knows they've come to see him: "Mmm . . . new faces to look at, new faces to smile back at me. What? Mum and Dad think I'm going to miss this by sleeping? I don't think so."*

Park her in her crib before she reaches dreamland. Many people think that you can't put a baby into her crib until she's fast asleep. That's simply wrong. Putting her down at the beginning of Stage 3 is the best way to help your baby develop the skills she needs to go to sleep on her own. There's another reason, too: If your baby falls asleep in your arms or in a rocking device and then wakes up in her crib, it's tantamount to my pushing your bed out into the garden while you're sleeping. You wake up and wonder, "Where am I? How did I get here?" It's the same for babies, except that they can't reason, "Oh, someone must have put me out here while I was asleep." Instead, they get disoriented, even scared. They end up not feeling comfortable or safe in their crib.

When I put a baby down, I always say the same words: "I'm going to put you in your bed for a sleep. You know how good you feel afterward." I observe her closely. She might fuss a bit before settling down, especially when she experiences a Stage 3 jolt. Parents tend to rush in at this point. Some babies will naturally quiet themselves. But if she cries, a gentle, rhythmic pat on the back will give her the assurance that she's not alone. But remember to stop patting when she stops fussing—if you continue longer than she needs you to, she will begin to associate patting with going to sleep and, worse, begin to *need* it to get to sleep.

TIP: I usually suggest putting a baby down on her back. However, you can also put her to sleep on her side by wedging her with two rolled-up towels or special wedge-shaped cushions that can be purchased at most drugstores. If she sleeps on her side, for her comfort, make sure it's not always the same side.

When the road to dreamland is a bit bumpy, use a pacifier to aid sleep. I like to use a pacifier during the first three months—the period when we're first establishing routines. This saves Mum from becoming a human pacifier. At the same time, I always caution limited use so that the pacifier doesn't turn into a prop. When used correctly, babies will suck ferociously for about six or seven minutes, then start to slow down a bit; eventually, they'll spit the pacifier out. That's because they have expelled the sucking energy they needed to release and are on the way to dreamland. At this point, some well-meaning adult comes along and says, "Oh, poor baby, you've spit your pacifier out," and tries to put it back in. Don't! If the baby needed her pacifier to continue sleeping, she'd let you know by making gurgling noises and squirming.

For many babies, if you've taken the above route to dreamland each time the *S* in E.A.S.Y. rolls around, that's all it will take to help your baby have a positive association with sleep. Repeating the journey builds security as well as predictability. You'll be amazed at how quickly your baby learns the skills she needs for sensible sleep. She will also look forward to sleep as a restorative, pleasant experience. Of course, there will be times when your baby gets overtired, has teething pain, or has a fever (see pages 211–213). But these are the exceptions, not the rule.

Bear in mind, too, that it takes twenty minutes for

Pacifier Use and Misuse: Quincy's Story

As I pointed out in Chapter 4, there's a very fine line between the use and misuse of a pacifier (pages 143–144). By the time babies are six or seven weeks old, if they haven't automatically spit out their pacifiers after falling asleep, parents can remove them. When a baby three months or older wakes up crying for his pacifier, I see that as a sign of misuse. This brings to mind six-month-old Quincy. His parents called because he kept waking in the middle of the night; only his pacifier calmed him. Inquiring further, I discovered what I had expected: When Quincy naturally spit out the pacifier, they kept going in and sticking it back into his mouth. Of course, he became dependent on the feeling of the pacifier, and its absence disturbed his sleep. I told his parents my plan: Take away the pacifier. That night, when he cried for his pacifier, I patted him instead. The second night he needed less patting. It only took three nights, and at that point Quincy was actually sleeping better, because he developed his own independent self-soothing technique. He started sucking his tongue. At night, he sounded a bit like Donald Duck, but during the day, he was a much happier little boy.

---

your baby to actually fall asleep, so don't ever try to rush things. If you do, she will get fussy and you will disrupt her natural three-stage process. For example, if she is disturbed during the third stage—say, by a loud bang, a dog barking, or a door slamming—it will move her toward waking, not sleep, and you have to start all over. It's no different from when an adult is drifting off and a telephone rings, jarring the silence. If the person gets annoyed or overstimulated, it's sometimes hard to fall back to sleep. It's the same with your baby. If this happens, she naturally will fuss, the cycle must start again, and it just might take another twenty minutes for her to drift off.

When You Miss the Window

Now, in the beginning, when you're not really familiar with your baby's cries and body language, it stands to reason that you might not catch him by the third yawn. That may not matter much if you have an Angel or Textbook baby; a little reassurance usually gets those types on track in fairly short order. But especially with a Touchy baby, and somewhat with a Spirited or Grumpy baby, you've got to have a few tricks up your sleeve in the event that you miss Stage 1, because at that point, Baby is already close to overtired. Or, as I suggested above, a loud noise might startle him, disrupting the natural process; if he's very distressed, he will need your help.

Most Sleep Problems Occur Because . . .

One of the following happens before bedtime
- Baby is nursed.
- Baby is walked around.
- Baby is rocked or jiggled.
- Baby is allowed to fall asleep on an adult's chest.

or . . .

- When Baby is asleep, parents rush in at the first little whimper. She might have fallen back to sleep on her own without their well-meaning interference. But she then becomes accustomed to her parents' rescuing her (more about this on page 211).

First, I'm going to tell you what *not* to do in either situation: Never bounce or jiggle. Never walk or rock him too wildly. Remember that he is already *over*-stimulated. He's crying because he's already had enough, and crying is his way of blocking out sound and light. You don't want to do anything to add to his arousal. Moreover, this is usually how bad habits first develop. Mum or Dad walks or rocks their infant to sleep. When he weighs fifteen pounds or more, they *try* to get him to sleep without such props. Understandably, Baby starts wailing at that point. It's his way of saying, "Hey, guys, we don't do things this way. You usually rock or walk me to sleep."

To avoid such a scenario, here's what you can do to help your baby calm down and block out the outside world.

Swaddle. Fresh from a fetal position, infants are not used to wide-open spaces. Plus, they don't know that their arms and legs belong to them. When they're over-tired, you need to immobilize them, because seeing their appendages flail about both scares the daylights out of them—they think someone's doing something *to* them—*and* the experience heaps more stimulation onto their already overloaded senses. Swaddling, one of the oldest techniques for helping a baby get to sleep, may seem dated, but even modern research confirms its benefits. To swaddle properly, fold the corner of a square receiving blanket down into a triangle. Lay your baby on top, positioning the fold level with his neck. Place one of his arms across his chest at a 45-degree angle and bring one corner of the blanket snugly across his body. Do the same with the other side. I suggest swaddling for the first six weeks, but after the seventh week, when Baby is first trying to get his hands to his mouth, help him out by bending his arms and leaving his hands exposed and close to his face.

Reassure. Let him know you're there to help him. Pat his back steadily and at an even pace, mimicking a heart-beat. You also can add a sound, *sh . . . sh . . . sh . . . sh,* which simulates the rhythmic whooshing Baby heard in the womb. Keep your voice low and soothing, and whisper into his ear, "It's okay," or "You're only going to sleep." As you put him down into his crib, if you've been patting, continue to pat. If you've been vocalizing a reassuring sound, keep doing it. That makes for a smoother transition.

Block out visual stimulation. Visual stimulation—light, moving objects—assaults a tired baby, especially a Touchy one. This is why we darken the room before putting Baby into bed, but for some, that's not enough. If your baby is lying down, place your hand over, not on, his eyes to block out the visuals. If you're holding him, stand still in a dimmed area or, if he's really agitated, in a totally dark closet.

Don't cave in. When a baby is overtired, it's very hard on the parents. It takes tremendous patience and resolve, especially if the baby has already gotten into a bad habit. Their baby is screaming; they keep patting; the cries get louder. Overstimulated babies tend to cry and cry until their high-pitched "I'm exhausted!" wails reach a crescendo. Then they'll stop for a moment, and start all over again. Usually, there are three such crescendoes before a baby finally calms down. What happens, though, is that by the second crescendo, parents have had it. Desperate, they revert back to whatever remedies they've used—carrying, the breast, that dreadful swing.

The problem is, if you keep caving in, your baby will continue to need your help to go to sleep. It doesn't take long for a baby to become dependent on a prop—a few times at most, because he's got such a small memory. If you've started off on the wrong foot, every day you continue will simply reinforce the negative behavior. I tend to get calls about sleep issues when babies have reached seventeen pounds and aren't quite so easy to carry round. The biggest problems manifest themselves around six to eight weeks. I always tell parents when they call, "You need to understand what's going on here and take responsibility for the bad habits you fostered. Then the hard part: Have the conviction and perseverance to help your baby learn a new and better way." (More about changing bad patterns in Chapter 9.)

This Bears Repeating: INDEPENDENCE IS NOT NEGLECT!

I never leave a screaming baby. On the contrary, I consider myself that baby's voice. If I don't help him, who will translate his needs? At the same time, I don't advocate holding or comforting a baby once you have met his need. The minute he's calm, put him down. Thus, you give him the gift of independence.

Sleeping Through the Night

I can't very well write a chapter about sleep without addressing the question of when babies start to sleep through the night. Following this section you'll find a chart indicating what you can expect *in general* from infants at various stages of development. Remember, though, that these are *rough guidelines*, based on statistical probability. Only Textbook babies will conform exactly (hence the label). There's nothing "wrong" with an infant whose sleeping habits don't conform—it only means that he or she is different.

Let's start this discussion by reminding you that your baby's "day" is twenty-four hours long. She doesn't know the difference between day and night, so the idea of sleeping through the night means nothing to her. It's something *you* want (and need) her to do. It's not a natural occurrence; you will train her to do it, teach her that there's a difference between day and night. Here are some reminders I give parents.

Employ the robbing-Peter-to-pay-Paul principle. There is no doubt that keeping your baby on an E.A.S.Y. routine helps speed his sleeping through the night, because it's a structured yet flexible routine. I hope you're also keeping track of your baby's feeds and naps—that way, you better understand his needs. If, for example, he has had a particularly fussy morning and sleeps an extra half hour into what's supposed to be his next feed, you let him (whereas with a schedule, you'd wake him). But you also use judgment. During the day, never let a baby sleep more than a feed cycle—in other words, no longer than three hours—because otherwise it will rob his nighttime sleep hours. I guarantee that any baby who has had six hours of uninterrupted sleep during the day will not sleep more than three at night. So if you find your baby doing this, you can be sure that his "day" has now become your night. The only way to switch him round is by waking him, thereby robbing Peter of the hours your baby is using up by sleeping during the day, in order to pay Paul—adding those hours to the nighttime sleep.

Tank them up. This might sound like a rather crude expression, but one of the ways we get babies to sleep through the night is by filling their tummies. To that end, when an infant is six weeks old, I suggest two practices: *cluster feeding*—that is, feed her every two hours before bedtime—and giving what I call a *dream feed* right before you retire for bed. For example, you give her the breast (or a bottle) at six and eight in the evening, and the dream feed at ten-thirty or eleven. With dream feeding, literally nurse or bottle-feed her in her sleep. In other words, you pick your baby up, gently place the bottle or breast on her lower lip, and allow her to eat, taking care not to wake her. When she's finished, you don't even burp her; just put her down. Infants are usually so relaxed at these feeds, they don't gulp air. You don't talk; you don't change her unless she's soaked through or soiled. With both these tanking-up techniques, most babies can sleep through that middle-of-the-night feed, because they have enough calories to keep them going for five or six hours.

> **TIP:** *Have Dad take over the dream feed. Most men are usually home at that time, and most love doing it.*

Use a pacifier. If it isn't allowed to become a prop, a pacifier can be very helpful in weaning a baby off the nighttime feed. If a baby weighs ten pounds and he's consuming at least twenty-five to thirty ounces of food during his daytime feeds or is getting between six and eight breastfeedings (four or five during the day; two or three clustered at night), he doesn't need an additional night feeding for nourishment. If he's still waking, he's using the opportunity for oral stimulation. This is where prudent use of a pacifier can pay off. If it normally takes your baby twenty minutes to feed at night, when he wakes up crying for the breast or bottle, and yet he only feeds for five minutes or takes barely an ounce, give him a pacifier instead. The first night, he'll probably stay up the entire twenty minutes with the pacifier in his mouth before falling back to sleep. The next night, it may cut back to ten minutes. The third night, he might fidget in his sleep at the time he'd normally get up for the feed. If he wakes, give him the pacifier. In other words, you're substituting the oral stimulation of the pacifier for the bottle or breast. Eventually, he won't wake up for it.

Baby Sleep

When they're asleep, babies, like adults, progress through cycles of sleep that are approximately forty-five minutes long. They first go into a deep sleep and then into REM, a lighter sleep featuring dreams, and, finally, come to consciousness. These cycles are barely noticeable to most adults (unless a vivid dream wakes us). Usually, we just turn over and send ourselves back to sleep without realizing we've woken.

Some infants do pretty much the same thing. You might hear them make grumpy little noises—which I call "phantom baby" sounds. And as long as no one disturbs them, they're off to dreamland again.

Other infants coming out of REM sleep aren't able to send themselves back to sleep as easily. Often, it's because their parents rush in too quickly from the moment they're born ("Oh! You're awake!") and they never have an opportunity to learn how to shift gears going in and out of these natural sleep cycles.

This is just what happened with Julianna's little boy, Cody. Cody was fifteen pounds, and Julianna, having observed him carefully, realized that his three A.M. feed was a habit: Cody would get up and suck on his bottle for ten minutes and then go back to sleep. When Julianna called me, she asked if I could come over—first of all, to see if her assessment was correct (although I already knew from what she had described that it was), and then to help get him to stop waking up at that hour. I spent three nights with the family. The first night, I lifted Cody out of the crib and, instead of a bottle, I gave him a pacifier, which, like his bottle, he sucked for ten minutes. The next night, I left him in the crib and gave him the pacifier, and this time he lasted just three minutes. The third night, sure enough, Cody made little restless noises at a quarter after three, but he didn't wake up. That was it; from then on, Cody slept until six or seven the next morning.

Don't rush in. At their best, babies often sleep fitfully (see the "Baby Sleep" sidebar opposite). That's why it's not wise to respond to every little noise you hear. In fact, I often tell parents to get rid of those bloody monitors that exaggerate every coo and cry. They turn parents into alarmists and worrywarts! As I've repeated throughout this chapter, one must walk a fine line between *responding* and *rescuing*. A baby whose parents respond becomes a secure child who's not afraid to venture forth. A baby whose parents continually rescue begins to doubt his own capabilities and never develops the strength and skills he needs to explore his world or to feel comfortable in it.

Normal Sleep Disturbances

Let me end this chapter by saying that notwithstanding any of the foregoing, sleep disturbances are, at times, inevitable. Normally good sleepers go through periods of restlessness and even have problems getting to sleep. Here are some of those times.

When solid food is introduced. Babies may wake up with gas once they begin ingesting solid food. Check with your pediatrician to see what foods to introduce and when. Ask which foods could possibly cause gas or allergies. Keep a careful record of every food you've introduced so that if problems occur, your pediatrician can study your child's food history.

When they start moving about. Babies who have just learned how to control their movements often get a tingling in their limbs and joints. You've probably experienced a similar phenomenon after you've worked out at the gym if you've been idle for some time. Even after your limbs have stopped moving, your energy level and circulation are still pumped up. The same thing happens to babies. They're not used to movement. Sometimes, once they're able to skooch about, they can get themselves into positions they can't get out of, and this, too, can disturb their sleep. They also may wake up confused, because they're in a different position. Just go in and reassure the baby with a rhythmic whisper: "Sh . . . sh . . . sh . . . sh . . . you're okay."

When they go through a growth spurt. During a growth spurt (page 131), babies sometimes wake up hungry. Feed your baby that night, but the next day give her more food during the day. The growth spurt may last for two days, but upping your baby's calories usually ends the sleep disturbance.

When they're teething. If it's teething and not some other problem, they drool, their gums are red and swollen, and sometimes they have a low-grade fever. One of my favorite home remedies is to wet one corner of a washcloth, stick it in the freezer, and when it's frozen solid, give it to Baby to suck on. I personally don't like store-bought items that you freeze, because I don't know what kind of liquid is inside. In England, we have Farley's Rusks, hard teething biscuits that melt down to nothing—they're fantastic, safe, and can be found in most British shops stateside. I like Infants' Motrin better than Infants' Tylenol for the pain because I've found that it lasts longer.

When they have a dirty diaper. One mum I know calls them "power poops"—and most infants wake up when they happen. Sometimes it even scares them. Change the diaper in dim light, to prevent your baby from getting revved up. Reassure her, and put her back to sleep.

> **TIP:** *Whenever your baby wakes in the middle of the night, for whatever reason, never be too playful or friendly. Be loving, take care of the problem, but be careful not to give your baby the wrong idea. Otherwise, she might wake up the next night wanting to play.*

One thing I always remind parents who worry about sleep is that whatever issues crop up, they won't last forever. If you look at the bigger picture, you're less apt to catastrophize over a few sleepless nights. For sure, it's the luck of the draw: Some babies simply *are* better sleepers than others. But no matter what your baby is like, at least *you* ought to get enough rest to withstand the onslaught. In the next chapter, I stress this and the many other ways you can take care of yourself.

What They Need/What You Can Expect

Age/Milestones	Sleep Needed per Day	Typical Patterns
Newborn: Don't have control over anything except their eyes	16–20 hours	Nap 1 hour in every 3; sleep 5–6 hours at night
1–3 months: More alert and aware of their surroundings; able to move head	15–18 hours, until 18 months of age	Three naps, 1½ hours each; 8 hours at night
4–6 months: Gaining mobility		Two naps, 2–3 hours each; 10–12 hours at night
6–8 months: More mobility; able to sit and crawl		Two naps, 1–2 hours each; 12 hours at night
8–18 months: Always in motion		Two naps, 1–2 hours each, or one big nap, 3 hours long; 12 hours at night

CHAPTER SEVEN
The *Y*—It's Your Turn

> Now quick! Lie down, and do so
> every time you reach for this book.
> The most critical advice we can give
> you today is simple: Don't stand
> when you can sit, don't sit when
> you can lie down and don't stay
> awake when you can sleep.
> —Vicki Iovine, in
> *The Girlfriends' Guide to Surviving
> the First Year of Motherhood*

> Think of yourself sometimes. Don't
> give everything to the children and
> leave nothing for yourself. You have
> to know who you are; you have to
> learn a lot about yourself, listen to
> yourself, and watch yourself grow,
> too.
> —One of 1,100 mothers responding
> to a survey by National Family
> Opinion in *The Motherhood Report:
> How Women Feel About Being Mothers*

My First Baby

It takes one to know one. One of the reasons parents
trust me is that I share my own early experiences as a
mother with them. I remember all too well the fears and
disappointment I felt with my firstborn, wondering how
prepared I was and whether I could really be a good
mum. I have to say, I had a wonderful support system in
place—my Nan, who practically raised me, my own
mother, and countless other relatives, friends, and neigh-

bors ready to pitch in. Still, it was a bit of a shock when delivery day finally arrived.

My mother and grandmother, of course, exclaimed how beautiful Sara was, but I wasn't too sure. I remember looking at her and thinking, "Wow, she's all red and crinkly." This wasn't at all how I had imagined she'd be. That memory is so vivid, I can almost put myself back there now, eighteen years later, feeling my disappointment because Sara's top lip didn't look exactly picture-perfect. I also can recall her bleating like a lamb and staring at my face for the longest while. My Nan turned to me then and said, "You've started your labor of love, Tracy. You will be a mum until the day you draw your last breath." Her words hit me like a cold splash of sea-water: I was *a mother*. Suddenly, I had the urge to run or at least call the whole thing off.

The following days seemed to be filled with endless fumbling and lots of tears and pain. I ached in my legs from holding them in an awkward froglike position during labor. My shoulders pinched from the midwife's having thrust my head onto my chest. My eye sockets were sore from the pressure of pushing, and worst of all, my breasts felt like they were going to explode. I remember my mum saying that I had to start breastfeeding straightaway, and the idea absolutely terrified me. At least my Nan helped me find a comfy position, but the truth of the matter was that *I* had to figure it all out. That, and learning how to diaper Sara, comfort her, really *be* with her, as well as trying to find a moment for myself, consumed most of my day.

Eighteen years later, most new mothers go through pretty much the same experience. (I suspect that eighteen years before me, it was no different, either.) It's not just the physical trauma, which would be enough to debilitate anyone. It's the exhaustion, the staggering cocktail of emotions, and the crushing feelings of inadequacy that overwhelm you as well. And that, lovey, is *normal*. I'm not talking postpartum *depression* (which I'll address later); I'm just talking about the time nature gives you to heal and to stay close to home in order to get to know your baby. The trouble is, some women barely take the time to feed themselves once the baby comes, which is a very defeating, if not dangerous, proposition.

A Tale of Two Women

To illustrate my point, let me tell you about two mums I worked with: Daphne and Connie. Both are high-powered women, self-starters who had worked for several years in their own businesses. In their thirties, both had uncomplicated vaginal deliveries and the further good fortune of giving birth to Angel babies. The difference—and it is an important one—is that Connie realized that her life would change when her baby arrived, while Daphne stubbornly clung to the notion that she could go on as usual.

Connie. Connie, an interior designer, was thirty-five when her daughter was born. An organized person by nature (probably a 4 on the Wing It/Plan It continuum; see pages 60–62), she had given herself the goal of having her nursery completely ready by her third trimester, which she did. When I arrived for our predelivery visit, I remarked, "Looks like you've covered everything. All we need to add here is a baby." Knowing that once the baby arrived, she might not have the time or desire to cook, something she normally loved to do, Connie also filled her freezer with delicious and nutritious home-cooked soups, casseroles, sauces, and other pop-'em-in-the-oven dishes. As she neared her due date, Connie called all her clients, letting them know that *someone* would be there in case of emergencies, but for the next two months, it wasn't going to be her. She and her new baby would have to come first. Interestingly, no one objected; in fact, they found her forthright approach refreshing and admirable.

Because Connie enjoyed very close and loving relationships with her family, it was understood that when the baby arrived, everyone would swing into action, which they did. Mum and Grandma cooked and did the errands. Connie's sister fielded business calls and even went into Connie's office to check on various projects.

The first week after Annabelle's birth, Connie stayed in bed practically all day, poring over her little girl, getting to know her. She slowed her own normally fast pace and gave herself plenty of time to breastfeed. She accepted the fact that she needed to take care of herself. When her mum left, she had a freezer full of food to draw from. She also had piles of take-out menus for evenings when it seemed like too much to even heat the oven.

Connie was smart about involving her husband, Buzz, too. While I see some women stand over their men, directing as they diaper or, worse, complaining that they're doing it wrong, Connie knew that Buzz loved Annabelle as much as she did. Maybe his diapers were a little loose. So what? She was encouraging him to be *a parent*. They divided up jobs and stayed out of each other's territory. As a result, Buzz felt more like a true parenting partner than a "helper."

Putting Annabelle on a structured routine helped Connie organize her own time. Still, her mornings flew, as they do for most new mums: By the time she got up, saw to Annabelle's needs, took her own shower, and got dressed, it was lunchtime. Every afternoon between two and five, though, Connie lay down. Whether she napped, read, or just collected her thoughts didn't matter; she needed time alone. Rather than rob herself of this precious free time, she did only tasks that were high-priority. With note writing or phone calls, she usually concluded, "It can wait."

Even after I left, Connie was able to continue her routine of rest and recuperation. She had anticipated my departure, as she had planned for everything else. Weeks and weeks before, Connie had lined up a group of good friends who would each take a turn daily, coming over to baby-sit from two to five. And she had already begun to search for a nanny who would take care of Annabelle when she went to the office.

When Annabelle was two months old, Connie gradually eased her way back to work, at first spending just enough time at the office to reconnect with clients and to make sure everything was on track. Rather than take on any new projects at that point, she worked only part-time. When Annabelle was around six months old and Connie had spent enough time with the new nanny to be comfortable with her choice, she increased her hours at the office. But by that time, Connie knew her daughter, was confident about her own parenting ability, and felt physically fit—if not back to her old self, at least a rested, healthy version of her new self.

Now back to work full-time, Connie still takes a cat-nap in her office every afternoon. She told me recently, "Tracy, motherhood has been the best thing for me because, among other reasons, it has forced me to slow down."

Daphne. If only Daphne, a thirty-eight-year-old entertainment lawyer in Hollywood, could have followed

Connie's example. She wasn't home from the hospital an hour before she got on the phone. Countless visitors traipsed through the house. A beautiful, well-appointed nursery was ready for the baby, but nothing had been taken out of its wrapping. By the second day, I overheard Daphne planning a business meeting that would take place in her living room. And by the third day, she announced her intention to "get back to work."

Daphne had a huge circle of friends as well as business associates, and within a week, she was booking lunches, as if to prove that having a baby wasn't going to affect her life at all. She was almost defiant. "I can have lunch. Tracy's here. And I've hired a baby nurse." She made appointments with her trainer and picked at her food, obviously concerned about her weight gain. She wanted to use the Stairmaster, too—a perfect metaphor for her hectic prebaby existence, where climbing the ladder of success was a way of life.

It was as if Daphne didn't realize she had a baby. Given her circumstances and her world—an industry in which people often call a project "my baby"—it made sense. To Daphne, childbirth was another project— or at least she'd have liked to see it that way. Getting pregnant, which was difficult for her, was the "in development" stage, and when the end product—the baby— finally came, she was ready to move on.

Not surprisingly, Daphne seized every opportunity to leave the house. If there was an errand to be done, no matter how mundane, she volunteered. Without fail, she'd forget (or purposely not buy) one or two items on the shopping list, which gave her yet another excuse for leaving the house.

Over those first few days, being at Daphne's house was like living with a tornado. She tried breastfeeding, but when she realized that, at least at the outset, she'd have to devote forty minutes to it, she said, "I think I want to try formula." Now, you know that I advocate *any* feeding method that works for Mum's lifestyle, but I also advise factoring in a number of considerations (see "Making the Choice," pp. 103–110). In this case, Daphne's only concern was what would give her more time for *her* day. "I want to get back to my old self," she announced.

Meanwhile, she gave mixed messages to her poor husband, Dirk, a hands-on dad who was more than willing to take up the slack. At times, she welcomed his participation. "You'll watch Cary while I'm out, won't you?" she'd say, flying out the door. Other times, though, she'd criticize the way he held the baby or dressed him. "Why did you put him in *that* thing?" she'd ask sharply, eyeing Cary's outfit. "My mother's coming over." Not surprisingly, Dirk grew resentful and became less involved.

I tried every trick in the book to get Daphne to slow down. First, I confiscated the phone. That didn't work because she had so many, including a cell phone. I ordered her to bed between two and five, but she'd invariably use the time for calls or visits. "I'm free between two and five. Come over," she'd tell friends. Or she'd schedule a meeting. Once Dirk and I conspired to hide her car keys. She went mad looking for them. When we finally confessed but refused to give in, she said defiantly, "Well, I'll just walk to the office, then."

All of this was classic denial. She might have kept up the front if it weren't for the fact that the nanny she'd hired to replace me failed to show up, and she had only two days more of my time at that point. Suddenly, reality hit her like a ton of bricks. Utterly exhausted, she became totally unsettled and finally broke down, sobbing.

I helped her see that all along she had been covering her insecurity with activity. I gently reassured her that she was going to be a good mother but that it would

Excuses, Excuses, Excuses!

From the day your baby is born, every day, ask yourself, "What did I do for me today?" Here are rationalizations of women who don't take time for themselves—and what I say to their excuses:

"I can't leave the baby alone." Get a relative or friend to come over for an hour.

"None of my friends are familiar with babies." Invite them over and show them what to do.

"I don't have time." If you follow my suggestions, you will make time. You're probably not prioritizing. Put the answering machine on instead of taking phone calls.

"No one takes care of my baby like I do." Rubbish—you're being controlling. Besides, when you've run yourself ragged, someone will *have* to step in.

"What if I'm not here?" Women who tend to be controlling are shocked to find their households do not fall apart without them.

"I'll take time when the baby is a little older." If you don't take time for yourself now, you won't feel important. You'll lose your own (nonmother) identity.

take time. Because she hadn't taken the opportunity to get to know her son or learn what he needed, she *felt* incompetent, but that didn't mean she was. Furthermore, she was exhausted, because she hadn't given herself time to heal. "I can't do anything right," she wept in my arms, and finally admitted her deepest fear: "How could I fail at what everyone else seems to do so well?"

I certainly don't mean to paint a bad picture of Daphne. My heart went out to her, and believe me, I've seen the same scenario often. A lot of mums go into denial, particularly those who leave thriving, high-prestige careers in favor of motherhood, or those who are superorganized. Their lives are thrown out of sync when the baby arrives. They want to believe that life will be exactly the way it always has been. And rather than feel the emotions that come with early motherhood or own up to their fears, they minimize the experience. In fact, prospective power mums often ask, "How hard could it be to have a baby?" or "How hard could it be to breast-feed?" When they get home, they find out that although they can run multimillion-dollar companies or shepherd complex programs through committees, motherhood poses challenges they never dreamed of. Thus, part of their denial manifests itself in an urgency to embrace something they already know how to do and are good at. Business or lunch with their cronies is a no-brainer compared to all they have to do and learn when they first come home with a new baby.

It's no better if a mother comes down on the other side of the continuum, insisting on doing *everything* herself. Joan, for instance, interviewed me and then announced, "I want to figure this out on my own." She tried . . . for two weeks, and then I got a desperate call. "I'm exhausted, fighting with my husband, Barry, all the time, and I feel like I'm not doing a good job of mothering either. This is way harder than I thought," Joan admitted. It wasn't so much that it was more difficult, I explained. It was just more work than she anticipated. I got her to take a nap in the afternoon, which gave Barry a chance to be with his daughter.

Giving Yourself a Break

To be sure, one of the most important bits of advice I give new parents during the first few days and weeks is to remember that you're a better parent than you think you are. Most don't realize that parenting is a learned art. They've read all the books and seen media portrayals, and they *think* they know what they're in for. Then the baby arrives. Unfortunately, just when they're at the beginning of the learning curve, they're also feeling worse than they've ever felt. That's the reason I suggested in Chapter 4 that breastfeeding mothers observe my forty-day rule (see page 126–127)—but the truth is, *all new mothers need to take time to heal*. In addition to the

---

Recovery Reminders

These may seem elementary, my dear Watson, but you wouldn't believe how many mums don't keep them in mind:

✓ Eat. Consume a balanced diet, at least 1,500 calories a day, 500 extra if you're breastfeeding. Don't watch your weight. Have food in the freezer or take-out menus on hand.

✓ Sleep. Take a nap every afternoon at least, more often if you can. Give Dad a turn.

✓ Exercise. Don't use equipment or train for at least six weeks; take long walks instead.

✓ Find a few moments for yourself. Ask your spouse, a relative, or a friend to take over so that you can truly be "off duty."

✓ Don't make promises you can't keep. Let others know you won't be available for at least a month or two. If you've already overbooked yourself, beg off: "I'm sorry. I underestimated what having a baby would mean."

✓ Prioritize. Cross nonessentials off the list.

✓ Plan. Line up baby-sitters; plan menus; make lists so that you shop only once a week. To resume prebaby activities, like a weekly book club, coordinate with your spouse, a relative, or a good friend.

✓ Know your own limitations. When you're tired, lie down; when you're hungry, eat; and when you're irritable, leave the room!

✓ Ask for help. No one can do this on her own.

✓ Spend time with your partner or a good friend. Don't center every minute around your newborn. All-baby-all-the-time is unrealistic.

✓ Pamper yourself. As regularly as you can, have a massage (from someone familiar with postpartum bodies), a facial, a manicure, and/or a pedicure.

---

physical trauma of childbirth, they're consumed with details they never thought about, more tired than they imagined they'd be, and overwhelmed by their emotions. For mothers who nurse, the difficulties of learning how and the problems that can arise from breastfeeding (see page 128–129) only compound the shock.

Even a woman like Gail, a former nursery school teacher and oldest of five, found herself astonished by the sheer weight of work and responsibility. She had cared for her younger siblings and regularly came to the rescue when her friends had their first babies. But when Lily was born, Gail plummeted. Why? First of all, this was *her* baby and *her* body—her soreness, her stiffness, her burning when she peed. And her hormones were raging. She was incensed when her toast got a little too brown, snapped at her mother for moving a chair, and was reduced to tears when she had trouble screwing on the top of a bottle.

"I can't believe *I* can't cope," Gail lamented.

She's far from unique. Another mother, Marcy, who met me at the door with a long list of questions, remembers her first few days: "It was like a bad movie. I was sitting at the dinner table, naked from the waist up because my nipples hurt too much to wear anything. My breasts were leaking, and I was crying as my mother and husband looked on in horror. All I could say was 'This sucks!' "

To me, the best rejuvenation of all is sleep. I send mums to bed between two and five every day. If they can't manage that, I tell them to take at least three one-hour naps each day during the first six weeks. I warn them not to waste this most valuable time by being on the phone, catching up on household chores, or writing notes. You can't give 100 percent if you're only operating with 50 percent of the sleep that you need. Even if you have help, even if you don't *feel* tired, you have this huge wound inside you. If you don't get enough rest, I guarantee that six weeks later you'll feel like a bus hit you. But don't let me be the one to say I told you so.

For women, it helps to talk to good friends who've been through it, as well as your own mother if you have a good relationship with her—she can be a great support and can remind you that this is a natural process. For men, talking to the guys might not be as satisfying. I've heard from the fathers in my group that new dads tend to compete with one another about how *bad* it is. "The baby kept me up half the night," one might say to the other. "Yeah?" responds his friend. "Well, mine was up all night. I don't think I had ten minutes' sleep."

For either gender, it's essential to take it slow and allow for mistakes and difficulties. Connie, for example, was kind to herself and patient. She recognized the importance of planning and support. She didn't rush to get onto an exercise machine. Instead, she took long walks, which increased her circulation *and* got her out of the house. Most important, Connie understood that her postbaby life was never going to be the same. That's not a bad thing—it's just different.

It also helps to take things in small bites. Even if there's a mountain of laundry staring at you, you don't have to do it all. Though many gifts have come in, people will understand if you don't send a thank-you note right away.

The truth is that when you have a baby, everything *does* change—your routines, your priorities, and your relationships. Women (and men) who don't accept this reality can be headed for trouble. Perspective, perspective, perspective—that's what a smooth postpartum recovery boils down to. The first three days last for only three days. The first month is just that. You're in this for the long haul. You'll have good days and not-so-good days; be prepared for both.

The Many Moods of Mum

I can often tell a mum's emotional temperature by the way she greets me at the door. Francine, for example, called me ostensibly for a breastfeeding consultation. When she greeted me at the door in a rumpled T-shirt decorated by patches of white spit-up, I knew breastfeeding wasn't her only problem. "I'm sorry," she apologized immediately, watching my eyes scan her attire. "This was the one day I wanted to be up and dressed and showered—because *you* were coming." Then she added, quite unnecessarily, "I'm having a bad day today."

She confided, "I feel like Dr. Jekyll and Mrs. Hyde, Tracy. One minute, I'm the best and most loving mother in the world to my two-week-old. The next, I feel like I want to leave the house and never return because it's all too much."

"That's okay, luv," I said, smiling. "That just means you're like every other new mother."

"Really?" she asked. "I was beginning to think something was wrong with me."

I reassured Francine, as I often must with new mums, that the first six weeks are a roller-coaster ride of emotions, and the only thing we can do is strap ourselves in and prepare for the ride. Given the mood swings, it's no wonder that many women feel they suddenly have multiple personalities.

Remember: They're mood *swings*, which is why within the course of a day, certainly a week, you might feel as if you're inhabited by a variety of personalities whose voices resonate inside you.

"This is pretty easy." At these moments, you feel like the quintessential natural mother—you can figure it all out pretty quickly and easily. You trust your own judgment, feel confident, and aren't particularly susceptible to parenting trends. You can also laugh at yourself and know that motherhood isn't something you're going to do perfectly all the time. You're not afraid to ask questions, and when you do, you easily retain the answers or can adapt them to suit your own situation. You feel balanced.

"Am I doing this right?" These are the anxiety-ridden moments when you feel inept and pessimistic. You may feel skittish about handling the baby, fearing that you might break her. The slightest glitch can upset you—in fact, you may even worry about events that haven't occurred. And at the extreme, perhaps when your hormones are raging most wildly, you imagine the worst.

"Oh, this is bad . . . really, really bad." At these moments, you moan and groan over your experience of childbirth and the ongoing saga of motherhood, and you're sure no one has ever felt this miserable—or else why would they have babies? It makes you feel better to tell everyone how painful the cesarean was, how the baby is keeping you up at night, how your husband is just not doing the things he promised he would. And when you're offered help, you're apt to play the martyr: "It's all right. I'll handle it."

"No problem—I'll just whip everything into shape." Successful women who leave thriving careers to become

mothers are most prone to moments like these. At such
times, you think you can impose your management
skills onto your baby, and you may be surprised, disappointed, or angry when your infant doesn't cooperate.
You're having a moment of denial, luv, believing that life
with Baby will continue to be just as it was before he arrived.

"But the book says . . ." During moments of confusion
and doubt, you read everything you can get your hands
on and then try to apply it to your baby. To deal with the
chaos, you make endless lists and use chalkboards and
organizers. While I applaud structure and order, it's not
good to be inflexible, letting your routine rule you
rather than guide you. For example, if a Mummy-and-
me class starts at 10:30 A.M. you might not enroll, because you're afraid it will disrupt your schedule.

Of course, it would be nice if the "This is pretty easy"
voice dominated and you felt like a natural mum 24-7,
but I assure you that most women don't. The best you
can do is take note of those voices, keep a journal of
your moods if you can't remember them, and then learn
to deal with the changes. If one voice shouts at you per-
sistently, telling you that you're never going to make it
as a mum, then it might be time to reassess.

Baby Blues or Real Depression?

Let me reiterate: Some negativity is *normal*. All in the
typical course of a postpartum period, women get hot
flashes, headaches, and dizzy spells; they may become
lethargic or weepy; they may have feelings of self-doubt
and anxiety. What causes these baby blues? Levels of
the hormones estrogen and progesterone drop radically

within hours of delivery, as do levels of endorphins, which have contributed to feelings of joy and comfort during pregnancy. This causes one's emotions to swing wildly. Clearly, the stress of new motherhood is also a factor. Moreover, if you're prone to PMS, it means that your hormones typically give you a wild ride; you can probably expect one after childbirth, too.

Baby blue days usually come in waves, which is why I call the force that propels them your "inner tsunami." A wave can drown out your sanity and sense of well-being for an hour or for a day or two, or it can continue on and off for three months to a year. Baby blue days can color how you feel about everything, most of all your infant. Those voices in your head are likely to chime in with "What have I let myself in for?" or "I can't manage the [you fill in the blank—diapering, breastfeeding, getting up in the middle of the night]."

> **TIP:** *If your baby is crying, you're alone with him, and you feel like you can't deal or, worse, you feel anger rising, put him in the crib and leave the room. A baby never died of crying. Take three deep breaths and then come back. If you're still agitated, phone a relative, a friend, or a neighbor and ask for help.*

When your inner tsunami is crashing onto the shoreline of your psyche, focus on the bigger picture. What's happening is normal—just go with it. Stay in bed if that makes you feel better. Cry. Yell at your partner if that helps. It will pass.

But how do you know when a little angst or a little insecurity is too much? Postpartum depression is a documented mental disorder—an illness. Its onset is often pinpointed as the third day after childbirth, continuing through the fourth week. However, I (and many psychiatrists familiar with the condition) feel that's far too narrow a time range. Some of the symptoms, including deep, unrelenting sadness, frequent crying and feelings of hopelessness, insomnia, lethargy, anxiety and panic attacks, irritability, obsession and frightening recurring thoughts, lack of appetite, low self-esteem, lack of enthusiasm, distance from partner and baby, and feelings of a desire to harm self or child can surface several months after delivery. In any case, such symptoms—a more severe manifestation of the baby blues—should be taken seriously.

It is estimated that 10 to 15 percent of new mothers have postpartum depression; one out of a thousand suffers a complete break with reality, known as postpartum psychosis. Other than hormonal changes and the stress of new motherhood, scientists are still unclear about why some women sink into a severe clinical depression after childbirth. One documented risk factor is a history of chemical imbalance. One-third of women with a history of depression experience depression postpartum as well; half of those who suffer from it after their first delivery relapse after subsequent births.

Sadly, even some doctors aren't aware of the risk. As a result, women often have no idea what's happening to them when the depression hits—a problem that could be avoided with information and education. Yvette, for example, had been put on Prozac for her depression. When she got pregnant, she stopped taking the drug. She had no idea how aggravated her condition would be after her delivery. Instead of feeling warm and compassionate about her baby, Yvette wanted to lock herself in the bathroom every time he cried. When she complained about "not feeling normal," no one listened to her. "Oh, that's just postpartum stuff," her mum said, negating Yvette's increasingly bad feelings. "Pull yourself together," her sister admonished, adding, "We've all been through it." Even Yvette's friends agreed: "What you're going through is normal."

Yvette called me to explain: "It takes every bit of strength for me to even take the trash out or get showered. I don't know what's wrong with me. My husband tries to help, Tracy, but I won't even let him talk to me

---

Sample Depression Scale Questions

From the Hamilton Depression Scale:

Agitation
0 = None
1 = Fidgetiness
2 = Playing with hands, hair, etc.
3 = Moving about, can't sit still
4 = Hand wringing, nail biting, hair-pulling, biting of lips

Anxiety Psychic
0 = No difficulty
1 = Subjective tension and irritability
2 = Worrying about minor matters
3 = Apprehensive attitude apparent in face or speech
4 = Fears expressed without questioning

From the Edinburgh Postnatal Depression Scale:*

Things have been getting on top of me:
0 = No, I have been coping as well as ever
1 = No, most of the time I have coped quite well
2 = Yes, sometimes I haven't been coping as well as usual
3 = Yes, most of the time I haven't been able to cope at all

I have been so unhappy that I have had difficulty sleeping:
0 = No, not at all
1 = Not very often
2 = Yes, sometimes
3 = Yes, most of the time

*Reprinted by permission of the Royal College of Psychiatrists

without biting his head off, poor man." I didn't take Yvette's ever-darkening moods lightly. I became especially concerned when she told me how she felt about little Bobby's crying. "When he screams, sometimes I yell back, 'What's wrong? What do you want from me? Why don't you shut up?' The other day, I got so frustrated, I felt myself rocking the baby's bassinet just a little too hard. That's when I knew I needed help. Truth be told, I wanted to throw him against a wall. I can understand why people shake their babies."

Now, there are days when a baby's seemingly perpetual crying gets on anyone's nerves, but what Yvette was feeling was already far beyond the edge of normal. It was appropriate for her obstetrician to advise her to go off her medication when she was pregnant—the drugs could have harmed her fetus. Women who normally suffer from depression often feel fine without their medication during pregnancy, because the higher levels of hormones and endorphins kick in. What was wrong and dangerous, however, was that no one warned Yvette about what might happen *after* her delivery, when the same chemicals that had kept her afloat were depleted.

As it turned out, childbirth led to a severe letdown in Yvette's case, and the symptoms of her depression returned tenfold. I advised her to visit her psychiatrist straightaway. Once she resumed her medication, she had an entirely different outlook on life and felt good about being a mum. Because of the drugs in her system, it was no longer advisable for her to breastfeed, but that didn't feel like much of a sacrifice compared to the composure and self-confidence she soon regained.

If you suspect that you have postpartum depression, consult your regular physician or a psychiatrist. In this country, psychiatrists often refer to the *Diagnostic and Statistical Manual* to determine whether a patient meets the criteria for various types of depression. However, this bible of the profession, which is updated every several years, did not even recognize postpartum depression until 1994. The current version, *DSM-IV*, contains a paragraph explaining that symptoms of various types of "mood disorders" could have "postpartum onset." Doctors also utilize psychiatric rating scales to determine the severity of depression—one of the most widely used is the twenty-three-item Hamilton Depression Scale—although such instruments are not specifically meant to diagnose postpartum depression. Some physicians here prefer the ten-item Edinburgh Postnatal Depression Scale, which was developed some twenty years ago in Scotland. The latter scale is far simpler and has been found to be about 90 percent accurate when it comes to spotting at-risk mothers. Both scales are designed to be administered by professionals, not as self-tests; but to give you an idea of what to expect, I've reprinted items from each one (see sidebar on page 232).

In the United States, most professionals agree, postpartum depression is underdiagnosed. Two medical students at the Mayo Medical School, in Rochester, Minnesota, proved this by studying the records of all women who gave birth for the year from 1997 to 1998. Whereas 1993 records indicated that in the same county, only 3 percent of new mothers surveyed were diagnosed with the condition, when the students asked all women who attended the clinic for their first postpartum visit to complete the Edinburgh questionnaire, the incidence rose to 12 percent.

If your baby blue days seem to linger, or if one bad day runs painfully into the next without much respite, seek professional help immediately. There is no shame in depression; it's a biological condition. It doesn't mean that you're a bad mum—it means you have an illness, no different from a flu. Consequently, and most important, you can get medical help as well as support from other women who've been through it.

Dad's Reaction

Fathers are often given short shrift during the postpartum period, because most of the focus and energy in the household are directed toward Mum and the new baby. That's as it should be, of course, but men are human. Research shows that some even exhibit symptoms of stress and depression. Dad can't help but react to the baby, to all the attention the newest family member is getting, to Mum's mood, to the visitors and new people traipsing about. In fact, just as mums have many moods, I've noticed certain "father feelings" that crop up when Baby arrives.

"Let me do it." Sometimes, especially in the first few weeks, Dad is a really hands-on kind of guy. He is totally involved from pregnancy through delivery and then is into the baby in a *big* way. He's open to learn and eager to hear that he's doing a good job. He has good natural instincts with his baby as well, and you can tell from his face that he just loves being with her. If your partner feels this way, Mum, count your blessings. If you're lucky, it will last until your baby goes to college.

"It's not my job." This is the reaction we'd expect from what we once thought of as a "traditional" father—a guy who prefers a hands-off approach. Sure, he loves his baby, but not when it comes to changing diapers or giving the baby a bath. In his view, that's a woman's job. He may lose himself in work immediately after the baby

is born, or he may be genuinely concerned that he now needs to make more money to support his growing family. Either way, he believes he has a bona fide excuse not to do the boring, dirty work of child care. In time, especially as the baby becomes more interactive, he may soften. I guarantee that he *won't* come round, though, if you harp on what he *doesn't* do, or compare him to other fathers ("Leila's husband changes Mackenzie's diapers").

"Oh, no—something's wrong." This guy is tense and stiff when he first holds the baby. He may have done all the childbirth and parenting classes with his wife, even suggested they take a CPR course, too, but he's still terrified about doing something wrong. When he gives a bath, he frets about scalding; after he puts the baby to sleep, he worries about SIDS (sudden infant death syndrome). And when it's all quiet on the home front, he starts to wonder if he can afford to send the kid to college. Successful experiences with his baby usually build Dad's confidence and help dissipate these feelings. Gentle encouragement and applause from Mum can help, too.

"Look at this baby!" This father is proud beyond belief. Not only does he want everyone to see his trophy baby, he may also inflate his own involvement. You'll hear him tell visitors, "I let my wife sleep in the middle of the night." Meanwhile, his exasperated wife is rolling her eyes behind his back. If this is his second marriage, even if he was a hands-off dad the first go-round, he's now the expert, frequently correcting his wife with a dismissive comment such as "That's not how *I* did it." Give him his due, Mum, especially if he seems like he knows what he's doing, but don't let him override your best instincts.

"What baby?" As I mentioned earlier, some mums go into denial when the baby comes. Well, luv, dads have their own version. Recently I was at a hospital visiting with Nell, barely three hours after her delivery, and innocently asked, "Where's Tom?" She replied—as if it were the most natural thing in the world—"Oh, he's home. He wanted to get some gardening done." It's not that Tom doesn't think child care is part of his domain; rather, this guy doesn't quite get the fact that the baby has arrived and that his life is going to change. Even if he perceives the change, he retreats to the comfort of doing something he is already good at. What he needs is a dose of reality, as well as Nell's encouragement. If, however, he resists, or if she doesn't make room for him to participate, he might become the kind of father I see watching TV in the living room, oblivious to the chaos around him. Mum, overwhelmed because she's juggling the phone and trying to make dinner, asks him, "Honey, would you hold the baby?" He looks up and says, "Huh?"

No matter what a man's initial reaction, most do change, although often in ways that don't please their wives. When mums ask me, "How do I get him to participate more?" they're disappointed because there's no magical answer. What I've found is that men become interested in their own ways and in their own time. An eager beaver may become less involved, while an unlikely nurturer suddenly throws himself into child care once his baby begins to smile, or sit, or walk, or talk. And most fathers tend to do best with concrete jobs that they feel they can do well.

"That's not fair," Angie cried when I suggested that she let her partner, Phil, opt for the chores he prefers. "*I* don't get to pick what I want to do. I'm 'on' no matter how I feel."

"That's true," I acknowledged, "but you have to deal with the man you've got. And if Phil won't bathe the baby, maybe he'll at least do the dishes after dinner."

The "secret" here is one of the underlying themes of this book: respect. If a man feels that his needs and wants are acknowledged, he more likely will respect yours. But in the beginning, you ought to expect a bit of juggling about as each of you struggles to find your footing.

What About *Us*?

When Baby makes three, the relationship between partners changes as well. In many cases, the reality rarely matches the dream. But it's usually problems *under the surface* that make a couple's connection come undone. Here are some of the more common issues.

Beginners' jitters. Mum feels overburdened. Dad doesn't quite know what to do to help. When he does step in, Mum may be impatient and snap at him. He's likely to back off.

"He puts the diaper on wrong," a mother will complain behind her partner's back.

"That's because he's learning, luv," I'll say. "Give him a chance." The truth is, everyone is a beginner in this enterprise. Both parents are on the steep part of the learning curve. I try to remind Mum and Dad of their first date. Didn't *they* have to get to know each other? In time, didn't a deeper understanding grow out of their increasing familiarity? It's the same with them and their new baby.

I like to give specific jobs to Dad—shopping, bath, the dream feed—that make him feel like he's part of the process. After all, Mum needs every bit of help she can get. I urge men to be their wife's ears and her memory. Besides the fact that there's so much new information to absorb, many women suffer from postpartum amnesia, a temporary condition that nevertheless drives them absolutely crazy. Or there may be a special need that a father can fulfill. For example, there was Lara (you met her in Chapter 4, page 102), a mum who found breast-feeding particularly stressful. Her husband felt very useless—as if there were absolutely nothing he could do to help her get through this difficult period. However, when I showed Duane what a proper latch-on looked like and instructed him to gently coach Lara if she was having trouble (the emphasis there is on *gently*), it made

He Said/She Said

In any two-parent partnership, each person has a different perspective. I often act like a UN translator, telling one what the other wants him or her to know.

Mum wants me to tell her partner

- How much the delivery hurts
- How tired she is
- How overwhelming breastfeeding is
- How much breastfeeding hurts (to demonstrate, I once pinched a dad's nipples and said, "Let me just hold on like this for twenty minutes")
- That she's crying or yelling because she's hormonal, not because of him
- That she can't explain *why* she's crying

Dad wants me to tell his partner

- To stop criticizing everything he does
- That the baby isn't made out of china and won't break
- That he's doing his best
- That it hurts him when she dismisses his ideas about the baby
- That he's feeling more pressure now to provide for his new family
- That he's depressed and overwhelmed, too

him feel like he was truly contributing. I also gave him the responsibility of making sure that she got her requisite sixteen glasses of water a day.

Gender differences. Whatever conflict occurs between Mum and Dad in those first few weeks, I inevitably remind them that they're in this together, although they may see their situation from very different points of view. As I pointed out in Chapter 2 (page 53), Dad tends to be a "fixer," when all Mum wants is an ear to listen, a shoulder to cry on, and two strong arms to embrace her. Often, couple troubles are rooted in such gender differences. I often find myself acting as interpreter, letting Venus know what Mars means and vice versa (see "He

---

Calling All Partners!

A few words of wisdom to the one who hasn't given birth and isn't spending all day at home with the new baby:

DO
- Take a week or more off work; if you can't afford to, save money to get someone in to do the housework
- Listen without having a solution
- Offer support lovingly and without comment
- Take no for an answer when she says she *doesn't* want your help
- Shop, clean, do laundry, and vacuum without her having to ask
- Recognize that she has a good reason when she says, "I don't feel like myself"

DON'T
- Try to "fix" her emotional or physical problems—ride them out
- Be a cheerleader or patronize her—for example, by patting her behind and saying "Good job," as if she's a dog
- Walk into your own kitchen and wonder aloud where something is kept
- Stand over her and criticize
- Call home from the store if they're out of smoked turkey to ask, "What should I get instead?"—figure it out yourself

---

Said/She Said," on page 239). Couples do best when they learn not only to translate but also not to take it *personally* when one sees things differently from the other. They should find strength in their dissimilarities, because then they have a broader repertoire to draw from.

Lifestyle shifts. With some couples, the major stumbling block is learning how to change the way they make plans. They may have lots of relatives who help out, or paid nannies, but they're not good at scheduling their time to include a dependent third party—because they've never had to. Michael and Denise, thirtysomethings who had been married for four years before starting a family, were a real power couple. He was an upper-level manager in a large corporation and an athlete who played tennis three times a week and soccer on the weekends. She was a studio executive who often worked from eight in the morning until nine at night, with time out only for her four-day-a-week exercise routine. Not surprisingly, they took meals mostly in restaurants, together or apart.

We met initially when Denise was in her ninth month. After hearing their typical week, I said to the two of them, "Let's make one thing clear here. Some things have to give, but not everything. To achieve the life you want after your baby is born, you've got to plan for it."

To their credit, Michael and Denise sat down and made lists of their needs and wants. What could they afford to give up for the first few months while they adjusted to parenthood? What was absolutely necessary to their emotional health? Denise decided to cut back at work, although she only allowed herself a month's worth of recovery time. Michael promised he would ask for some extra time from his company, too. They overscheduled themselves a bit at first—it's hard for some

couples to cut back in this way. But when Denise realized what a toll childbirth had taken on her entire being,
she extended her leave another month.

Couple Care 101

♥Schedule time together—a walk, date night, a trip to the ice
  cream parlor
♥*Plan* a childless vacation, even if you can't actually take one for a
  while
♥Hide surprise messages for your mate
♥Give an unexpected present
♥Send a love letter to the office, telling her/him all that you adore
  and appreciate
♥Always be kind and respectful to one another

Competition. This is, by far, one of the most problematic
couple issues I see. Take George and Phyllis, both in
their early forties when they adopted one-month-old
May Li. They vied with each other to see who could get
her to take more of the bottle, who was better at calming the baby. When George diapered May Li, Phyllis
would say, "You've got it on too low. Let me do it."
When Phyllis was bathing her, George would offer instructions from the sidelines: "Watch her head. Careful—you'll get soap in her eyes." Each read books about
baby care and would then quote word for word to the
other, not so much in service of doing what was best for
their child but more as a way of saying, "See? I'm right."

George and Phyllis called me because May Li
screamed much of the time. By then, the adults were
convinced their baby had colic, but they couldn't agree
on what to do. When one tried something, the other crit-
icized. To remedy the situation, I first explained to this
couple what I thought was really happening, and it
wasn't colic. May Li was crying constantly because no
one was listening to what she was saying. Her parents

were so busy challenging each other, they weren't observing her. I suggested putting May Li on E.A.S.Y. and gave Phyllis and George tips about slowing down so that they could begin to really pay attention to their daughter (see Chapter 3). Perhaps most important in this couple's case, I also divvied up the baby chores and told them, "You each have your own domain now. You are not to oversee, comment, or criticize what the other one does in his or hers."

Whatever the cause, if difficulties between partners persist, it spills over into every area of a couple's life. They may argue over chores; they may refuse to coordinate and cooperate. And, most likely, their sex life, already suspended for several weeks (or months), will be hung out to dry.

Sex and the Suddenly Stressed-out Spouse

Talk about your he said/she said issues. Sex is *the* number one topic on every father's to-do list, and usually at the bottom of most mums'. Indeed, the first question he asks when she comes home from the gynecologist after her postpartum checkup is "Did he say we could have sex?"

Meanwhile, the question itself makes her seethe inside, because instead of asking how *she* feels or wooing her with flowers, her husband wants a third-party opinion about their sex life, as if *that* would sway her. If she was disinclined to have sex before the question, she becomes even more resolute after.

So she takes a deep breath and says, "No, not yet." The implication is that the doctor said she's not ready, but of course it's her saying that. Some women also use the baby sleeping in the marital bed as an excuse. Others elevate the old "I've got a headache" to new heights: "I'm exhausted." "I'm in pain." "I can't bear to have you look at my body this way." All of these statements have more than a kernel of truth, by the way, but a sex-phobic woman wears them like armor.

Postbaby Calisthenics

I said no exercise for six weeks, but there's one you can do as early as three weeks postpartum, and it goes like this: **Squeeze and hold, one, two, three!**

Pelvic floor exercises, often known as Kegel exercises, named for the doctor who identified the fibrous tissues within the lining of the vagina, are done to strengthen the muscles that support the urethra, bladder, uterus, and rectum and, not so incidentally, tone the vagina. It's as if you're urinating and then try to stop—those are the muscles you'll tense and relax. I suggest doing them three times a day.

This will be a challenge at first—you'll feel as if there are *no* muscles there. You might even feel a bit sore. Start slowly, with your knees together. To test whether you're working the right muscles, insert a finger into your vagina and you'll feel the squeeze. As you get better at isolating the muscles, try it with your legs apart.

In my groups and on my visits, desperate fathers ask for my help. "What can I do, Tracy? I'm scared we'll never make love again." Some even beg me, "Tracy, *you* talk to her." I try to emphasize that there's nothing magical about six weeks, which is usually when a woman has her first ob-gyn checkup. That's generally how long it takes for an episiotomy or C-section to heal, but that doesn't mean all women recover fully by six weeks, or that your woman is emotionally ready for sex.

Moreover, sex after childbirth *does* change. We do parents an injustice when we don't warn them. Men who want sex straightaway often don't realize the extent to which a woman's body transforms with childbirth: Her breasts are sore, her vagina has been stretched, her labia have been extended, lower levels of hormones can make her dry. Breastfeeding can complicate the picture further. If a woman formerly liked to have her nipples stimulated, she may find it painful now, or repugnant—her breasts suddenly belong to her baby.

Given all these changes, how can the *feeling* of sex not be different? Fear plays a role as well. Some women worry that they're "too stretched out" to have or give pleasure. Others anticipate pain, and that alone makes them tense up, even at the mere suggestion of lovemaking. When a woman has an orgasm and her breasts simultaneously let forth a spray of milk, she may feel embarrassed, or afraid that her mate finds it distasteful.

And some men do. It's not exactly erotic to be showered by mother's milk. Depending on the man and how he viewed his wife *before* she got pregnant, he may have trouble seeing her in her new role as a mother, and may even be skittish about touching her. In fact, some men have admitted to me that they were turned off when they saw their wives in the delivery room or when they first witnessed breastfeeding.

So what does a couple do? There's no instant solution here, but some of the suggestions I dispense usually at least take the pressure off both parties.

Talk about it openly. Rather than allowing emotions to bubble under the surface, admit how you really feel. (If you have trouble finding the right words, look at the box on page 248—some of those universal concerns might ring true for you.) For example, Irene called me in tears one day from her car phone: "I just had my six-week checkup, and the doctor said I could have sex. Gil has been waiting for the doctor to give us the green flag. I can't disappoint him—he's been so good with the baby. I owe him that much, don't I? What can I say to him?"

"Let's start with the truth," I suggested. I knew from previous conversations that Irene had had a particularly long labor and a large episiotomy. "First of all, how are *you* feeling?"

"I'm scared that it will be painful to make love. And honestly, Tracy, I can't bear the thought of his touching me, especially down there."

Irene was relieved to hear that so many women feel the same way. "You have to tell him your fears and feelings, darling," I told her. "I'm no sex therapist, but the idea of your feeling like you 'owe' him sex is also not a good thing."

Now, the interesting part of this story is that Gil was in one of my Daddy-and-me classes, where sex is always, pardon the pun, a hot topic. Earlier that week, I had explained to the guys that a man can and should be honest about his desires, but he also needs to understand the woman's vantage point. I added that there's a big difference between a woman's being physically ready and her being emotionally willing. Gil was quite understanding and receptive to the idea that he needed to talk to Irene, recognize her feelings, and, most important, wine and dine his wife, not as a means to an end, but to show her how much he appreciated her, loved her, and wanted to be with her. That's authentic caring, and women find that a lot more erotic than being "convinced."

Look at your sex life before you became parents. This point was driven home to me one day when I dropped by to visit Midge, Keith, and their almost three-month-old daughter, Pamela, whom I'd taken care of for the first two weeks.

Keith pulled me aside while his wife was in the kitchen putting up a pot of tea. "Tracy, Midge and I haven't had sex since Pam was born, and I'm getting impatient," he confided.

"Keith, let me ask you: Did you have sex a lot before the baby was born?"

"Not really."

"Well, luv," I said to him, "if your sex life wasn't that good before the baby, it's certainly not going to improve afterward."

The conversation reminded me of the old joke about the man who asks his doctor if he can play the piano after surgery. "Of course," says the doc. "Gee, that's great," the man says, "because I never could play before." All kidding aside, couples need to have realistic expectations about their sex lives. It stands to reason that the issue of postbaby sex affects a couple more if they've been bonking three nights a week and suddenly stop than if they did it once a week or once a month.

Keep your priorities straight. Decide *together* what's important to you now, and allow for reevaluation in a few months. If you *both* decide that lovemaking is important, make time and space for it. Plan a date night once a week. Get a baby-sitter and get out of the house. I always remind the men in my groups that a woman's idea of romance often has nothing to do with sex. "You may want a roll in the hay," I say, "but she wants conversation, candlelight, and cooperation. She'll find it sexy if you do the wash without having been asked!" And, as my Nan always says, "You get more with sugar than

TIP: Mum, when you and Dad take an evening out, don't talk about the baby. You've physically left your little bundle of joy at home, where she should be. Unless you want subconscious resentment to build on Dad's part, leave her home emotionally as well.

you do with vinegar." Buy her flowers; handle her emotions with care. But if your woman is not physically and emotionally ready, back off. Pressure is not an aphrodisiac.

Lower your expectations. Sex is intimate, but not all intimacy is sex. If you're not ready for lovemaking, find other ways to be intimate. For example, go to a concert together and hold hands. Or consider a "make-out session" where you do nothing but kiss for an hour. I always admonish men to be patient. Women need time. Also, a man should not take a woman's reluctance personally. In fact, I suggest that guys try to imagine what it must be like to carry and then expel a little being. I mean, how soon afterward would they want sex under those conditions?

Sex After Childbirth

How Women Feel	How Men Feel
Exhausted: "Sex just feels like one more chore."	**Frustrated:** "How long do we have to wait?"
Overwrought: "Everyone seems to be taking from me."	**Rejected:** "Why doesn't she want me?"
Guilty: They're depriving their child *or* their spouse.	**Jealous:** "She cares more about the baby than me."
Ashamed: "If the baby is in the next room, I feel like I'm sneaking."	**Resentful:** "The baby takes all her time."
Uninterested: "It's the last thing on my mind."	**Angry:** "Isn't she ever going to be back to normal?"
Self-conscious: They feel fat and "weird" about their breasts.	**Confused:** "Is it okay to ask her to have sex?"
Wary: "If he kisses me on the cheek, says 'I love you,' or puts an arm around my waist, it feels like an expectation—the first stage of lovemaking."	**Duped:** "She said if the doctor said it's okay, we would have sex, but it has been weeks since then."

Work: Going Back . . . Without Guilt

Whether a woman leaves a high-powered career, a cozy office job, a volunteer position, or even a beloved hobby behind because she wants to have a baby, there usually comes a time—for some women a month after delivery, for others several years later—when the question "What about me?" begins to niggle around her brain. Of course, some women already have a game plan in place during pregnancy about when they'll return to work or resume a particular project they've undertaken. Others play it by ear. Either way, they deal with the same two questions: "How will I do this without feeling guilty?" and "Who will care for the baby?" At least in my mind, the first question is a simpler one, so let's deal with that right off.

Guilt is the curse of motherhood. As my granddad used to say, "Life is not a rehearsal. There are no pockets in shrouds." In other words, you can't take it with you, so guilt is a waste of our precious time on earth. I don't know when, where, or why you Americans invented guilt, but it's an epidemic here in the States. Maybe it's part of American perfectionism, but the way I see it, you're damned if you do, damned if you don't. Some women in my classes feel utterly inadequate because they're "just mums" or "just housewives." Working mums, though, whether going off to impressive careers or to menial jobs that simply pay the bills, feel just as bad about themselves, but for different reasons. "My mother thinks I'm horrible for working," such a woman might say. "She tells me I'm missing the best years of my baby's life."

Women who make the decision to work outside the house consider a great many elements before making the decision, among them the fact that they love their child.

But it's also a matter of money, emotional satisfaction, and self-esteem. Some mums confess that they would go crazy if they didn't have something that is *just theirs*—whether or not they get paid for it. I encourage them to love and care for their babies. But that doesn't mean they can't also pursue *their* dreams. Working doesn't make women bad mothers. It makes them women who are empowered enough to say, "This is how it's going to be."

Clearly, some women have no financial choice but to work. Others work for their own self-satisfaction. Whether or not pay is involved, though, the point is that these women are doing things that feed their grown-up selves. And they needn't apologize, any more than the mother who is contentedly managing her home. I remember once asking my own mother, "Did you ever want to *do* anything?" She gave me an annoyed look and said, "*Do* anything? I'm a home manager. What do you mean, '*do* anything'?" I never forgot the lesson.

The truth of the matter is that even though some dads are rigorously hands-on at home, many mums still shoulder the greatest portion of the child-rearing load—all the more if they're single parents who haven't got the luxury of a partner coming home at night. There's nothing wrong with wanting at the very least to be able to answer phone calls, to have lunch with friends, to feel like you're something other than Mother. But because you're bombarded by advice, overwhelmed by the responsibility, and, at the core of it all, confused, you easily fall into the guilt trap. I hear overwrought mums all the time, floundering between the two extremes—total immersion and laissez-faire. "I love this baby," they tell me, "and I want to be the best mother I can be. But do I have to give up *my life*?"

TIP: Say this mantra to yourself when you're feeling guilty: "Having time for me is not hurting my baby."

If you don't take this time to do whatever it is that nourishes *your* soul, life becomes *all baby*. And face it: There's only so much you can do with an infant, only so many conversations you can have about your new bundle of joy. And instead of feeling guilty, it's better to use your energy to come up with solutions that make your situation, whatever it is, better. If you want or need to work twelve hours a day, figure out ways to make your time at home more meaningful. For example, don't pick up the phone when you are with your kids. Take it off the hook or let the answering machine field all calls. Don't work on weekends. And when you're at home, keep your mind at home rather than in the office. Even babies sense when you're not really there.

Now, as far as the other big question goes—who's going to look after the baby—the answer is either unpaid help or paid help. Below I look at each.

Your Neighbors, Friends, and Relatives: Creating a Circle of Support

I come from a tradition of forty days of lying in, which means that for the better part of six weeks after Sara was born, I was expected only to take care of my new baby. With my Nan, my mum, and a bevy of female relatives and neighbors around me, my household was taken care of, my meals were prepared. I never felt pressured to perform. When I had Sophie, the same circle of support kept three-year-old Sara busy and cared for, so that I could get to know her little sister.

This is quite typical in England, where having a baby

is very much a communal affair. Everyone pitches in, from Grandma to the aunties to Nelly next door. We also have the added benefit of a health care system that builds in professional help in the form of home health aides, but it's that network of women, kin and friends alike, who help a new mum the most. They show her the ropes. After all, who's better qualified? They've been through it.

Circles of support are commonplace in many cultures; there are rituals to help women through pregnancy and labor as well as traditions that honor their fragility as they move through the passage to parenthood. New mothers are bolstered physically and emotionally, cooked for and nurtured, absolved of normal household duties so that they're free to watch their baby and to recover from childbirth. Sometimes, as in Arab countries, the husband's mother is designated to feed the new mum and look after her.

Sadly, not many women in the United States live in communities where this is typical. Mums here rarely get much neighborly assistance, and relatives often live clear across the country. If a woman is lucky, though, some members of the family at least come to visit, and a few good friends are willing to come round with a pie or a hot meal. Or a new mum may be a member of a religious group or community organization whose members come to her aid. In any case, it's important to at least try to create your own circle of support, one person if not several, who will cheer you on and insist that you take it easy.

Assess your relationships with various family members. Are you close to your own mum? If so, there's no one who knows you better. She loves her new grandchild, so she has the baby's safety at heart. She has experience, too. When I work in a household with a

Maintaining Your Circle of Support

Here's how to make the most of unpaid help:

- Don't expect people to read your mind—*ask* for help.
- Especially in the first six weeks, ask people to shop, cook, bring in food, clean, do laundry—so that you have time to be with and get to know your baby.
- Be realistic. Ask of people only what they can actually do—don't send a forgetful dad to the grocery store without a list; don't ask your mum to baby-sit at the time when you know she has a regular tennis game.
- Write down your baby's schedule so that others understand what the day is like and can work around it.
- Apologize when you snap . . . because you will!

cooperative grandma or grandpa, it's wonderful. I give everyone a to-do list, anything from vacuuming to sticking stamps on envelopes—things Mum shouldn't even be thinking about at this point.

However, this idyllic picture changes dramatically when a mum doesn't have harmonious family relationships. Parents can sometimes interfere or be judgmental of the younger generation. Especially when it comes to breastfeeding, Grandma may be as inexperienced as the new parents. Her criticism can be delivered subtly, in comments such as "Why are you holding him for so long?" or "*I* didn't do it that way." What's the point of asking for help under those circumstances? You already have more stress on your plate than you can easily handle. I'm not saying you ought to bar your mum from the house, but it's a good idea not to depend on her and to know her limits. (See "Maintaining Your Circle of Support," on this page.)

New mums often ask me how to field unsolicited advice, especially when relationships are strained to begin with. I advise them to keep advice in perspective. This is a sensitive time. You're just getting your footing. If someone suggests a technique or practice that's different from what you're doing, even if the advice is meant to help, it can *feel* like criticism. So before you immediately conclude that you're under fire, consider the source. Chances are the person is genuinely trying to be helpful and may have some good pointers to share. Let yourself listen to all sorts of suggestions—from your mum, your sister, your aunt, your grandma, and your pediatrician, as well as from other women. Take it all in and then decide what's right for you. Just remember: Parenting is not a subject of debate. *You don't have to argue or defend yourself.* After all, how you raise your family is going to be nowhere near how I raise mine. That's what makes every family unique.

> **TIP:** *Respond to unsolicited advice by saying, "Wow, that's really interesting—it sounds like it really worked for your family," even though in your head you may be saying, "I'm going to do it my way."*

Hiring a Nanny—Not a Ninny

I hate to sound like a British chauvinist in this chapter, but compared to England, the nanny business in this country is fraught with flaws. Back home, being a nanny—or a governess, as we often say—is a recognized profession, regulated by strict laws. A nanny hopeful must train for three years at an accredited nanny college. I was surprised when I came here to find that you need a license to file nails but nothing to look after children. The screening process is therefore left to parents or agencies. Because I generally work with parents in the first few weeks, I'm often involved in nanny selection. I can tell you, it's a difficult matter at best—and very stressful.

TIP: *Give yourself at least two months, ideally three, to conduct a nanny search. If, for example, you plan to go back to work when your baby is six or eight weeks old, that means you have to start when you're pregnant.*

Finding the right nanny is an arduous process. But this child is your most precious—and irreplaceable—possession; hiring someone to care for her should be a top priority. Put all your insight and energy into the search. Below are some other points you need to consider.

What do you need? The first step, obviously, is to assess your own situation. Do you want a full-time live-in worker, or a part-timer? If the latter, will she keep regular hours or come as you need her? Also think about your own boundaries. If someone is going to live with you, will any areas of your home be off-limits? Will she eat meals on her own or at the family table? Do you expect her to "disappear" when Baby is sleeping? Will you provide her with her own room? Her own TV? Unlimited telephone and kitchen privileges? Use of recreation areas, like a gym or pool? Is housework in her job description? If so, how extensive is it? Many highly experienced nannies won't do any more than keep the baby's clothes laundered, and some refuse even that. What reading and writing skills will she need? At the least, she needs to be able to read directions, take messages, and fill in a daily "nannilog" (see page 260). But will you also want her to be computer literate? Do you want or need her to drive? Must she have her own car, or can she use yours? Would you like someone who has training in first aid and CPR? Someone with nutritional savvy? The more details you focus on, before you even begin your search, the better equipped you'll be to conduct the interviews.

> **TIP:** Write a job description of everything you want your nanny to do. That way, you'll be clear on what you want, and when prospective nannies come to call, you can share every detail—not only duties related to the baby and to your household, but also salary, days off, restrictions, vacations, bonuses, and overtime.

Agencies may or may not be helpful. There are a good many reputable agencies, but they usually charge fees equal to 25 percent of the nanny's annual salary. The better agencies carefully screen their nannies and can save you the time it takes to eliminate undesirable applicants. However, some fly-by-night operations do more harm than good. They don't check references carefully; some even lie about a person's qualifications and history. The best way to find a good agency is word of mouth. Ask friends about their experiences. If no one you know has used an agency, look in parenting magazines or the yellow pages. Ask them how many nannies they place each year—a good-sized agency will put between a thousand and fifteen hundred to work a year. Ask about their fee and find out what it includes—among other points, how extensive are background checks? What happens if the nanny doesn't work out? Are there any guarantees? If they don't find someone to your satisfaction, you shouldn't have to pay a fee.

Pay close attention during the interview. Find out what *the nanny* is looking for in a job. Does it match your description? If not, discuss the differences. What kind of training has she had? Ask her to talk about previous jobs and why she left them (see "Nanny Red Flags," on the next page). What are her thoughts on affection, discipline, visitors? Try to get a sense of whether she's a take-charge kind of person or whether she's looking for your direction. Either is fine, depending on what *you* want from a nanny. You certainly wouldn't be happy if you ended up with a dictator when you were hoping for an assistant. Beyond baby care, does this woman have the skills that you require, such as driving, and personal attributes that will make for a good working relationship? Ask about her health. Particularly if you have animals, allergies might be an issue.

Nanny Red Flags

- *She's had many recent positions.* Perhaps she works only in short stints, or she also could have problems getting on with employers. In contrast, when someone has held only one or two long-term positions in three years, it usually indicates competence and commitment.
- *She's had no recent positions.* That might be because she's been ill or is unemployable.
- *She talks badly about other mums.* One I interviewed went on and on about how the woman at her last job was a bad mum because she worked too late every night. Why she hadn't discussed that with *her employer* is beyond me.
- *She has toddlers of her own.* Her kids' germs will come to work with her, or she might have emergencies of her own, leaving you in the lurch.
- *She needs a green card.* This may not be an insurmountable problem if you're willing to help. But if you don't factor this in, your beloved nanny could risk deportation.
- *Your gut feeling is bad.* Trust yourself. Don't hire anyone you don't feel good about.

Is she the right person for you? Chemistry is important. That's why a nanny your friend loved might leave you cold. So ask yourself, "Do I have in mind a particular type of person?" Bear in mind that no one is perfect, except perhaps the mythical Mary Poppins. Among factors to consider might be age and agility. If you live in a house with many stairs, or a fourth-floor flat, you may need someone fairly young and spry—a good idea if you've also got a toddler underfoot as well. Or, for a variety of other reasons, you may wish to have an older, more settled person. Are you looking for someone of a certain ethnic background, like or dissimilar to your own? Remember that nannies bring their cultural traditions with them—her views on feeding, discipline, and how one demonstrates affection, for instance, may be different from yours.

Do your own background check. Ask each prospect to supply at least four references from former employers as well as her Department of Motor Vehicles record, which tells you something about how responsible she is. Call every one of her references, but also *visit* at least two to meet them in person. If someone offers a glowing testimonial, it's best to meet *that* person, too.

Do an at-home visit. Once you've narrowed your search, arrange to meet on *her* turf. Meet her children, if possible. Although it's not always an indication of how she'll interact with your baby, especially if her children are older, you'll at least get a sense of her warmth and her standards of cleanliness and care.

Bear in mind your own responsibilities. This is a partnership of sorts—you're not hiring a slave. The job description works both ways, so don't pile on extra responsibilities. If you didn't hire her to do housework, for example, you shouldn't expect her to do it once she's on the job. Give her all the resources she needs to do her job well—instructions, pocket money, everyday telephone numbers, phone numbers to be used in case of emergency. Remember, too, that she has personal needs of her own—for days off and time with her own family and friends. If she's from out of town, help her cultivate a social life by offering information about local churches, neighborhood centers, or health clubs. You don't want her to be lonely on the job. If all-baby-all-the-time isn't good for you, it's equally undesirable for your nanny to be deprived of contact with other adults.

Reassess her performance regularly and correct mistakes immediately. The best way to sustain a good relationship with anyone is through honest communication. With nannies, it's vital. Ask her to keep what I call a daily "nannilog" (see page 260), so you will know what has gone on in your absence. Also, if your baby behaves unusually at night or has some sort of allergic reaction, you'll then be in a better position to assess why. Be candid and direct whenever you make suggestions or ask her to do something differently. Have these conversations in private, and be sensitive in your delivery. Instead of saying, "That's not how I told you to do it," you might get the same message across by phrasing it in a more positive manner: "This is the way I'd like you to change the baby's diaper."

Monitor your own emotional reaction. Unspoken fears about having someone else take care of your baby can color your opinion of your nanny's conduct. Jealousy is a normal and common reaction. Even when my own mother took care of Sara, I was a bit envious of their relationship. I hear from many working mums as well that although they're overjoyed to have found someone who's so wonderful and trustworthy, it hurts to think that person will get to witness their baby's first smile or first step. My advice is to talk about these feelings with your partner or a good friend. Know that there's no shame in having them; almost all mothers have been there. Just remember that you're the mum, and there's no substitute for that.

Keeping a Nannilog

Ask your nanny to keep a simple daily record of what happens when you're not there. Below is a sample. Tailor your own nannilog to suit your circumstances. Put it on your computer, so that you can modify it as your baby grows and changes. It should be detailed but brief, so that it doesn't take your nanny much time to complete.

Foods

Bottles at _____   _____   _____   _____
New food introduced today: _____
Baby's reaction: ❑ Gas   ❑ Hiccups   ❑ Vomiting   ❑ Diarrhea
Details: _____

Activities

Indoors: ❑ Gymini for _____ minutes   ❑ Playpen
Other:_____
Outdoors: ❑ Walk to park   ❑ Class (e.g., Gymboree)   ❑ Pool
Other:_____

Milestones

❑ Smiled ❑ Lifted head ❑ Rolled over ❑ Sat up ❑ Stood up ❑ Took first step
Other:_____

Appointments

Doctor_____
Play dates_____

Extraordinary Occurrences

Accidents_____
Temper
tantrum_____
Anything else out of the ordinary_____

CHAPTER EIGHT

Great Expectations: Special Circumstances and Unforeseen Events

> Great emergencies and crises show us how much greater our vital resources are than we had supposed.
>
> —William James

The Best-Laid Plans

When planning a family, of course we all would *like* to count on an easy conception, an uneventful pregnancy, an effortless delivery, and a healthy baby. But that's not always what Mother Nature has in store.

You might, for instance, come up against a fertility problem and have to adopt or use an assisted reproductive technology (ART), an umbrella term for a variety of alternatives that aid or bypass traditional conception. Among these is surrogacy, in which another woman actually carries your baby to term. Clearly, adoption, both domestic and foreign, is more prevalent than surrogacy (see the "Chances Are . . ." sidebar, next page, for specifics), but during my tenure in the States, I've had the privilege of knowing eight sets of parents who've used "carriers," as they're sometimes called.

Once pregnant, you might be beset by circumstances you didn't foresee. You may be told that you're carrying twins or triplets—a blessing, to be sure, but also a daunting prospect. Other problems can occur during your pregnancy that necessitate bed rest. If you are over thirty-five, especially if you've taken fertility drugs, you probably will have to be more cautious than a younger mother-to-be. A preexisting condition, such as diabetes, might put your pregnancy into the high-risk category as well.

Chances Are . . .

Adoption: In the 1990s, there were approximately 120,000 adoptions annually. Approximately 40 percent are kinship adoptions, but 15 percent are through public agencies, 35 percent are private (agencies, doctors, lawyers), and 10 percent are from abroad.

Surrogacy: There are no official records, but it is estimated by the Organization for Parenting Through Surrogacy (OPTS) that between 10,000 and 15,000 babies, or more, have been born via surrogacy since 1976.

Multiples: The overall twinning rate is 1.2 per 100 live births, triplets 1 in 6,889. Those figures rise dramatically with fertility drugs: with Clomid, the chance of twinning rises to 8 per 100, triplets 0.5 per 100; with Pergonal, twins are 18 per 100, triplets 3 per 100.

Premature Births: There are approximately 300,000 births a year, or 10 percent of all pregnancies, occurring at 37 or fewer weeks (40 being normal). Your chances of early delivery rise if you're older than 35, carrying twins, or have one or more of the following conditions: extreme stress, a chronic medical problem such as diabetes, an infection, or a complication during pregnancy, such as placenta previa.

Finally, your delivery can be marked by complications. Your baby (or babies) might arrive early, or something might happen during childbirth that requires an extended hospital stay. It's particularly hard when you don't get to hold your newborn straightaway. For instance, Kayla had to leave the hospital empty-handed because Sasha was born three weeks early. Tiny and fragile, Sasha had fluid in her lungs and was put in the neonatal intensive care unit (NICU) for the next six days. Kayla, an avid athlete, recalls, "It was like you're all set up to play the game and someone comes in and says, 'Never mind—it has been postponed.' "

Admittedly, entire books are written on the subjects of infertility, adoption, multiple births, and birth problems. Here, though, I'm most concerned with your ability to apply the concepts I've covered throughout this book, *regardless* of how your baby was conceived or delivered, and in spite of whatever problems occur.

The Trouble with Trouble

Although the situations I touched on above represent vastly different scenarios, and I will discuss them separately in the pages that follow, there also are common threads that run through all special circumstances and unforeseen events. Your reaction can affect your decisions, color the way you see and hear your baby, and impact your ability to institute a structured routine. Whatever your situation, whatever the trouble that you encounter, here are some of the most universal feelings that arise. Knowing what to expect can help you sidestep the pitfalls.

You're likely to be more exhausted, more emotionally overwrought, and therefore more anxious about everything. If you've had a difficult pregnancy or a high-risk birth, you're utterly spent by the time the baby arrives— so much more so if you've had twins or triplets. Or if something unexpectedly goes wrong during delivery, it sends shock waves through your body that reverberate for days and weeks to come. Hence, as exhausted as *any* woman is after childbirth, unforeseen circumstances can leave you even more debilitated. What's more, the ongoing strains can affect not only your parenting ability but your relationship with your partner as well.

There is no magical pill that will make this all better; heightened emotions go with any crisis (see the "Emotional Roller Coaster" sidebar, page 278). The antidote is to get the rest that you need and accept all the help that's offered. Be aware of what's happening to you and know that it will pass.

When You *Should* Worry

If your baby has any of these symptoms, call your pediatrician

- Dry mouth, lack of tears, or dark urine (may signal dehydration)
- Pus or blood in the stool, or a persistent green color
- Diarrhea lasting more than eight hours, or if it's accompanied by vomiting
- High fever
- Severe abdominal pain

You're likely to be more fearful of losing your baby, even after he or she arrives. If you've tried for six or seven years to conceive, if your pregnancy or delivery has been difficult, your level of anxiety, which has probably been high to begin with, may increase once the baby arrives. Even with adoption, you're likely to misinterpret even the usual glitches and mishaps as potential disasters. You may listen obsessively to the baby monitor and jump at every creak and squeak your baby makes. You may convince yourself that you're going to "do something wrong." Kayla and Paul were afraid of "killing the baby," she admits. Sasha initially latched on with no problem. However, at three weeks old she bobbed off the breast crankily—by then, she had become a more efficient feeder and could empty the breasts more quickly.

But Kayla immediately interpreted this behavior as "a problem."

Again, the remedy is self-awareness. Know that you're on edge, that you might not be seeing clearly. Rather than jump to dire conclusions, make a reality check. Call your pediatrician, the nurses in the NICU, or friends who have babies a little older than yours to see what's "normal." A sense of humor doesn't hurt, either. Kayla recalls, "Whenever I'd say something totally neurotic to Paul, like 'You can't diaper her like *that*,' or scream at him, 'I have to nurse her *now*,' even when Sasha wasn't hungry or crying, he'd say, 'You're turning into that old FM station, hon.' That stood for 'freaky mummy.' Usually I would hear myself at that point and calm down." Kayla relaxed into motherhood by the time Sasha was three months old, which I find is typical of many anxiety-ridden mums.

You might wonder, "Did I do the right thing?" So much of what you've done to have a child has been deliberate, hard work. If you've tried for years to get pregnant, suffered through an agonizingly long adoption process, and had disappointments along the way, when you're finally a parent you may wonder whether all that effort was really worth all this effort, or if you've bitten off more than you can chew, as with twins or triplets, a common by-product of fertility treatments. Sophia, who had a baby through a surrogate mother, was grateful that the whole process went smoothly—finding the surrogate, Magda, impregnating her with Fred's sperm, and seeing her through the next nine months. However, once the reality of caring for her new baby set in, Sophia plummeted. Technically, *her* hormones weren't affected by a pregnancy, but she recalls, "There was great joy in

Becca's birth, but I went through a lot of emotional swings, a lot of self-doubt."

Sophia's ordeal is more common than mothers are often willing to admit. They might be embarrassed by such feelings, even ashamed, and therefore reluctant to talk about them. As a result, many mothers don't realize just how typical their emotions are. Deep down inside, of course, no one really wants to give her baby back. Nevertheless, the emotions can be downright overwhelming. And because this wall of silence keeps women isolated, it's hard to believe that eventually the negativity and fear will pass. By the time Becca was approaching her third-month birthday, Sophia had comfortably slipped into motherhood, a day at a time.

If you identify with Sophia's story, take heart. You *can* ride these feelings out, especially if you remind yourself that they won't last forever. Get support—a counselor, a group, other parents who've been through the same thing. Whether it's an adoption, the arrival of multiple babies, a difficult delivery, or an infant whose needs seem inordinate, there are people who can help you.

You're likely to be more dependent on outside validation than on your own judgment. If you went to a fertility clinic, you probably developed call-in relationships with many professionals on the staff. Or if you had a low-birth-weight baby, you may have become dependent on the NICU nurses in the hospital. Once the baby came home, if you're like many women, you became a slave to the clock and the scale. You time every meal, asking yourself, "Am I breastfeeding long enough to give him the nourishment he needs?" and you measure his progress in ounces. You're accustomed to constantly calling doctors and nurses for direction, but now you feel isolated and at sea.

I'm not saying that professional input and precise measures are unnecessary—in the beginning, it's important to make sure your baby is on track. But parents tend to rely on these supports long after their infant is out of trouble. Once you see your baby gaining, weigh her once a week instead of once a day. Don't stop calling for help by any means, but before you make the call, take a moment and try to figure out what *you* think is wrong and what *you* think is a good solution. Using experts to *confirm* rather than rescue will give you increasing confidence in your own judgment.

You may have trouble seeing your baby as the unique human being she is. Sometimes parents unwittingly become stuck in the parent-of-a-sick-baby mode. Fears and worries cloud their vision, and they can't see beyond their own emotions or their baby's early arrival or difficult birth. If you find yourself referring to your infant as "the baby," this may be a sign that you're not seeing her as a human being. Remember that just because your little one had a struggle coming into the world, she's no less of an individual. Now, this may be hard to remember when viewing a three- or four-pound baby who's swaddled in an incubator in the NICU and has tubes running in and out of him. Still, you must start the dialogue: Talk with your baby, notice her reactions, and try to discern who she is. Once you bring her home, and especially once she reaches her original due date (which is usually the basis for how we determine the true "age" of a preemie), continue this careful, slow observation.

A similar phenomenon can happen with multiples—they become "the babies." In fact, studies note that parents of twins tend to look *between*, not at, their babies.

Take care to regard your precious bundles as individuals; look them straight in the eye. I assure you, each will have his or her own distinct personality and needs.

You may resist a structured routine. Of course, a premature or low-birth-weight baby has to be fed more often and sleeps more than a normal baby. Certainly, we want a sick infant to get better, so we may have to administer medications. But there comes a point, usually when the baby has reached five and a half pounds, when it's not only possible to put your baby on E.A.S.Y., but also advisable. The problem, again, is that you might continue to see your infant through anorexic eyes. Months after his birth, you don't realize that Baby has caught up to his peers.

With adoption, too, parents sometimes resist a structured routine because they feel skittish about putting their new baby through too many changes. They try to follow the baby instead—a course of action that invariably leads to chaos. As I said earlier in this book, he's a *baby,* for goodness' sake. Why let him take the lead? In some of the more extreme cases of overprotection, the baby is so sheltered and so revered that he becomes, as one couple jokingly call their son, "King Baby." Needless to say, I'm not about to tell parents not to cherish their children—quite the opposite, in fact. But I hate to see the balance so skewed that Baby rules the roost.

Such parenting pitfalls are present, naturally, in any home, but Mum and Dad are more likely to stumble when their infant's earliest days were marked by extraordinary circumstances. Now let's look at some of the specific issues you might encounter as well.

Special Delivery:
Adoptions and Surrogacy

"Special delivery" is what Mum and Dad get when they pick up their baby at a hospital, an agency, a lawyer's office, or an airport. Often this moment comes at the end of a long, hard road that includes applications, home visits, endless phone calls, meeting with a prospective birth mum or surrogate, and even disappointment when an arrangement doesn't work out or is canceled at the last minute.

> **TIP:** *If you're adopting a baby, ask the birth mum or surrogate to play a tape of your voice, so that at least the child gets to hear you in utero.*

When a woman is pregnant, she has nine months to prepare herself. Although she may have second thoughts along the way, the gestation period gives her ample time to get used to the idea. Not so here, where the news of your special delivery can be rather sudden and the experience of having a baby placed in your arms is often shocking: "I remember seeing the women walking to the gate," said one adoptive mother, "each with a baby in her arms, and I thought, 'Oh, my God. One of those is *mine*.'" Adding additional stress is the fact that adoptive couples then usually have to travel with their new babies, so there's a double adjustment—the impact of that first moment, followed by the stunning experience of bringing the infant home.

Granted, an adoptive mother doesn't have the physical aftershock of pregnancy and delivery. She can at least maintain her normal life, relieving tension by jogging or whatever it is she normally does. Charlotte, a real-estate broker who had twins by surrogacy, was able to run around like a spring chicken until the moment her boys were born. At the same time, because the burden of care often falls on the new mum's shoulders, the emotional toll can be quite heavy.

Although all "special deliveries" have in common the fact that someone else carries your child and you must legally adopt him or her, there are some important differences between these types of arrangements as well. For one thing, with surrogacy, the legal arrangements can be trickier than adoption, for which there are decades of precedents. Additionally, you're literally putting all your eggs in one basket—not only because you're counting on one woman, but also because one out of ten surrogacies ends in miscarriage. With adoption, you have a wider range of prospective mothers, and you can deal with agencies in this country and abroad. Although either plan involves costs, those associated with surrogacy, the less traditional option, can exceed adoption fees, especially if the surrogate is impregnated in a lab, which is not always the case. Sophia and Magda, for example, met in a beautiful hotel overlooking the sea and shared tea and cookies; then Sophia used a turkey baster to impregnate Magda with Fred's sperm!

The underlying motivation of the mother who provides the baby makes for quite different situations, too. A surrogate mother makes a conscious decision to help out an infertile couple by carrying their baby. She often has as much to do in the selection process as the adoptive parents, and there can even be a biological tie, as when a sister or aunt volunteers to be a carrier. With adoption, the birth mother is giving up a baby because she either is too young *or* too old and/or doesn't have the financial or emotional resources to care for her own child. She may or may not have a prior or ongoing connection to the adoptive parents; she may not even know who they are.

With surrogacy, the adoptive parents often are involved in the pregnancy, and they know exactly when they're getting their baby. Some, as in Sophia's case, get close to the surrogate, even get to know her children, and the surrogate's family ultimately becomes part of their family. "I was the first one to hold Becca," recalls Sophia, who was in the delivery room when Magda gave birth, "and that night I took her back to the hotel and slept with her."

The course of a smooth-running surrogacy arrangement can make the whole process quite real and slightly more predictable than traditional adoption, where parents might not know precisely when to expect their little miracle. I remember getting a call from Tammy on a Sunday; she had applied for a baby and was inquiring about my availability. To her shock and mine, the following Thursday—four days later—she called again: "Tracy, they told me I'm getting my baby tomorrow." Talk about not having much time to prepare! Tammy had to fly a thousand miles to pick up the baby from the hospital following a series of medical tests that are usually performed on adopted babies to make sure there are no existing problems. She had never met the mother and had little to go on except a clean bill of health and the love that instantly poured from her heart for this tiny, helpless being in her arms.

Meeting Your Specially Delivered Baby

When you bring your little bundle home, here are some things to keep in mind.

Keep up a dialogue. Clearly, one of the first things an adoptive mother must do is *talk* with her new baby. If the baby has already heard your voice in utero, so much the better, but in many cases, this isn't possible. Actually introduce yourself. Tell your child how lucky you feel to have her. If you've adopted a baby from another culture, it may take her longer to acclimate to your voice. Your pitch, your intonation, and the pattern of your speech *will* sound different from what she's used to. That's why I generally suggest, whenever possible, to find a care-taker of the same nationality as your new baby.

Expect a rough first few days. Coming "home" can be very disorienting to a baby who suffers the usual traumas of birth and, in addition, is bombarded by a bevy of strange voices and has to endure a long trip. Therefore, many adopted infants are exceptionally ill-tempered when they arrive home. This was the case with Hunter, Tammy's special delivery. To allay his fears and make him feel comfortable in his new surroundings, Tammy pretty much stayed up for the first forty-eight hours with little Hunter, napping only when he napped. She talked to him nonstop, and by the third day he was less fretful. Now, you could attribute his crankiness to the long plane ride, but I also think he missed his birth mother's voice.

Don't get discouraged because you can't breastfeed. This is a sticking point for many adoptive mums who either want the experience themselves or would like their baby to get the nutritional benefits of mother's milk. The lat-ter can be accomplished if the surrogate or birth mother is willing to pump her milk for the first month or so. I know many families for whom breast milk has been frozen and overnighted clear across the country. And if it's the *feeling* of breastfeeding that an adoptive mother wants, she can at least simulate the experience by using a supplemental feeding unit (see page 138).

Take a few days to observe your baby before starting E.A.S.Y. It's important to get your baby onto a structured routine as quickly as possible, but with adoption, you have to spend a few days just observing. Of course, it depends, too, on *when* your bundle arrives. With surrogacy, there's a chance you'll be with the baby immediately after birth, and in such a case you proceed just as any birth mother would. But with other types of adoption, there's usually a gap, anywhere from a few days to a few months (more, of course, if you're getting a toddler or older child, but here we're concerned with infancy). Babies who are two, three, or four months old are often put on schedules in the orphanage or foster home where they are cared for. Still, because of the additional stress on your little newcomer, you'll need to give him or her time to adjust. The main thing to remember is that you must listen. Your baby will tell you what he needs.

Even with a newborn arriving straight from the hospital, you need to watch carefully, to gauge what he's like and what he needs. With Tammy's son, for example, by the fourth or fifth day, Hunter began feeling at home, and it was clear that he was a Textbook baby. He ate well, was fairly predictable in his moods, and slept for nearly two hours at a stretch, so it wasn't hard for Tammy to get him into an E.A.S.Y. routine.

The experience of each adopted baby is different, however. You need to take into consideration all that *your child* has been through. If your infant seems particularly disoriented, it's good not only to keep talking to him, but also to have a lot of close contact. Carry him around. In fact, for the first four days, you can replicate his prenatal environment by putting him in a wearable infant carrier and keeping him literally close to your heart. Don't do this for more than four days, though. Once your baby seems calmer and more responsive to your voice, then you can start him on E.A.S.Y. Otherwise, you risk the kind of accidental parenting problems I describe in the next chapter.

If your baby is a little older and has become accustomed not to the E.A.S.Y. routine, but to someone else's idea of a schedule, which involves his falling asleep after each meal, you can gently switch him round, but here, too, you must give it a few days. First, take the time to see how much she's eating. Most adopted babies are put on formula, and they drink from bottles. Since we pretty much know that formula typically breaks down at the rate of one ounce per hour, you can make sure she's taking enough at each feed to see her through a three-hour period. If she's falling asleep on the bottle because that's what she's been trained to do, wake her (see tip on page 111). Play with her a bit to keep her up after the feed. Within a few days, she'll be on E.A.S.Y.

Remember that you're no less a parent than a woman who gives birth. Through surrogacy or traditional adoption, Mum initially may feel like she doesn't really deserve this baby or know what to do with it, but after the first three months, a mum who has adopted is no different from one who has given birth to a baby herself. Women needn't apologize for adopting. After all, being a parent is an action, not a word. If you've been with a baby, sat with him at night when he's sick, and in every way played out the role of parent, you don't need a biological tie to earn the title of mother or father.

In the back of many an adoptive parent's mind is the question "Will this child want to find his birth mother when he grows up?" That's something to anticipate but not to worry about. You need to respect your child's right to research his past—these are his roots, his decision. In fact, I guarantee that the more you dread his curiosity, the more inquisitive he'll be.

Be open. Make the idea of adoption a regular part of the dialogue with your baby, so that you don't have to figure out the "right time" to tell her about her origins. With surrogacy, I suggest using a plant analogy. You have a concrete yard, and your next-door neighbor has soil. You give your neighbor the seeds, and when the plants sprout, you take them back onto your patio. You then continue to water the plants and help them to grow.

By "open," I don't necessarily mean keeping in touch with the birth mother or surrogate. That's a complex and very personal decision, best made by couples after careful consideration of their particular situation. Regardless of your conclusion, however, it's important to be honest with your child about his or her beginnings. In Charlotte's case, for example, she hasn't kept in touch with the surrogate, who used Charlotte's egg and Mack's sperm to conceive (a process known as gestational surrogacy, as opposed to traditional surrogacy, in which only the father's sperm is used). As soon as the babies were born, Charlotte and Mack cut off contact, because they viewed Vivian solely as a host. "She took them the distance for nine months, and now they're ours," Charlotte explains. Still, there's a photo of Vivian in the boys' room, and the family talks about her. "Your daddy and I are so lucky," Charlotte will say to her sons, "because even though I couldn't have babies in *my* tummy, we found Vivian, a wonderful woman who could carry you in *her* tummy and take care of you until you were ready to be born." She's been telling them their birth story from the day they arrived.

Don't be surprised if you get pregnant. No, it's not an old wives' tale, although no one is quite sure why seemingly infertile women suddenly conceive after adopting a child. Regina, who was told she could never have children of her own, adopted a newborn. A few days later, lo and behold, she got pregnant. Perhaps she no longer felt pressured to get pregnant; perhaps not. In any case, she now has two babies—nine months apart. Regina is so grateful to her adopted son, so sure that he "helped" her conceive, she calls him her "miracle baby."

Early Arrivals and Shaky Beginnings

Speaking of miracles, there's nothing quite so amazing—in retrospect, that is—as watching a premature infant or one born with medical problems, who you're afraid might not make it through the first night, blossom into a normal baby. I know, because my younger daughter arrived seven weeks early. She was in the hospital five weeks. In England, we're allowed to stay with them, so I stayed for the first three weeks, after which I spent the next two weeks going back and forth—home to Sara at night, back to Sophie every day.

Because I've been on the roller coaster myself, my heart truly goes out to parents of preemies and others whose babies are placed in an NICU. One day you have hope; another day you're paralyzed with fear because her lungs have shut down. I know the obsession with every ounce of weight gain, the concerns over infection, the fear of retardation and other problems that can occur. You see your baby lying in the NICU and you feel utterly useless. You're recuperating yourself, your hormones are spiraling out of control, and yet you must also face the possible death of your child. You hang on the doctor's every word, but half the time you forget what he or she said. You try to convince yourself that even in the bad news, there is some good news, some hope. But every hour, you're wondering, "Will she survive?"

Of course, some babies don't—about 60 percent of serious complications or infant deaths are due to the consequences of premature birth. It depends, of course, on *how early* Junior arrived (see sidebar on page 279). Furthermore, surviving infants can develop ongoing problems or require surgery, which only heightens one's anxiety. But a good many of these infants not only survive but thrive, and within a few months, they're virtually indistinguishable from their peers. Still, when parents come home with a preemie, even though they're told their baby is over the worst of it, their nerves are so raw that it's hard for them to believe that life will ever be the same. Here are some guidelines that can help you survive as well as your baby.

Wait until your baby's due date before treating her like a normal baby. The hospital will allow you to take your baby home when she's five and a half pounds, but if that occurs before your original due date, you need to continue treating her with kid gloves. Your goal is to get your baby to eat and sleep as much as possible and not to be stimulated. This is the only time I recommend feeding on demand.

Remember: Technically, your baby is still supposed to be *inside,* so do what you can to replicate those conditions. Swaddle her in a fetal position. Maintain the room temperature at around 72 degrees. You may have

The Emotional Roller Coaster of a High-Risk Birth

The stages of accepting death and dying first identified by Elisabeth Kübler-Ross have since been used to explain the normal course of adaptation to any crisis.

Shock: You will feel so dazed that it's hard to digest details or think clearly. It's best to have a friend or family member by your side to remember information and ask questions.

Denial: You don't want to believe this is happening—the doctors must be wrong. Seeing your baby in the NICU ultimately makes you face reality.

Grief: You mourn the perfect baby and the ideal birth. You feel sad for yourself, sadder still that you can't bring your baby home. You ache inside; every moment is torture. You cry often—and the tears help you go on.

Anger: You ask, "Why us?" You may even feel guilty, fearing that you could have done something to prevent the problem. You may direct your anger at your partner or family until you get to the next stage.

Acceptance: You realize that life must go on. You understand what you can and cannot change or control.

TIP: Remember this important lesson: It's not what happens to you in life, but how you deal with it that matters.

noticed that in the NICU, they sometimes cover babies' eyes so as to cut down on visual stimulation. At home, therefore, it's best to keep her room dark. Don't expose your baby to black and white toys—her brain isn't fully formed yet and shouldn't be bombarded. Where you would take care not to expose any infant to bacteria, with a preemie you must be even more rigorous about cleanliness; pneumonia is a very real risk. Sterilize all bottles.

Survival Rates for Preemies

Weeks are counted from the last menstrual period. Based on infants in NICUs, estimates may vary in individual cases.

23 weeks	10–35 percent
24 weeks	40–70 percent
25 weeks	50–80 percent
26 weeks	80–90 percent
27 weeks	More than 90 percent
30 weeks	More than 95 percent
34 weeks	More than 98 percent

A baby's chances for survival increase 3–4 percent *per day* between 23 and 24 weeks and 2–3 percent per day between 24 and 26 weeks. After 26 weeks, because survival rate is already high, the daily rate of increase is not as significant.

Some parents also take turns sleeping with their preemies on their chest at night. This "kangaroo care," as it's called, has proven beneficial in helping preemies' lungs and hearts. A study in London found that compared to babies in incubators, babies laid skin to skin on Mum's chest gained weight faster and had fewer health problems.

Give bottles instead of, or as well as, the breast. Until a baby is five and a half pounds, his or her feeding regimen will be decided by a neonatal specialist. Once your baby comes home, though, that lifeline drops away. One of your major concerns, of course, will be weight gain. How you feed your baby is something you need to discuss with your pediatrician. But the reason I like to give bottles, ideally of expressed breast milk, is that I can see how much the baby is taking in. Moreover, some babies have trouble on the breast. Depending on how early your baby arrived, he may not have yet developed the sucking reflex, which doesn't happen until around thirty-two or thirty-four weeks after conception; if he was born earlier than that, he won't know how to nurse.

When Baby Can't Come Home

If your baby arrived early or developed any kind of problem in the hospital, you may have to come home before her. Here are some strategies to make you feel more involved and, I hope, less helpless:

- Pump your milk within six to twenty-four hours and bring it to the NICU. Whether you ultimately plan to breastfeed or not, your milk is good for your baby. However, if your milk hasn't come in, your baby can also thrive on formula.
- Visit your baby daily and try to have physical contact, but don't live at the hospital. You need your rest, too, especially once your baby comes home.
- Expect to feel depressed. It's normal. Cry and talk about your fears.
- Take it a day at a time. There's no point in worrying about a future you can't control. Focus on what you can do *today*.
- Talk to other mothers who have had problems. Your baby may be in trouble, but she's not the only one who needs help.

Monitor your own anxiety and find an outlet for it. You want to hold your baby constantly to make up for the time you missed. When he sleeps, you're so scared that he might not wake up. These feelings and countless other protective urges are understandable given what you've been through. However, anxiety *won't* help your baby. Quite the contrary—studies have shown that infants intuitively sense their mother's emotional distress and can be adversely affected by it. It's absolutely vital that you find adult support—people to whom you can voice your deepest fears and who will encourage you to cry in their arms. It can be your partner. After all, who understands your fears more? But because you're both in the same predicament, it's also helpful for each of you to have other individuals on whom you can rely.

Physical exercise can be helpful in expending stress,

too. Or you may be someone who is calmed by meditation. Whatever works, do it, and keep it up.

When your baby is out of the woods, stop seeing him or her as a preemie or a sick baby. If your baby arrived early, or if she went full term but was born with a problem, your biggest hurdle can be your own inability to get over that sense of foreboding that accompanied the experience. You may still be operating with the mind-set of a parent who has a weak or sick child. Indeed, when parents call me with eating or sleeping problems, the first question I ask is, "Was he a preemie?" My next question is, "Did he have any kind of problems at birth?" Usually, the answer to one or both questions is yes. Focused on weight gain, parents tend to overfeed, and they continue to weigh the baby long after he's passed into the normal range. I've seen babies as old as eight months who are still sleeping on their parents' chest, still waking in the middle of the night for a feed. The antidote here is E.A.S.Y. Putting your baby on a structured routine is beneficial to him and infinitely kinder to yourself. (In the next chapter, I tell some of these parents' stories and explain how I helped them solve the problem.)

Your Double Bundle of Joy

Luckily, thanks to the wonders of ultrasound technology, women carrying more than one baby are rarely taken by surprise these days. If you're pregnant with twins or triplets, there's a good chance you'll be consigned to bed rest for at least the last month of your pregnancy, if not the last trimester. What's more, multiples have an 85 percent probability of arriving early.

Hence, I advise parents to start in the third month to prepare the nursery. But even that can be too late. I recently had a mum who was put on bed rest fifteen weeks into her pregnancy. She had to rely on others to get everything ready for her twins.

Because their pregnancies were hard and their deliveries often end with a C-section, not only do mothers of multiples have twice or three times the work once the babies arrive (I won't even talk about quads!), they also have a greater need to recuperate. However, I can tell you that the *last* thing a mother of twins wants to hear is "Oh, you're really in for something." Besides the fact that such comments usually come from people who have had only *one* baby at a time, it's a rather obvious and unhelpful point to make. I prefer to say, "You're in for twice the joy, and you've got a built-in playmate for your child."

When twins arrive early or are under five and a half pounds, take the same precautions I suggest above for early deliveries. A major difference, of course, is that you have two babies to worry about instead of just one. Twins don't always come home together, because one may weigh less or be considerably weaker than the other. Either way, though, I keep them together in the same crib. Gradually, at around eight to ten weeks, or whenever they start to explore and grab at things, including their sibling, I begin the process of separating them. I start by moving the babies farther and farther apart over a period of two weeks. Finally, I move each into individual beds.

Once your babies are past the point of possible complications, it's best to stagger their routines. Sure, it's possible to feed two babies at once, but then it's harder to focus on the babies as *individuals*. Also, it's harder on you. And where you might be able to handle simultaneous feeding, other tasks, like burping and diapering, have to be done separately.

The most pressing issues with twins or triplets are the seemingly nonstop work for Mum and the need for her to make the time to be with each of the babies separately. Not surprisingly, then, mothers of multiples are

	Haley	Joseph
Eat	6–6:30 A.M.: Feed (As they get older feeding takes less time; you can wake Joseph earlier and end up with extra time for yourself)	6:40–7:10 A.M.: Feed
	9–9:30 A.M.	9:40–10:10 A.M.
	12–12:30 P.M.	12:40–1:10 P.M.
	3–3:30 P.M.	3:40–4:10 P.M.
	6–6:30 P.M.	6:40–7:10 P.M.
	Until he sleeps through the night, dream feeds at 9 and 11 P.M.	Dream feeds at 9:30 and 11:30 P.M.
Activity	6:30–7:30 A.M. Diaper change (10 min.) and plays independently while Barbara feeds Joseph	7:10–8:10 A.M. Diaper change (10 min.) and plays independently while Barbara puts Haley down for nap
	9:30–10:30 A.M.	10:10–11:10 A.M.
	12:30–1:30 P.M.	1:10–2:10 P.M.
	3:30–4:30 P.M.	4:10–5:10 P.M.
	After 6 P.M. feed, let Haley play while Joey eats dinner	Baths for both at 7:10 P.M., when Joey finishes his feed
Sleep	7:30–8:45 A.M. nap	8:10–9:25 A.M. nap
	10:30–11:45 A.M. nap	11:10–12:25 A.M. nap
	1:30–2:45 P.M. nap	2:10–3:25 P.M. nap
	4:30–5:45 P.M. nap	5:10–6:25 P.M. nap
	Into bed straight after bath	Into bed straight after bath
You	Not yet, Mum!	After she puts Joey down, Mum rests for at least 35 minutes or until Haley wakes up for his next feed

instantly receptive to a structured routine, because it simplifies their life.

Barbara, for instance, was delighted when I suggested that she put her babies, Joseph and Haley, on E.A.S.Y. Joseph had to stay in the hospital an extra three weeks because of his low birth weight. Heartbreaking though it was to leave him, it gave Barbara an opportunity to get Haley's routine going. Because Haley had been on a three-hour feeding schedule in the hospital, it was fairly simple for us to keep him on track. Then, when Joseph came home, we started his feeds forty minutes after his brother's, staggering each one's schedule accordingly. I've reprinted Joseph and Haley's E.A.S.Y. schedule on page 283.

Although Barbara chose not to supplement her babies' feeds with formula, I often suggest that mums do. It's very hard to keep pumping and feeding when you're recovering from a C-section. Of course, it's even harder when the twins arrive after a first child, as was the case with Candace, whose twins, a boy and a girl, arrived when her older daughter, Tara, had just turned three. Oddly enough, Candace's twins were able to leave the hospital before their mum, who had delivered them vaginally and lost a great deal of blood in the process. Her doctor made her stay three extra days, until her dangerously low platelet count increased. Candace's mother and I took care of the babies, putting them on E.A.S.Y. straightaway.

When Candace came home, she was ready to leap into the fray: "Luckily, I had gone full term, and I had been in good physical shape to begin with." Candace also believes that she didn't "stress out" because this wasn't her first child. She also was aware of Christopher and Samantha's personalities right from the start and was therefore able to deal with them as separate little beings.

"He was so mellow, even in the hospital nursery—they had to tickle him to cry. She came out with fire. To this day, even when you change her diaper, she acts as if you're torturing her."

Candace's milk didn't come in for the first ten days, and at six weeks her supply still wasn't sufficient, so her twins happily remained on a combination of formula and breast milk. Understandably, with the added complication of three-year-old Tara underfoot, Candace had her hands full. "I took every Wednesday to spend with Tara, but on the days I was home all day, it was an endless cycle of breastfeeding, pumping, changing diapers, and putting them to sleep, with a half-hour break—until it started all over again."

Perhaps the most surprising aspect of multiples is that once you get over the initial adaptation period, twins and triplets are often *easier* to care for because they amuse each other. All the same, Candace has discovered what most mums of twins must accept: There are times when you have to let the babies cry. "I used to think, 'Oh, no, what am I going to do?' But you just deal with them one at a time, because that's all you can do. It's not like they're going to die from crying."

Amen to that, I say. In fact, as a final note to this chapter, this thought bears repeating: *It's not what happens to you in life that matters, but how you deal with it.* Keep in mind, too, that a good many unexpected situations and birth traumas become distant memories in a matter of months. Perspective is key when one deals with normal parenting issues as well as unusual circumstances, even trauma. In the next chapter, we'll look at some of the problems that arise when parents *don't* manage to keep a sane and sensible outlook.

CHAPTER NINE

Three-Day Magic: The ABC Cure for Accidental Parenting

> If there is anything that we wish to change in the child, we should first examine it and see whether it is not something that could be better changed in ourselves.
>
> —Carl Jung

"We Have No Life"

When parents don't start as they mean to go on, they may end up doing what I call accidental parenting. Take Melanie and Stan. Their son, Spencer, who was three weeks premature, was initially fed on demand. Although he quickly recovered from his birth trauma, Melanie fretted over his health during the first few weeks at home. She also took Spencer into bed with her because it was easier to nurse him several times in the middle of the night. During the day, whenever Spencer cried, his parents worked as a team; they rocked him and lulled him to sleep by taking him in the car or by walking around with him. Eventually, they got into the habit of soothing him with "kangaroo" parenting, allowing him to fall asleep *on* one of them. Melanie became a human pacifier; whenever Spencer seemed upset, she offered him a breast. Of course he would stop fussing at that point—his mouth was full.

Eight months down the line, these well-meaning parents realized that their adorable little boy had taken over their lives. Spencer couldn't get to sleep unless Mum or Dad trotted him round the room—and by then he weighed close to thirty pounds, not six! Their dinner was often interrupted. Melanie and Stan never found the "right" time to move Spencer from their bed to his own crib. One night Melanie would sleep in their bed with Spencer, and Stan would go into the guest room to get a proper night's rest; the following night, Dad would be on duty. Understandably, Melanie and Stan never resumed having a sex life, either.

Clearly, this couple didn't *intend* for their family life to turn out this way—hence the term "accidental parenting." What's worse is that they sometimes fought about it, each blaming the other for what happened. At times, they even resented their baby, who was, after all, only doing what they had trained him to do. By the time I visited their home, you could cut the tension with a knife. No one was happy, least of all Spencer. He had never asked to be put in charge!

Melanie and Stan's story is typical of the calls I get—sometimes as many as five to ten a week—from parents who didn't start as they meant to go on. They make comments such as "He won't let me put him down" or "She only eats for ten minutes at a time," as if the baby is deliberately resisting what's best. What really has happened is that *the parents* unintentionally reinforced a negative behavior.

My purpose in this chapter is not to make you feel bad but to teach you how to turn back the clock and undo the unwanted consequences of accidental parenting. And believe me, if your baby does something that upsets your household, disrupts your sleep, or prevents you from having a normal everyday life, there is always *something* that you can do about it. However, we must start with these three basic premises.

1. Your baby isn't doing anything willful or spiteful. Parents are often unaware of the impact they have on their children, and that, for better or for worse, they shape their babies' expectations.

2. You can untrain your baby. By analyzing your *own* behavior—what *you* do to encourage your baby—you'll be able to figure out how to change whatever bad habits you've unwittingly encouraged.

3. Changing habits takes time. If your baby is under three months old, it usually takes three days, or even less. But if your baby is older and a particular pattern has persisted, you will have to make changes in steps. It will take more time—usually each *step* takes three days—and require a fair amount of patience on your part to "fade out" whatever behavior it is you're trying to change, whether it's resistance to nap time or feeding difficulties. You have to be *consistent,* though. If you give up too soon, or if you are inconsistent, trying one strategy one day and another the next, you'll end up encouraging the very behavior you're trying to change.

The ABCs of Changing Bad Habits

Often, parents who find themselves in situations like Melanie and Stan's feel desperate. They don't know where to begin. Therefore, I've devised a strategy to enable parents to analyze their part in the problem and, in doing so, help them figure out how they can change a difficult pattern. It's a simple ABC technique.

"A" stands for the antecedent: what came first. What were you doing at the time? What did you do for your baby—or not do? What else was going on in his environment?

"B" stands for the behavior: your baby's part in what's happening. Is she crying? Does she look and sound angry? Scared? Hungry? Is what she's doing something that she usually does?

"C" stands for the consequences—what kind of pattern has been established as a result of *A* and *B*. Accidental parents, unaware of how they may be reinforcing a pattern, keep doing what they always did—for example, rocking the baby to sleep or thrusting a breast in his mouth. The action may stop the present behavior for a few minutes, but it will strengthen the habit in the long run. The key to changing the consequence, therefore, is to *do something different*—introduce a new behavior in order to allow the old one to fade out.

Let me give you a concrete example. Take Melanie and Stan, which admittedly was a very difficult case, because Spencer was eight months old and quite used to his parents' attention in the middle of the night. In order to get their life back, Melanie and Stan had to take several steps to undo the effects of their accidental parenting. Using my ABC method, though, I first helped them to analyze their situation.

The *antecedent* in this case was an ever-present fearfulness that arose—understandably—from Melanie and Stan's initial concern for their premature baby. Wanting to nurture Spencer, one of his parents always rocked him and held him on his or her chest. Moreover, to soothe him, his mum gave him her breast. Spencer's *behavior* was consistent, too; he was often cranky and demanding. This pattern became firmly entrenched, because every time Spencer cried, his parents rushed in, doing what they always did. The *consequence* was that Spencer, at eight months old, could neither self-soothe nor get to sleep on his own. To be sure, this was not how Melanie and Stan had planned to raise their son. But in order to change the situation, a by-product of their accidental parenting, they had to do something different.

Taking It One Baby Step at a Time

I had to help Melanie and Stan retrace what was actually a series of antecedents that contributed to Spencer's behavior, and then break down the solution into steps. In other words, we worked backward to undo what had been done. Let me take you through the process.

Observe and figure out a strategy. First, I just observed. I watched Spencer's behavior in the evening after his bath when Melanie tried to put him into his crib, freshly diapered and dressed in PJs. He clung to his mum in terror if she so much as neared the crib with him in her arms. I told Melanie that he was saying to her, "What are you doing? This is not where I'm supposed to be sleeping. I'm not going in *there*."

"Why do you think he is so scared?" I asked. "What happened before?" The antecedent to Spencer's panic was clear: Melanie and Stan had been desperate to break him of his habit of sleeping on their chests. After reading every sleep book they could purchase and talking to friends whose babies had had sleep problems, the parents had decided to "Ferberize" Spencer, not once but three times: "We tried to leave him to cry it out, but each time he cried so hard and long that my husband

and I found ourselves crying with him." The third time, when Spencer cried so intensely it caused him to vomit, his parents wisely abandoned this strategy.

The first thing we needed to do—or should I say *undo*—was clear: Get Spencer to feel safe in his crib. Because he was understandably so terrified of being alone in his own bed, I told Melanie we had to be very patient and cautious not to do anything that would remind him of his trauma. Only after that was accomplished could we deal with Spencer's nighttime behavior and his need to nurse every two hours.

Do each step slowly—you can't rush the process. In Spencer's case, it took a full fifteen days to get him over the terror of going into his crib. We had to break down this process into smaller steps, too, starting with nap times. First, I had Melanie walk into Spencer's bedroom, lower the blinds, and play some soothing music. She was only to sit in the rocking chair, holding Spencer. That first afternoon, even though she was nowhere near the crib, Spencer kept looking toward the door.

"This will never work," Melanie said anxiously.

I told her, "Yes, it will, but we have a long way to go. We need to take baby steps."

For three days, I stood by Melanie's side and we repeated the same sequence: go into his room, draw the blinds, and put music on for quiet time. First Melanie stayed only in the rocking chair, gently singing to Spencer; the lullaby helped distract him from his fear, but he kept his little eyes riveted on the door. Then she stood up with Spencer in her arms, taking care not to scare her little boy by moving too close to the crib. For the next three days, Melanie gradually inched closer to his crib until she could actually stand next to it without Spencer squirming. On the seventh day, she put him in his crib but held on to him, bending down close to his body. It was almost as if she was still holding him, but now he was lying down.

This was a real breakthrough. Three days later, Melanie was able to walk into the room with Spencer, darken it, put on the music, sit in the rocking chair, then move over to the crib and put him in. But she continued to lean over him and to reassure him that she was right there and he was safe. At first, he stayed close to the side of the crib, but after a few days, he eased up a bit. He would even allow himself to get distracted and actually move away from us toward his toy rabbit. The moment Spencer sensed that he had strayed too far, though, he'd quickly return to his sentry post at the side of the crib, ever vigilant.

We repeated this ritual, every day moving him along another baby step. Instead of holding him, Melanie stood by the side of the crib; eventually, she could just sit there. By the fifteenth day, Spencer was going into his crib willingly and lying down. As soon as he started to fall asleep, though, he would wake himself and sit up. Each time, we simply laid him back down. He'd start to relax again but would still cry a little, even as he started to cycle through the three stages of sleep (see page 197). I told Melanie not to rush in—that might interrupt his sleep process and he'd have to start over. Finally, Spencer learned how to make the journey to dreamland on his own.

Solve one problem at a time. Mind you, we had helped Spencer through his fear, but during the *daytime only.* We hadn't even attempted to change his other nighttime issues—he was still sleeping with Mum and Dad, still waking up for feeds. When you're dealing with a multi-layered issue, such as this one, it takes time and patience. As we say in England, "One swallow doesn't make a summer." But once I saw that Spencer no longer regarded his bed as an unfamiliar place, I knew that he was feeling secure enough for us to tackle the other problems.

"I think it's time to stop the feedings in the night," I told Melanie. Normally, Spencer, who had already started solids, would nurse at seven-thirty in the evening, go into his parents' bed, and then sleep on and off until one in the morning, at which point he woke every two hours for a nip on the breast. The *antecedent* here was that whenever Spencer stirred in the middle of the night, Mum, thinking he was hungry, would feed him, even though he took only an ounce or two each time. The *behavior*, his constant waking, was reinforced by Melanie's naive willingness to whip out a boob. The *consequence* was that Spencer expected to feed every two hours—a regimen more appropriate for a preemie than an eight month old.

Again, we had to take on the problem in stages. The first three nights, the rule was no feeding until four o'clock, then no food till six, at which time he could have a bottle. (Fortunately, this was a little boy who had been taking both breast and bottle, so he easily accepted the change.) Because his parents stuck to the plan, giving him a pacifier when he woke the first time instead of Melanie's breast, and putting him on a bottle for the six o'clock feed, Spencer was fine with the new plan by the fourth night.

After a week passed, I told Melanie and Stan it was time for me to sleep over, so that I could give the parents a rest and, just as important, teach Spencer to send himself back to sleep in his own crib without Mum, Dad, *or* a bottle. He was consuming solid food and plenty of milk during the day, so we knew he didn't *need* food during the night. And he had been taking naps willingly for around ten days. It was now feasible to introduce the idea of sleeping on his own—and through the night.

Expect some regression, since old habits die hard; you must commit yourself to the plan. The first night we put Spencer in his crib after his bath, we did the same ritual we had been doing during the day. It worked like a charm . . . or so we thought. He seemed tired when he got into his crib, but just as we were about to place him onto the mattress, his eyes pinged open and he started to fuss. He pulled himself up on the crib sides, and we laid him down and sat down in the chair next to the crib. He cried again and stood up. We laid him down again. After laying him down thirty-one times, he finally stayed down and went to sleep.

That first night, he woke at exactly one o'clock, crying. When I went into his room, he was already standing. I gently laid him down. So as not to stimulate him, I didn't say a word or even look him in the eye. A few minutes later, he fussed again and stood up. And so it went. He'd cry and pull himself up; I'd lay him down. After doing this little ballet forty-three times, he was exhausted and finally fell back to sleep. At four, he cried out again. Spencer was so true to his pattern, you could have set a clock by this kid. And again, I laid him down. This time my little jack-in-the-box popped up only twenty-one times.

(Yes, luv, I actually *count* when I do this. I'm often asked to deal with sleep problems, and when mums ask me, "How long will it take?" I want to at least give them an accurate range. I've had to count into the hundreds with some babies.)

The next morning, when I told Melanie and Stan what had happened, Dad was skeptical: "This will never work, Tracy. He won't do that for us." I winked and nodded, promising I'd come back for the next two nights. "Believe it or not," I said, "we are over the worst."

As it turned out, the second night, it took only six times of laying Spencer down to get him to sleep. At two o'clock, when he stirred, I crept into his room, and just as he was starting to lift his shoulders off the mattress, I gently laid him back down. I had to do that only five times, after which he slept until 6:45 that morning, something he had never done. The following night, Spencer stirred at four but didn't get up, and slept until seven. Since then, he has continued to sleep for twelve-hour stretches through the night. Melanie and Stan finally have their life back.

"He Won't Let Me Put Him Down"

Let's look at another common problem using our ABC method: the baby who needs to be carried all the time. Such was the case with Sarah and Ryan's three-week-old Teddy, whom you met in Chapter 2 (page 54). "Teddy doesn't like to be put down," Sarah lamented. The *antecedent* was that Ryan, who'd been traveling when Teddy was born, was so delighted to be with his son that whenever he came home, he constantly carried him around. Sarah also had a nanny from Guatemala, a culture in which babies are held a great deal. Little Teddy's *behavior* was utterly predictable, and I've seen hundreds of babies exactly like him: I'd put him on my shoulder, and he'd be happy as a lark. But the minute I began to put him down—mind you, he would be no more than eight to ten inches away from my chest at this point—he'd start to cry. If I stopped, reversed direction, and lifted him toward my shoulder, he'd immediately cease crying. Sarah, who always gave in, thinking that Teddy wouldn't "let her" put him down, only reinforced the pattern. The *consequence* of this sequence was—you guessed it—Teddy always wanted to be held.

Now, there's nothing wrong with holding your baby or nuzzling him. And, by all means, a crying baby ought to be properly soothed. The problem, which I've mentioned earlier, is that parents often don't know when the comforting ends and the bad habit begins. They continue to hold the baby *way past meeting his need*. Then the baby decides (in his baby mind, of course), "Oh, this is what life is like: Mum or Dad carries me all the time." But what happens when Baby gets to be a bit heavier or when his parents have work that isn't easily accomplished with an infant in tow? Baby says, "Hey, wait a minute. You're supposed to be holding me. I'm not going to just lie here by myself."

What do you do? Change the consequence by changing what *you* do. Instead of holding him endlessly, pick him up when he starts to cry, but put him down as soon as he is calm. If he cries again, pick him up. When he quiets, lay him down again. And so on and so on. You might have to pick that baby up twenty or thirty times or more. In essence, you're saying, "You're fine. I'm here. It's okay to be on your own." I promise this won't go on forever—*unless* you go back to your practice of comforting past his need.

The Secret to this Three-Day Magic

Although parents sometimes think what I do is magic, it's really common sense. As you see from a situation like Melanie and Stan's, you might have to plan for a few weeks of transition time. On the other hand, we managed to change little Teddy's need for constant holding in two days, because the antecedent—Dad's and the nanny's carrying him much of the time—had been going on for only a few weeks.

I employ my ABC strategy to analyze precisely what kind of three-day magic I'll need. Often, it comes down to one or two techniques, all of which involve encouraging the old behavior to fade out. In three-day increments, you withdraw whatever it was you once did—fade out the old—in favor of something that builds your child's independence and resourcefulness. The older babies get, of course, the harder it will be to discourage the old behavior. In fact, most of my calls for help come from parents with babies five months or older.

In the "Troubleshooting Guide" on pages 310–312, I offer a quick review of the most common bad habits I'm asked to help change. However, in each case there are common threads.

The ABCs of Change

Remember: Whatever bad habit you're trying to break is a **consequence** (C) of what you've done—the **antecedent** (A)—which has inadvertently caused the **behavior** (B) you now want to eliminate. If you keep doing the same thing, it will only reinforce the same consequence. Only by doing something different—by changing what *you* do—can you break the habit.

Sleep problems. Whether it's a baby who doesn't sleep through the night (after three months) or one who has trouble falling asleep independently, it's always a matter of, first, acclimating her to her own bed, and then teaching her to sleep in it without your soothing. In worst-case scenarios, typically when accidental parenting has gone on for several months, the baby may be afraid of her own bed. Sometimes it's a case of her being used to your holding or rocking her. The consequence is that she never learned how to fall asleep on her own.

I had one baby, Sandra, who was utterly convinced that her "bed" was a human being's chest. When I held her, it was as if there were a magnet in my chest and one in hers. Every time I tried to lay her down, Sandra cried. It was her way of saying to me, "This isn't how *I* go to sleep." At first, it was impossible to lay her even next to me. My job was to teach Sandra another way of sleeping, and I told her as much: "I'm going to help you learn how to go to sleep on your own." Of course, she was skeptical and not particularly interested in learning at first. I had to pick her up and put her down 126 times the first night, 30 the second, and 4 times the third. I never left her to "cry it out," nor did I revert to the kangaroo technique her parents had been using to calm her, which would have only perpetuated Sandra's sleep difficulties.

Feeding problems. When bad eating habits are the problem, the antecedent is usually some form of parents' misreading their baby's cues. Gail, for instance, complained that it took Lily an hour to nurse. Even before I visited her, I suspected that Lily, then a month old, was not actually eating for the entire sixty minutes; she was pacifying herself. Gail found breastfeeding so relaxing—she probably had high levels of oxytocin—that she herself often fell asleep. She'd pass out in midfeed and then jolt awake after a ten-minute catnap, only to find Lily still sucking away. Although I've made many mums throw their timers in the trash, in this case, I trotted one out and suggested that Gail set it for forty-five minutes. More important, I told her to *observe carefully* how Lily was suckling. Was she really eating? Paying close attention, Gail realized that Lily was pacifying herself at the end of each feed. So when the timer went off, we replaced Mum's nipple with a pacifier. In three days, we got rid of the timer, too, because Gail became much more attuned to her baby's needs. As Lily grew, she didn't need the pacifier, either, because she found her own fingers.

With feeding problems, your baby's behavior might be that she suckles continuously, long after she's taken in the nourishment she needs, as Lily did. She also might bob on and off the breast—her way of trying to tell you something like "Mum, I'm a better eater now and it takes me less time to drain your breast." If you don't understand what she's saying, you're apt to try to coax her back onto your breast, and she'll continue to suck, because that's what babies do. Or she might wake in the middle of the night for feeds when, in fact, she no longer needs them. In any of those situations, your baby learns to use the breast or the bottle as a pacifier, a consequence that serves neither you nor your child well.

No matter what the behavior, the first thing I do is suggest a structured routine. With E.A.S.Y., there's less guesswork because parents know when babies are supposed to be hungry, and they can then look for other reasons for their infant's crankiness. But I also encourage parents to observe what's going on, to assess whether their baby really needs to eat, and if not, to then gradually fade out unnecessary extra feeds and to teach their child other ways of self-soothing. I may cut extra feeds shorter at first, allowing the baby to spend less time on the breast or take fewer ounces. I might switch to water, or use a pacifier to make the transition complete. In the end, the baby won't even remember the old habit, which is why it looks like magic.

"But My Baby Has Colic"

Here's where my three-day magic is really put to the test. Your baby wails and pulls his legs to his chest. Is he constipated? Does he have gas? Sometimes he seems to be in so much pain, you think your heart is going to break. Your pediatrician and other mums who have been through a similar experience say it's colic—and everyone warns you ominously, "There's not a thing you can do about it." In part that's accurate; colic has no real cure. At the same time, *colic* has become a much-overused term, a catchall word to describe almost any difficult situation. And many of those difficult situations *can* be made better.

Give Yourself a Break

In a roomful of mothers, even if none of the babies is crying, it's easy to recognize the mum with the colicky infant. She's the one who looks the most exhausted. She thinks it's her fault that somehow she ended up with a "bad" baby. Nonsense. If your baby has true colic, it's a problem, to be sure, but you didn't cause it. And in order to ride it out, *you* need as much support as your baby does.

Instead of laying blame—which, sadly, some couples do—you and your partner need to relieve each other. With many babies, the crying comes like clockwork—say, from three to six every day. So take turns. If Mum is on duty one day, Dad should handle the next day.

If you're a single mom, try to enlist a grandparent, sibling, or friend to stop by during the witching hour. And when relief comes, don't sit there listening to your baby cry. Get out of the house. Take yourself for a walk or a ride—do anything that gets you out of the environment.

Most important: Although it *feels* like your baby's colic is forever, I assure you that it *is* going to pass.

I grant you, if your baby suffers from colic, it can be a nightmare—for the baby *and* you. It is estimated that 20 percent of babies suffer from some form of colic, and of those, 10 percent are considered severe cases. In a colicky baby, the muscle tissue that surrounds the wee thing's gastrointestinal or genitourinary tract begins to contract spasmodically. The symptoms usually start with fussing and then lead to prolonged bouts of crying, sometimes for hours on end. Typically, the attacks come at approximately the same time every day. Pediatricians sometimes use the "rule of three" in diagnosing colic—three hours of crying per day, three days a week, for three weeks or more.

With Nadia, a classic colic baby, for example, she smiled most of the day and then from six to ten every night she'd cry, sometimes steadily, sometimes on and off. Just about the only thing that offered relief was to sit with her in a dark closet, which cut down the external stimulation.

Poor Nadia's mum, Alexis, was almost as distressed as her baby and even more sleep-deprived than your average new parent. She needed help as much as Nadia did. Just managing her emotions was a full-time job. To be sure, sometimes the best advice I can give parents of a colicky baby is "Be kind to yourself" (see the sidebar on page 300).

Colic often appears suddenly in the third or fourth week and seems to disappear just as mysteriously at around three months. (There's really no mystery. In most cases, the digestive system matures and the spasms abate. At that age, too, babies have greater control over their limbs and can find their own fingers to self-soothe.) However, in my experience, some of what is labeled colic may be a by-product of accidental parenting—a mum (or dad) desperate to calm a crying newborn slips into a pattern of either rocking her infant to sleep or giving him breast or bottle for solace. This seems to "cure" the child, at least for a bit. In the meantime, the baby begins to expect this kind of comforting whenever he's upset. By the time he's a few weeks old, the consequence is that nothing less will calm him, and everyone assumes it's colic.

Many parents who tell me their baby has colic have stories similar to that of Chloe and Seth, whom you met in Chapter 2 (page 58). On the phone, Chloe had told me that Isabella had been suffering from colic: "She cries almost all the time." Seth greeted me at the door with his round-faced, cherubic baby, who immediately settled in my arms and sat contentedly on my lap for the next fifteen minutes while her parents filled me in.

Tummyache Techniques

Food management is the best way to avoid gas pains, but at some point your baby probably will have a tummyache. Here are the strategies I've found most effective.

- The best way to burp any baby, especially one with gas, is to rub upward on the left side (where her stomach is) using the heel of your palm. If after five minutes Baby hasn't given you a burp, put her down. If she then starts to pant, squirm, roll her eyes, and make an expression that resembles a smile, she has gas. Pick her up, making sure her arms are over your shoulder and her legs straight down, and try burping her again.
- While your baby is lying on his back, pull his legs up and gently do a bicycling motion.
- Lay your baby across your forearm, facedown, and use your palm to put gentle pressure on her tummy.
- Make a cummerbund by folding a receiving blanket into a four- or five-inch band and wrap it snugly around your baby's middle—but not tight enough to cut off her circulation (if she goes blue, it's too snug).
- To help your baby expel the gas, hold him against you and pat his bottom. This gives him a focus point so that he knows where to push.
- Massage her tummy in a backward C motion (not a circle) so that you trace the colon—left to right, down, and then right to left.

As you may recall, Chloe and Seth, a darling young couple, were stalwart wingers. At the mere mention that a routine might go a long way toward helping their cranky five-month-old daughter, I half expected them to make the sign of the cross, as you would to keep a vampire at bay! They wanted to let it all hang loose, but let's look at the consequences of imposing their laissez-faire lifestyle on sweet little Isabella.

"She's a little better now," said Chloe. "Maybe she's finally outgrowing the colic." Mum went on to explain that Isabella had been sleeping in her parents' bed since birth and was still waking regularly throughout the night, screaming. During the day, it was more of the same. Isabella even screamed when she was nursing, which, Chloe said, happened every hour or two. I asked what the parents did to calm her.

"Sometimes we put her in a snowsuit, because it stops her from moving around so much. Or we'll put her in the swing and put the Doors album on for her. If it's really bad, we'll take her for a drive, hoping that the movement will soothe her. When it's not working," Chloe added, "I'll climb into the backseat and put my breast in her mouth."

"We can hold her off sometimes by changing the activity," Seth offered.

These delightful, caring parents had no idea that almost everything they were doing for Isabella worked *against* what they were trying to achieve. Applying the ABC technique revealed a situation that had been compounded and reinforced over a five-month period. Because Isabella wasn't on anything that remotely resembled a structured routine, her parents were constantly misreading her cues, interpreting every cry as "I'm hungry." The antecedent was overfeeding and overstimulation—and the baby's behavior—her part in perpetuating the pattern—was screaming. The consequence was an overtired baby who had no idea how to switch herself off. Misunderstanding her cues and thinking they had to invent new ways to "hold her off," her parents unwittingly contributed to her distress and only compounded the problem.

Almost on cue, Isabella started making little cough-cough cries—clearly (to me at least), her way of saying, "Mummy, I've had enough."

"See?" said Chloe.

"Uh-oh," Seth chimed in.

"Now hold on, Mum and Dad," I said in a baby voice, speaking for Isabella, "I'm just tired."

Then I explained, "The trick is to put her down *now,* before she gets herself too upset." Chloe and Seth led me upstairs to their bedroom, a sun-filled room with a queen-size bed and lots of pictures on the walls.

One easily remedied problem was immediately apparent: The bedroom was too bright and had too many stimulating diversions, and so there was no way for Isabella to switch herself off. "Do you have a bassinet or carriage?" I asked. "Let's try to put her to sleep in there."

I showed Chloe and Seth how to swaddle Isabella with a receiving blanket (see page 205). I left one arm out, explaining that at five months she had control over her arms and might be able to find her own fingers. I then stepped from the bedroom into a darkened hallway, and, with their tightly swaddled baby in my arms, patted rhythmically. In a soothing voice, I reassured Isabella, "It's okay, little one, you're only tired." In a few moments, she calmed down.

Her parents' amazement turned to skepticism as I then lowered Isabella into her little bassinet, continuing the patting. She was quiet for a few minutes and then began to cry. So I picked her up again, soothed her, and put her down when she was quiet. This happened two more times, and then, to her parents' astonishment, Isabella fell asleep.

"I don't expect her to sleep very long," I told Chloe and Seth, "because she's accustomed to catnapping. Your job now is to help her extend those naps." I explained that babies go through approximately the same forty-five-minute sleep cycle that adults do (see page 210). A child like Isabella, though, whose parents always rush to her side every time she makes a peep, hasn't yet learned the skills to send herself back to sleep. They have to teach her. If she wakes up after only ten or fifteen minutes, instead of assuming that she's had her nap and is now awake, they must gently coax her back to dreamland, as I had done. Eventually, she'll learn how to send herself back to sleep, and her naps will lengthen.

"But what about her colic?" Seth asked, obviously concerned.

"I suspect your baby doesn't really have colic," I explained, "but even if she does, there *are* things you can do to make it better for her."

I tried to help these parents realize that if Isabella did have true colic, the lack of structure in their household would only intensify whatever physical problem she had. But I believed that her discomfort was caused by accidental parenting. The consequence of Isabella's being fed every time she cried was that she learned to use her mum's breast as a pacifier. And because she was feeding so frequently, she was only "nipping" and, as a result, getting mostly the lactose-rich quencher portion of Chloe's milk, which can cause gas. "She even snacks all night," I pointed out, "which means her little digestive system never rests."

On top of all that, I explained, their baby wasn't getting a good, restorative rest—day *or* night—so she was constantly tired. And what does an overtired baby do to shut out the world? Cry. And when she cries, she swallows air, which could either cause gas or aggravate whatever is already trapped in her stomach. Finally, in response to all this, these well-meaning parents heaped on more stimulation—car rides, the swing, the stereo (and the Doors, no less). Instead of helping Isabella learn how to calm herself, they had inadvertently taken away her self-soothing skills.

I left them with this advice: Put Isabella on E.A.S.Y. Be consistent. Continue the swaddling. (At around six months, it would be okay to release both of Isabella's arms, because by then she would be less likely to scratch herself or pinch her own face with flailing hands.) Cluster-feed her at six, eight, and ten o'clock, so that she has the calories to make it through the night. If she wakes up again, don't feed her—give her a passy instead. Comfort her when she cries, but also reassure her.

I suggested taking these changes in steps, tackling the daytime sleep first, so that Isabella wouldn't be as overtired and cranky. Sometimes, just dealing with naps has a beneficial effect on nighttime sleep as well. In any case, I warned them that they might have to go through several weeks of crying as they made this transition. Given their situation, however, what could they lose? They had already suffered months of agony seeing their baby in such discomfort. At least now they could perceive a ray of hope.

What if I was wrong? What if Isabella really did have colic? The truth is, it doesn't matter. Although pediatricians sometimes prescribe a mild antacid to relieve the gas pains, nothing actually cures colic. But I do know that proper food management and the promotion of sensible sleep usually ease a baby's discomfort.

Moreover, overfeeding and a lack of sleep can cause behavior that looks like colic. Does it matter if it's "real" colic? Your infant is in discomfort all the same. Think what it's like for an adult. How would you feel if you stayed up all night? Cranky, I'm sure. And what happens to a lactose-intolerant grown-up who drinks milk? Babies are human beings and they suffer from the same gastrointestinal symptoms we do. Trapped gas is a nightmare for an adult, and it's even worse for a baby, who can't hold herself or massage her stomach or use words to tell us what's wrong. At least on E.A.S.Y., Mum and Dad can deduce what's needed.

In Seth and Chloe's case, I explained to them that by giving their baby proper feeds rather than allowing her to snack all day, it will help them analyze Isabella's needs. When she cries, they will be able to think more logically: "Oh, she couldn't be hungry. We just fed her a half hour ago. She probably has gas." And as they start to really tune into Isabella's facial expressions and body language, they will recognize the difference between a cry of distress ("Mmm . . . I see her grimacing and pulling her legs up") and fatigue ("She's yawned twice"). On a structured routine, I assured them, Isabella's sleep patterns will improve and she will no longer be a nonstop cranky baby. After all, not only will she be getting proper rest, but her parents will be able to figure out what she needs *before* her crying escalates out of control.

"Our Baby Won't Give Up the Breast"

This is a complaint I often hear from fathers, especially if they're turned off by breastfeeding in the first place, or if their wives are continuing to nurse past the first year.

It can lead to a very bad family situation if Mum doesn't realize that *she* is the reason Baby stubbornly clings to her breast. My feeling is that when mothers prolong nursing, it's almost always for *them,* not for the baby. A woman often loves the role, the closeness, and the secret knowledge that only *she* can calm the baby. Aside from finding breastfeeding peaceful or personally fulfilling, she might just relish the idea of her child being so dependent upon her.

Adrianna, for instance, was still nursing two-and-a-half-year-old Nathaniel. Her husband, Richard, was beside himself. "What can I do about this, Tracy? Whenever Nathaniel's upset, she gives him her breast. She won't even talk to me about it, because she says the LaLeche League told her it's 'natural' and that it's good to comfort a child on your breast."

I then asked Adrianna what she felt. "I want to comfort Nathaniel, Tracy. He needs me," she explained. However, because she knew that her husband had become increasingly less tolerant, she admitted that she had begun hiding it from him. "I told him I had weaned Nathaniel. But recently we were at a friend's Sunday barbecue, and Nathaniel started tugging at my breast, saying, 'Tata, tata' [his baby word for breast]. Richard shot me a look. He knew that I had lied to him. He was furious."

Now, my job is not to change a woman's mind about nursing. As I said earlier in this book, this is a very individual and private matter. But I did advise Adrianna to at least be honest with her husband. I stressed that my primary concern is for her family *as a whole.* "It's not for me to say whether you should wean Nathaniel or not, but look at how this is affecting everyone," I said. "You've got a baby *and* a husband to consider, but it seems like the baby is taking over." Then I added, "If, behind Richard's back, you're reinforcing the idea to Nathaniel that he *can* nurse, you're setting your little boy up to be deceitful, too."

Talk about accidental parenting. I suggested to Adrianna that she look at what was going on, consider her own motives for breastfeeding, and take a peek into the future. Did she really want to risk the consequences of lying to Richard and setting a bad example for Nathaniel? Of course she didn't. She simply hadn't thought it all through. "I'm not sure it's Nathaniel who *needs* breastfeeding anymore," I told her honestly. "I think it's you. And that's something you ought to look at."

To her credit, Adrianna did some important soul-searching. She realized that she was using Nathaniel as an excuse not to make decisions about work. She had been telling everyone how "eager" she was to get back to the office, but secretly she harbored a far different fantasy. She wanted to take off a few more years to be with Nathaniel, maybe to have another baby. She finally talked to Richard about it. "He was unbelievably supportive," she later told me. "He said we didn't need my income and, besides that, he was proud of the kind of mother I was. But he wanted to feel like he was a part of the parenting equation, too." This time Adrianna meant it when she told Richard she would wean Nathaniel.

She first stopped nursing him during the day. She simply said to him one day, "There's no more tata—only at bedtime." Whenever Nathaniel tried to lift her shirt, which he did several times a day for the first few days, she repeated, "It's all gone," and gave him a sippy cup instead. After a week, she then stopped the nursing at night. Nathaniel tried to convince his mum by saying, "Five more minutes," but she kept telling him, "No more tata." It took another two weeks of this nagging for

Nathaniel to give it up, but when he did, that was it. Adrianna told me a month later, "I'm really surprised. It's as if he has no recollection of ever nursing. I can't believe it." Even more important, Adrianna has her *family* back: "I feel like Richard and I are on a second honeymoon."

Troubleshooting Guide

The following is not meant to be an exhaustive list of every problem you might encounter, but these are the kinds of long-term difficulties I'm often asked to interpret and correct. If your baby has more than one, remember that you have to take *one at a time*. As a guide, ask yourself, "What do I want to change?" and "What do I want in its place?" When both feeding *and* sleeping issues are involved, the two are often interrelated, but it is impossible to work on either one, for example, if your baby is frightened about being in his own crib. When trying to figure out what to do first, use your common sense— the solution is often more obvious than you think.

Consequence	Likely Antecedent	What You Need to Do
"My baby likes to be held all the time."	You (or a baby nurse) probably liked to hold her . . . in the beginning. Now she's used to it, and you're ready to get on with your life.	When your baby needs comforting, pick her up and calm her, but then put her down the minute she stops crying. Tell her, "I'm right here—I didn't go anywhere." Don't extend the length of time you hold her past *her* need for comfort.
"My baby seems to take almost an hour to feed."	She may be using you as a human pacifier. Are you on the phone when you feed her or otherwise not paying attention to *how* she's eating?	At first, a baby's sucking is usually ferocious and quick, and you'll hear her gulping down the quencher. As she finally gets to the rich hind milk, she'll take long, harder, strokes. But when she's pacifying, you'll see her bottom jaw going, but you won't feel the pulling. Tune in so that you know how *your* baby feeds. Don't let feeds go longer than forty-five minutes.

Consequence	Likely Antecedent	What You Need to Do
"My baby is hungry every hour or hour and a half."	You may be misreading her cues, interpreting every cry as hunger.	Instead of giving her the bottle or breast, change her scene—she might be bored—or give her a pacifier to satisfy her need to suck.
"My baby needs a bottle [or the breast] to go to sleep."	You may have conditioned him to expect it by giving him the breast or a bottle before bedtime.	Put your baby on E.A.S.Y. so that he doesn't associate sleep with breast or bottle. Also see pages 207–211 for hints about helping a baby learn how to sleep independently.
"My baby is five months old and doesn't sleep through the night."	Your baby may have switched day for night. Think back to your pregnancy: If she kicked a lot at night and slept during the day, she came in with that biorhythm. Or you allowed her to take long daytime naps in her first few weeks, and now she's used to it.	It's important to switch your baby around by waking her every three hours during the day. (See page 208). The first day she'll be lethargic, the second day more alert, and by the third you've changed her biological clock.
"My baby can't get himself to sleep without our rocking him."	You may be missing his sleep cues (see page 200) and he's getting overtired. Because you've probably rocked him to calm him, he hasn't learned to fall asleep on his own.	Look for the first or second yawn. See page 199 if you've missed it. If you've been doing this for a while, he links rocking with sleep. As you phase out the rocking, you'll have to substitute other behavior: Either stand still when you hold him or sit in a chair without rocking. Use your voice and patting instead of movement.

Consequence	Likely Antecedent	What You Need to Do
"My baby cries all day."	If it's literally *all* day, it could be a matter of overfeeding, fatigue, and/or overstimulation.	Babies rarely cry that much, so it's best to consult your pediatrician. If it is colic, that surely isn't your doing; you'll have to ride it out. But if it's not colic, you may need to change your approach. See pages 307–313 for a story that might sound familiar. In either case, putting a baby on E.A.S.Y. and promoting sensible sleep (pages 190–198) usually helps.
"My baby always wakes up cranky."	Temperament aside, some babies are cranky when they wake up because they haven't had a proper amount of sleep. If you're getting your baby up when she's just shifting sleep gears (see page 210), she may not be getting enough rest.	Don't rush into her room the minute she makes a peep. Wait a few moments to allow her to fall back to sleep on her own. Extend her naps during the day. Believe it or not, this will make her sleep better at night, because she won't be so overtired.

Adrianna learned a valuable lesson about introspection and balance. Being a parent requires both. Many of the so-called problems I see, arise because mums and dads don't realize how much of themselves they project onto their babies. It's always important to ask yourself, "Am I doing this for my baby or for *me*?" I see parents hold their babies when they no longer need to be held, nursing long after their babies cease to need breast milk. In Adrianna's case, she was using her toddler to hide from herself; without realizing it, she was hiding from her husband as well. Once she was able to really look at what was going on, to be honest with herself and her mate, and to see that in fact she did have the power to change a bad situation into a good one, she was automatically a better parent, a better wife, and a stronger human being.

EPILOGUE
Some Final Thoughts

> Step with care and great tact
> and remember that Life's
> a Great Balancing Act.
> Just never forget to be dexterous
>   and deft.
> And *never* mix up your right foot
>   with your left.
> And will you succeed?
> Yes! You will indeed!
> (98 and ¾ percent guaranteed.)
> —Dr. Seuss in *Oh, the Places You'll Go!*

I want to end this book with a very important reminder: Have fun. All the baby-whispering advice in the world is useless if you're not having a good time being a parent. Yes, I know it can be hard, especially in the earliest months, especially when you're exhausted. But you must always keep in mind what a special gift it is to be a parent.

Remember, too, that raising a child is a lifelong commitment—something you must take more seriously than any mission you've ever accomplished. You are responsible for helping to guide and shape *another human being,* and there is no greater, higher assignment.

When the going gets particularly rough (and I guarantee that, even with an Angel baby, at times it will), try not to lose perspective. Your child's babyhood is a wondrous age—scary, precious, and all too fleeting. If you doubt for a moment that you'll someday look back with longing at this sweet, simple time, talk to parents of older kids who will attest: Taking care of a baby is but a tiny blip on the radar of your life—clear, sharp, and sadly irretrievable.

My wish for you is to relish every moment, even the tough ones. My goal is to give you not merely information or skills, but something even more important: confidence in yourself and in your own ability to solve problems.

Yes, dear reader, you can empower yourself. Mum or Dad, Granny or Granddad—whoever has this book in hand—these secrets are no longer mine alone. Use them well, and enjoy the wonder of calming, connecting, and communicating with your baby.

INDEX

THE PHENOMENAL NATIONAL BESTSELLER

SECRETS OF THE BABY WHISPERER FOR TODDLERS

TRACY HOGG

WITH MELINDA BLAU

Unnerved by the ceaseless demands of your toddler? Concerned that your two-year-old isn't developing on schedule? Starting with the simple but essential premise that there is no such thing as a "typical" child, Tracy guides you through her unique programs, including:

• H.E.L.P. (Hold back, Encourage exploration, Limit, Praise): the mantra that will remind you of the four elements that are critical to fostering your child's growth and independence, while at the same time keeping him safe.

• Using T.L.C. (Talk, Listen, Clarify) to communicate with your toddler, to figure out what she is really thinking, and to best help her express herself.

• And more!

Practical, reassuring, and written with wit and energy and boundless enthusiasm for real children and their everyday behavior, this book will be your constant companion during the magical, challenging toddler years.

Published by Ballantine Books
Available wherever books are sold